JUN 5 1997

D0777781

SEX SCANDAL

SERIES Q

Edited by

Michèle Aina Barale,

Jonathan Goldberg,

Michael Moon, and

Eve Kosofsky

Sedgwick

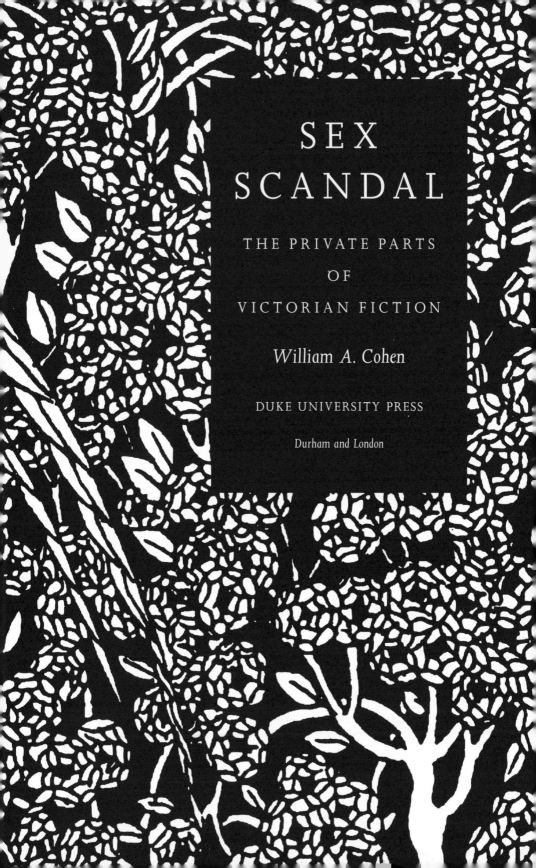

SEX
SCANDAL

THE PRIVATE PARTS
OF
VICTORIAN FICTION

William A. Cohen

DUKE UNIVERSITY PRESS

Durham and London

Several chapters of this book were previously published
in slightly different form. Chapter 2: ELH 60, no. 1 (Spring
1993): 217–59, copyright 1993 by The Johns Hopkins
University Press. Chapter 5: *Novel: A Forum on Fiction* 28,
no. 3 (Spring 1995): 235–56, copyright 1995 by Brown
University, and reprinted with the permission of the
copyright owner. Portions of chapter 6 appeared in "Willie
and Wilde: Reading *The Portrait of Mr. W. H.*," *South Atlantic
Quarterly* 88, no. 1 (Winter 1989): 219–45, copyright 1989 by
Duke University Press. Reprinted in *Displacing Homophobia:
Gay Male Perspectives in Literature and Culture*, ed. Ronald R.
Butters, John M. Clum, and Michael Moon (Durham: Duke
University Press, 1989), 207–33.
© 1996 Duke University Press. All rights reserved. Printed
in the United States of America on acid-free paper ⊗
Typeset in Joanna by Tseng Information Systems, Inc.
Library of Congress Cataloging-in-Publication Data appear
on the last printed page of this book.

FOR H & H

CONTENTS

ACKNOWLEDGMENTS

The moment the subject of scandal arises, the question of how to avoid it comes up as well. Since the surest means of keeping oneself from becoming scandal's victim is to be dutiful, a book that focuses on scandal might be expected to worry over the routine of meeting its own obligations. Such worry might be warranted were there not so much pleasure to be had in this particular diligence. It is to the readers for whose eyes these pages were initially written, in the form of a doctoral dissertation, that I owe my foremost intellectual debts. D. A. Miller, Catherine Gallagher, and Thomas W. Laqueur made immeasurable contributions to my thinking and writing, providing valuable guidance through both their comments on my work and the model of their own scholarship. Without the steadfast dedication of Laura M. Green and Elizabeth Young at every phase of its composition, this project would have been inconceivable. Members of the Victorian dissertation group at Berkeley supplied thoughtful comments on the work as it emerged, and continue to provide intellectual community. I am grateful to Laura C. Berry, Catherine Robson, Daniel Hack, Christopher Craft, and Kerry Walk for their contributions. Susan S. Lanser, Kathryn Bond Stockton, Hilary Schor, Jeff Nunokawa, and Joseph Litvak generously read and commented upon later versions of the manuscript, and Henry Abelove's advice has been important in bringing it to fruition.

I am always mindful of the emotional and intellectual support I derive from my family, and I can only express the gratitude I feel for their faith in me. Christopher Haines, James E. Gregory, and Serge Seiden exhibited an exceptional measure of compassion and confidence in the years during which this book was completed. Other friends who provided a convivial environment for my work include Eric Cavallero, Matthew Lore, Darrell Moore, Greg Mullins, Frank K. Saragosa, David Shengold, William Sherman, and Yonatan Touval. For encouragement in the completion and subsequent publication of chapter 2, I am grateful to Mary Poovey. She, along with Philip Weinstein, Susan Snyder, and Kaori Kitao, cultivated the intellectual roots of this work at Swarthmore College.

For financial support of this project, I wish to acknowledge the Mabelle McLeod Lewis Memorial Fund; the Doreen B. Townsend Center for the Humanities at the University of California, Berkeley; the Graduate Division of the University of California, Berkeley; and the Office of Graduate Studies and Research at the University of Maryland, College Park. Work on this book was completed at the Center for the Humanities at Wesleyan University, and I am thankful to the Andrew W. Mellon Foundation for supporting my residency there.

SEX SCANDAL

ONE

Victorian Britain is mainly remembered for two things: sexual prudishness and long novels. This book considers the relationship between
these two achievements—the one, which inhibited the Victorians from
speaking, and the other, which occasioned their extraordinary volu-
bility. The period from 1860 to 1900 witnessed both the consolidation
of modern sexual categories and the height of the long novel's cultural
authority. In these years, prudishness drove fiction in contradictory directions, compelling it to generate and to prohibit discussion of sexuality. Sex scandals, both as they appear in novels and as they form a
cultural context for literary production, supply the clearest means of
making legible these conflicting tendencies. Newspaper scandal stories
show the nineteenth-century imagination of sexuality at its most dramatic and public. In so doing, they elucidate the operations of the novel,
which offers a formally structured and covert aspect of this imagination. Through the combined effects of newspapers and novels, sexuality
in the nineteenth century became the subject routinely and paradoxically signaled by its ineffability—a subject that consequently produces
volatile effects at the moments when it approaches explicit articulation.
Like the novel, the scandal story, which publicly broadcasts information
ordinarily kept secret, supplies a rich vein of cultural material through
which to investigate language about sexuality.

Sex scandal is a Victorian phenomenon, but anyone within range of the mass media today needs hardly be told that it is not only Victorian. Nineteenth-century scandals establish the terms for, and supply the history of, the manifest absorption of contemporary Anglo-American culture in sensational stories of sexual exposure. Our own press tends to ignore the fact that scandal even *has* a history, treating each new case as if it sprang up sui generis.[1] The moment of scandal is a long one, and if its origins reach back in Europe and America at least to the eighteenth century, scandal stories continue today to propel mass aesthetic forms and popular-press reporting. While the discursive status of sexuality has indisputably changed in this period, sexual transgressions still provoke the most sensational media spectacles. Even if, as we often imagine, we have become inured to hearing news about sex, we are still shocked — or, at least, we are told that others are shocked — by sexual disclosures. Media reports insist that the public is outraged by the revelation of sexual secrets not necessarily because people *are* outraged, but because a consensus that sex ought not to be talked about in public continues powerfully to hold sway.

Foucault's analysis of power and pleasure in volume 1 of *The History of Sexuality* remains the most compelling demonstration we have that sexuality is constructed in language.[2] Even without Foucault, we might have suspected from the Victorians that silence about sexuality composes a strategic form, not an absence, of representation.[3] Anyone concerned with the language of sexuality must therefore pay attention to the manifold processes through which sex is made silent and its silence laden with meaning. The unspeakable status of sexuality is not added to sex, as a result of censorship or repression, but is the very condition for its modern discursive formulation. Consequently, rather than entertain

1. There have been remarkably few attempts to theorize scandal, and even studies that take it as their explicit subject provide no general account of the phenomenon; for instance, R. B. Martin, *Enter Rumour: Four Early Victorian Scandals* (London: Faber and Faber, 1962), and H. Montgomery Hyde, *A Tangled Web: Sex Scandals in British Politics and Society* (London: Futura, 1986). The criticism that does exist tends more to participate in the practices of scandalmongering journalism than to attempt an analysis of such operations; see, for example, Colin Wilson and Donald Seaman, *Scandal! An Encyclopedia* (London: Weidenfeld and Nicolson, 1986).

2. Michel Foucault, *The History of Sexuality*, vol. 1, trans. Robert Hurley (New York: Vintage, 1978).

3. For informative analyses of nineteenth-century sexual discourses, as well as capacious reviews of scholarship in the field, see James R. Kincaid, *Child-Loving: The Erotic Child and Victorian Culture* (New York: Routledge, 1992); and Roy Porter and Lesley Hall, *The Facts of Life: The Creation of Sexual Knowledge in Britain, 1650–1950* (New Haven: Yale University Press, 1995).

the question of ultimate causality—*why* is sex scandalous?—which presumes that sex can be explained (usually by naturalized categories of psychology or economy), this study pursues the question of *how* sex was made scandalous—or, better, how scandal helped to make sex, and how this process paradoxically produced it as unutterable.

Foucault leaves largely untouched the most professionalized institution for imaginative writing in the nineteenth century, and the principal beneficiary of this discursive situation: literature.[4] The readings I undertake in this book show that sexual unspeakability does not function simply as a collection of prohibitions for Victorian writers. Rather, it affords them abundant opportunities to develop an elaborate discourse—richly ambiguous, subtly coded, prolix and polyvalent—that we now recognize and designate by the very term *literary*. Like other restrictions upon expression, the conventions of sexual unspeakability serve writers as a productive constraint, contributing to a certain historical formation of the literary. Literature in turn supplies a culturally privileged repository for the production, and recognition, of sexuality as unspeakable. I emphasize the term *unspeakable* throughout this book, for it usefully condenses two meanings: something *incapable* of being articulated as well as something *prohibited* from articulation.[5] The term is especially apt for a literary project insofar as it indicates that, despite their exclusion from spoken language, sexual subjects might nonetheless find their way into written matter. This inscription is not always intentional, but its meanings are secreted in particular forms of writing where they could not be made in overt enunciations.[6]

4. D. A. Miller, *The Novel and the Police* (Berkeley: University of California Press, 1988), cites this as "perhaps the most notable reticence in Foucault's work" (viii, n. 1).

5. Elisabeth Lyon offers a brief and provocative discussion of the term in her introduction to the special issue "Unspeakable Images" of *Camera Obscura* 24 (September 1990): 5–6. Lyon writes of how, in the definition of the word *unspeakable*, "desire and prohibition are plotted, from pleasure to displeasure to interdiction, from the subject to the law" (5). On the sexual unspeakability of the Victorian novel, see Ruth Bernard Yeazell, "Podsnappery, Sexuality, and the English Novel," *Critical Inquiry* 9 (December 1982): 339–57, who writes, invoking Foucault, that "the silences of the novel are part of its discourse" (357). Eve Kosofsky Sedgwick writes of the ways in which the unspeakable in Henry James's writing serves to cover the secret of the homosexual closet in *Epistemology of the Closet* (Berkeley: University of California Press, 1990), 201–5 (see also 163–67), and "Is the Rectum Straight?" *Tendencies* (Durham: Duke University Press, 1993), 75–77.

6. Ann Banfield, *Unspeakable Sentences: Narration and Representation in the Language of Fiction* (Boston: Routledge & Kegan Paul, 1982), suggests that a syntax that literally cannot be spoken may designate the literary itself in the modern period.

If the requirements for discretion about sexuality supply a resource for literary writers, the same might also be said of scandalmongering journalists, who must convey the sexual content of their stories without offending their readership. Given all the fanfare of revelation and indignation associated with scandal, it may seem odd to argue that it makes anything less, rather than more, speakable. One might propose that the Victorians were in some full sense capable of talking about sex — and nowhere would this garrulousness be more evident than in a sex scandal.[7] But in bringing forth sexual activities for public consideration, scandal announces them in such a way as to establish their status as private, rather than — as scandal discourse itself encourages us to believe — radically to violate that status. However pious and disciplinary the public narrative scandal produces about private sexual transgression, though, its effects cannot be predicted according to formulas for ideological containment.[8] While it inculcates an understanding of normative behav-

---

7. On Foucault's model, scandal is one of the discourses that exercises power, for power accommodates the resistance scandal offers. Miller writes, "Modern social organization has made even 'scandal' a systematic function of its routine self-maintenance" (*Novel and the Police*, xii). Foucault's notion of power is infinitely variegated and decentralized:

> Discourses are not once and for all subservient to power or raised up against it, any more than silences are. We must make allowance for the complex and unstable process whereby discourse can be both an instrument and an effect of power, but also *a hindrance, a stumbling-block, a point of resistance* and a starting point for an opposing strategy. Discourse transmits and produces power; it reinforces it, but also undermines and exposes it, renders it fragile and makes it possible to thwart it. (*History of Sexuality*, vol. 1, 100–101; emphasis added)

It is worth noting in this context that an older sense of scandal is precisely "hindrance" or "stumbling-block"; the earliest English work I have identified on the subject, H. H. Hammond, *Of Scandall* (Oxford, 1644), states that scandal "signifies any *Obstacle* or *hindrance* laydd in a mans way . . . a *stone* or *blocke* in the way, at which men are apt (if they be not carefull, or if they goe in the darke) to stumble and fall." Here, scandal is taken in a religious sense — "*Scandall* signifies either some *sinne*, the *occasion of farther sinne* in others; or else some what else, which though it be not sinne, yet occasions sinne in others, though very indirectly sometimes" — and its modern meaning, "*slander or calumny or defamation*," is treated as "a sense which is vulgar amongst us in English" and is too rare to "deserve to be taken into consideration" (emphasis in original).

8. For an analysis of problems endemic to the so-called subversion/containment paradigm, especially in the context of performativity, see Joseph Litvak, *Caught in the Act: Theatricality in the Nineteenth-Century English Novel* (Berkeley: University of California Press, 1992), which is at many points relevant to this study. Litvak "attempt[s] to gesture beyond, or perhaps beneath, the dichotomy of subversion versus authority, indicating the need for more plural and discriminate ways of analyzing theatrical (and literary) poli-

ior in its audience, scandal also provides the opportunity to formulate questions, discuss previously unimagined possibilities, and forge new alliances. A social drama that enhances the power of one group may at the same time disempower others; while it gratifies some, it terrorizes others. And while scandal teaches punitive lessons, often deliberately intended to induce conformity in its audience, its thrilling terrors always pose the danger of inciting disobedience to the norms they advertise.

The scandalousness of an act hinges upon the degree of secrecy requisite to its commission. The Victorian scandals most revealing about the imagination of sexual privacy are therefore those that concern the sexual activity construed as most insistently covert, sex between men. Male-male sex is literally unspeakable: sodomy—which, by the midnineteenth century, is identified principally as sex between men—is defined (in Latin) by English law as the crime not to be named. The period under consideration here saw categories of sexual identity emerging in medical, legal, and social-scientific thinking; the male homosexual occupied a cardinal place in this classification, and hence in the larger process of folding sexual into personal identity.[9] While misdirected and uncontrolled male sexuality generated public displays of disgust and horror, the Victorian ideology that desexualizes women also provoked numerous scandals. Feminist scholars have demonstrated the scandalousness of women who were seen in public to be overly or inappropriately sexual, and this project builds upon that work in analyzing the concurrent mechanisms of exposure that surround deviant male bodies, and in considering the differences that gender makes there.[10] While the willful effort to deny female sexuality resulted in celebrated adultery,

---

tics. . . . The authority-subversion dualism itself, at least as it is often deployed . . . fails to be very useful, not to say very interesting" (115).

9. See Jeffrey Weeks, Coming Out: Homosexual Politics in Britain, from the Nineteenth Century to the Present (London: Quartet, 1977), and Sex, Politics and Society: The Regulation of Sexuality Since 1800, 2d ed. (London: Longman, 1989). The most thoroughgoing analysis of the conditions for the emergence of modern sexual identities, and of their effects, is Sedgwick, Epistemology of the Closet.

10. Newspaper sex scandals that focus on female subjects abound, and feminist scholars have convincingly demonstrated the scandalousness of the exposed and publicized female body; see, for example, Mary Poovey, Uneven Developments: The Ideological Work of Gender in Mid-Victorian England (Chicago: University of Chicago Press, 1988), chap. 3, on Caroline Norton; and Judith R. Walkowitz, City of Dreadful Delight: Narratives of Sexual Danger in Late-Victorian London (Chicago: University of Chicago Press, 1992), chap. 6, on Mrs. Weldon.

divorce, and illegitimacy cases, ironically it largely precluded lesbian scandals, which were less unspeakable than unthinkable; indeed, the refusal of lawmakers to believe in the possibility of sex between women is supposed to have exempted it from statutory prohibition.[11] Male homosexual scandals, by contrast, serve as an especially incisive point in Victorian culture for the production of sexual discourse, and the actual scandals I consider at length are consequently trials for sex between men.

In the Victorian period, scandals of all sorts proliferated in the popular press. In part as a result of the repeal of the stamp tax in 1855 and the paper duty in 1860, the number of newspapers in Great Britain multiplied, and they became cheaper, more widely available, and more national in scope. This burgeoning medium generated stories for popular consumption on a scale that had not been possible before, and the character of both newspapers and news itself changed significantly.[12] The papers' greater availability, coupled with increasing literacy, made scandals publicly accessible in new ways. As much as scandalous news may have exploded in the second half of the nineteenth century, however, this is not to argue that there were no scandals before 1855, nor that, characteristic as it is of this era, scandal is uniquely Victorian. Events from earlier periods, such as the South Sea Bubble, the Queen Caroline affair, and numerous notorious divorce cases, certainly fall under the rubric of scandal. Such antecedents notwithstanding, I suggest that scan-

---

11. For exceptions to the rule in the period prior to this one, see Emma Donoghue, *Passions Between Women: British Lesbian Culture, 1668–1801* (New York: HarperCollins, 1995).

12. Richard Altick's is the classic documentation of these shifts in *The English Common Reader* (Chicago: University of Chicago Press, 1957). Altick suggests the contents of the Radical Sunday papers, especially popular for shared reading in coffeehouses before the repeal of paper duties: "Exposés of governmental corruption, ministerial obstinacy, the stupidity or knavery of politicians, the greed of employers, and the sexual immorality reportedly endemic in the ruling class had a powerful appeal to multitudes who cared little for their specific political implications but relished their sensationalism" (345). Raymond Williams charts the growth of the popular press in *The Long Revolution* (New York: Columbia University Press, 1961), writing that "undoubtedly, in this period [1855–96], an attention to crime, sexual violence, and human oddities made its way from the Sunday into these daily papers, and also into older papers" (195). See also Lucy Brown, *Victorian News and Newspapers* (Oxford: Clarendon Press, 1985). On the more general capacity of newspapers (along with novels) to build consensus for nationalist ideologies, see Benedict Anderson, *Imagined Communities: Reflections on the Origin and Spread of Nationalism*, rev. ed. (London: Verso, 1991), who writes of the "profound fictiveness" of "the newspaper as cultural product" (33).

dal assumes its modern form only once several conditions are met: that news media are national and accessible; that they distance the subjects of their stories from their audience enough to effect a divide between the exposed private life and the anonymous public reading about it; and that the audience itself is conceived in terms sufficiently capacious to encompass a wide range of class, gender, and geographical positions.

The term *scandal* is often used, in vaguely metaphorical ways, with regard to any public outrage.[13] My concern here, however, is with a social phenomenon that has determinable characteristics and a consistent structure. In terms of form, scandal is a densely plotted narrative, with relatively fixed constituent parts: an accuser exposes an indiscretion or iniquity in the life of an accused and broadcasts that secret for public consumption, and the accused responds with denials.[14] Even if it does not come to an actual trial, scandal still relies on the tripartite juridical model of plaintiff, defendant, and jury. The public interest evinced in a case is itself the product of several factors: the quality of the charges (how titillating they are felt to be), the symbolic status of the actors (how prominent a class or celebrity position they occupy), and the destructiveness of the proceedings (how much damage they have potential for). Dissemination and consumption of the scandal depends upon a popular press that finds it profitable to make news out of stories

13. The anthology *Victorian Scandals: Representations of Gender and Class*, ed. Kristine Ottesen Garrigan (Athens, Ohio: Ohio University Press, 1992), for instance, lacks a systematic definition of its announced subject matter; the essays cover topics that probably fall within the domain of scandal (the wrongful confinement of women by their husbands, a prominent case of breach of marital promise) along with several that do not (debates over the education of women, the representation of the actress). The afterword by Thaïs E. Morgan, however, addresses some questions about the general operations of scandal in the period.

14. Harriet Bridgeman and Elizabeth Drury, *Society Scandals* (Newton Abbot: David & Charles, 1977), make the only attempt I know of to delineate its properties.

> Gossip and its more succulent and mature relation, scandal, are judgements made of a contemporary, exaggerated by the desire to entertain an audience or to injure the subject. The best scandal begins as rumour and develops gradually. It must falter through lack of information or invention, twist and turn and involve new and well known personalities. It is wittily delivered, contributing to the stature of its originator. It is engrossing because it entails a moral or social outrage; because it is competitive; because it strikes a blow at the socially secure or successful or because there are serious implications—a criminal offense or the possibility of severe disgrace or punishment. (7)

These generalizations are perceptive and mainly accurate.

about private life, and more generally upon conditions that Alexander Welsh has described as forming a knowledge industry.[15]

In temporal terms, scandal is composed of two discrete moments: the first comprises the alleged event that transgresses community moral standards and is therefore hidden; the second publicly recapitulates that earlier moment, lending the scandal its narrative form. The following letter from the Cleveland Street affair of 1889–90, which implicated prominent aristocrats in a homosexual prostitution ring, highlights this twofold process, displaying the distribution of the term *scandal*. In the letter, the director of public prosecutions expresses to the attorney general his dismay over the decision not to prosecute a nobleman for involvement in a male brothel:

> The moral effect of [the evidence] leaves no reasonable doubt that Lord Arthur Somerset was a frequent visitor at 19 Cleveland Street *for immoral purposes*. The public scandal involved in a criminal charge against a man in his position in society is undoubted—but in my opinion the public scandal in declining to prefer such a charge—and in permitting such a man to hold Her Majesty's Commission and to remain in English Society is much greater.
>
> In my opinion the attempt to avoid such publicity—even if such attempt was justifiable—which in my judgement it is not—must absolutely fail—and the public scandal will then be infinitely aggravated.
>
> Whatever may be said, and much may be said—as to the public policy of allowing *private* persons—being full-grown men to indulge their unnatural tastes—in private—or in such a way as not necessarily to come to public knowledge—in my judgement, the circumstances of this case demand the intervention of those whose duty it is to enforce the law . . . and no consideration of public scan-

---

15. In *George Eliot and Blackmail* (Cambridge, Mass.: Harvard University Press, 1985), Welsh examines the relationship between secrecy and information/knowledge, refracted through Eliot's later novels, particularly as embodied in the blackmailer's threat to reveal someone else's private life and destroy his or her reputation. In a section especially useful for this project, "The Pathology of Information," Welsh documents the preconditions for blackmail: "The growth of knowledge and communication in the nineteenth century, the rise of publicity and division of public and private life, and attitudes toward evidence attendant upon the commitment to crime prevention" (29). Generally speaking, blackmail is the antidote to scandal (when it works) or its precursor (when it does not).

dal—owing to the position in society or sympathy with the family of the offender should militate against this *paramount duty*.[16]

The first potential scandal, over Lord Arthur's "immoral" behavior, works in the usual way, by transforming hidden information into public knowledge, but the case is made difficult by the Crown's reluctance to prosecute a man who holds "Her Majesty's Commission." Yet his secret, once revealed, cannot be ignored, and so another scandal—over a failure to act—hangs before the government. Not to expose the nobleman's actions would precipitate a "public scandal" about government protection of him; whether or not the case comes to trial, then, an exposé is certain. In giving past private indiscretions the form of a popular narrative, scandal enables so-called public morals to exercise social control, even as it threatens to run out of the control of those who wield it.

As scandal recasts secret activities into a public story of exposure, it makes questions about truth almost impossible to answer, however deliberately it mobilizes truth-determining institutions (police interrogation, trial procedures, legislative inquiries). For while the motor that keeps the scandal machine running is the detective and legal work of verifying accusations, conclusive demonstration of the truth is inimical to a scandal's sustenance. Unlike criminal charges in general, exoneration is rarely possible from charges of scandalous behavior. A scandal's success is measured not by its accuracy but by its popularity and the damage it does to the accused's reputation. A scandal has public effects regardless of a final determination of its truth or falsity, and it captures public attention only to the extent that such a determination is deferred.

While scandal does not by definition concern sex, in its quintessential and paradigmatic form it focuses on sexual transgression. Financial and political scandals abound in the nineteenth century, and they are related to sex scandals insofar as they too rely on the public exposure of private information that damages its subject's reputation. At a moment when distinctions between private and public life are increasingly scrutinized, however, and in which private subjectivity is consolidating around a core of sexual identity, scandals about sex come to be the characteristic type of the genre. The intensification of social purity movements, which drew on evolving medical and scientific ideas about sexuality, partly explains the preponderance of sex scandals in the second half of the nine-

16. Quoted in Lewis Chester, David Leitch, and Colin Simpson, *The Cleveland Street Affair* (London: Weidenfeld and Nicolson, 1976), 72–73 (emphasis in original).

teenth century.[17] In large measure through the agency of scandal, these movements extended a reign of moral conservatism and effected reform of the laws that govern sexual conduct. A variety of social dramas that involve the crossing of public and private boundaries are subsumed by sex scandals in this era, and scandals that explicitly concern sexual misconduct frequently turn out to simplify or to serve as a cover for the violation of other social boundaries. Even the most licentious scandal rarely arises solely in the wake of a sexual transgression; most cases involve the crossing of rigid class, national, or racial lines, as well as the highly ossified gender divide, which organize Victorian society.[18]

The forbidden status of sexual subjects, and the public enchantment by them, allows sex to dramatize other kinds of social conflict, and to make otherwise boring subjects seem interesting. Every journalist knows that the surest way to ruin politicians and celebrities is to raise a scandal over their private sexual indiscretions, however irrelevant such behavior is to the performance of their public roles. The adultery trial that destroyed Irish Home Rule leader Charles Stewart Parnell in 1890 is the outstanding example of a politically consequential scandal in the Victorian era, and it was performed on a stage of sexual misconduct. If the period's most important political scandal was sexual, the one most famous for being sexual may itself have been politically motivated— for Oscar Wilde's 1895 trials were, by some accounts, the direct result of a partisan conspiracy.[19] Political ends are not the only ones to which

17. See Frank Mort, *Dangerous Sexualities: Medico-Moral Politics in England Since 1830* (London: Routledge, 1987).

18. In *Allegories of Empire: The Figure of Woman in the Colonial Text* (Minneapolis: University of Minnesota Press, 1993), Jenny Sharpe writes about reporting of the Indian sepoy mutinies of 1857:

> Operating behind a screen of decency that demanded it withhold details, the English press generated a narrative desire around what it did not say. The editorials divulged information in hints and innuendos, while the stories accompanying them were pieced together from the testimonies of eyewitnesses who were often not present at the scenes they describe. . . . The sensationalist stories, which are to be found in private letters, newspapers, and popular histories, all circle around a single, unrepresentable center: the rape of English women. Upon declaring the sepoy crimes to be "unspeakable," the Mutiny reports offer a range of signification that has the same effect as the missing details. (61–62, 66)

Sharpe's discussion of the politics of this scandal in the colonial setting accords with my analysis of the relationship among scandal, sexual unspeakability, and ideological fictions on the domestic front.

19. Lord Alfred Douglas and others had evidence that the Liberals scapegoated Wilde in exchange for protection of high-ranking homosexual politicians within the party. See

sexual means can effectively be used. The most prominent Victorian scandalmonger, journalist W. T. Stead, was undeniably sanctimonious, but his primary motivation for generating *causes célèbres* was to bolster sales of the paper he edited, the *Pall Mall Gazette*. On the grounds of sexual immorality, Stead demolished the promising career of Liberal M.P. and cabinet minister Sir Charles Dilke in the wake of a series of divorce trials in 1886, and it remains uncertain whether he was motivated by politics, profit, or prurience.[20]

While the press is the vehicle for such cases, and it profits from them, journalists serve a public culture that thrives on seeing secrets exposed. Beyond the moral outrage that typically confronts the accused person, the representation of scandal itself often becomes scandalous, redoubling the effect as it collapses into the originating event. Public indignation over such lurid narratives may explain why nineteenth-century scandals often reach the court in the form of libel cases and why news media are so frequently held responsible for creating the scandals they report. The press cultivates various techniques to protect itself against the backlash of such charges. An attitude of self-righteous piety like Stead's, for example, justifies sensationalistic reporting as a duty, and capitalizes on the shock ostensibly felt by the public. By contrast, the pose of urbane moral agnosticism frequently struck by the press simply assumes as its own the indifference to truth that belongs to the form of scandal itself; representatives of this position claim not to be surprised by the revelations they nevertheless trumpet as scandalous.

Whatever their inspiration and the means of their rationalization, scandals provide the opportunity for new types of knowledge about sexuality to circulate publicly. Victorian sex scandals, no less than those of today, are replete with the expert testimony of doctors and other spe-

---

Regenia Gagnier, *Idylls of the Marketplace: Oscar Wilde and the Victorian Public* (Stanford: Stanford University Press, 1986), app. B.

20. On Stead's role in the Dilke affair, Roy Jenkins, *Victorian Scandal* (New York: Pyramid, 1965), writes:

> It is impossible to read the files of [Stead's] paper for the weeks after the February trial without believing that his main interest was to print anything which would keep the case alive, and enable him to go on exploiting its sensationalism for some time to come. The *Pall Mall's* circulation had been dropping . . . and it badly needed to attract new readers. . . . [Stead] became seized with an abiding but self-righteous vindictiveness towards Dilke. He saw himself as the chosen instrument of public morality, protecting the innocent citizens of Britain against the impudent attempts of a shameless adulterer to climb back into their favour. (218)

cialists. If a case such as Dilke's appears in political history to be that of a man wronged in the public sphere, the fact that it occasioned reports of "French vices," such as ménage à trois, and of the loose sexual mores of London's high society, suggests how distinct its political effects were from its contributions to sexual ideology. Newspaper reports of the case made public the series of affairs carried on by four sisters in the aristocratic Eustace Smith family, who exchanged both lovers and venereal diseases. Such intelligence doubtless contributed to puritanical middle-class fantasies about the sexual depravity of the *haute monde*, but it may also have fostered notions of female sexual assertiveness, no matter how negative the portrayal of these particular characters. Similarly, the series of stories entitled "The Maiden Tribute of Modern Babylon," which preceded the Dilke affair in Stead's columns, both fulminated against the ease with which a young English girl could be purchased and included explicit directions for obtaining one. While the case eventuated in changes in the age-of-consent laws, it also feasibly put the idea of buying a virgin into the heads of men to whom it might otherwise never have occurred.[21]

Although scandal makes public the details of private life, the privacy at issue must be that of a person in whom the public has some reason to be interested. Usually the subjects of scandal elicit public curiosity because they are themselves, or are linked to, celebrities (that is, public figures), although those who symbolize a population under scrutiny for other reasons also become the subjects of scandal. The buggery trial I discuss in chapter 3, for instance, concerns young men who were not previously known to a wide audience, but both their connection to noblemen and their own symbolic status, as middle-class youths whose gender presentation had gone inexplicably wrong, made them the object of intense public attention. A case that ran concurrently in the newspapers with this one, however, the Mordaunt divorce, is representative of stories that make news primarily because of the fame of their participants. This case arose in 1870 when a young woman told her husband, a baronet and Conservative M.P., that she had committed adultery with several men, among them the Prince of Wales, and that their only child was illegitimate and infected with venereal disease. The husband, Sir

21. See Jenkins, *Victorian Scandal*, chap. 15, on Dilke; and Walkowitz, *City of Dreadful Delight*, chaps. 3–4, on the "Maiden Tribute." Walkowitz writes, "The 'Maiden Tribute' and its imitations, Stead's critics argued, actually encouraged the crimes it had set out to expose. . . . His publication simultaneously incited an interest in the sexual and helped to mobilize a new offensive against the obscene" (124–25).

Charles Mordaunt, sued for divorce, and his wife's family responded by pleading that she had been insane when she made the admission. When the case went to court for the first of five eventual trials, the Prince of Wales appeared on the stand as corespondent to deny the charges. In the divorce court, the presiding judge made the following comments on the public fascination with scandal:

> There are those who will lament that matters of this kind, aris-ing between husband and wife, should become topics of public discussion; and there may be some who think that such public dis-cussion, carrying with it, as it does, knowledge of immorality and matters which every one would wish should be kept from the eyes of many, is not desirable. It may be said, and I dare say has been said, that the avidity of the public to take part in the interest of this trial is a thing that is to be deplored, as showing a desire to participate in the investigation of immoral questions. But, gentle-men, I am not quite sure whether that is a correct description of the reason why this trial has occupied so much attention. Those who stand in high places are always objects of attention. It is un-fortunately true that in the proceedings of this court there is not a week or a day that passes which would not furnish materials that to such depraved tastes would be equally acceptable. It is on account of the position in society held by those who are implicated in this matter that it has excited and occupied so much of the public at-tention. And surely it is natural that those who stand in high places should be conspicuous; and those who are conspicuous naturally attract attention. It is that circumstance, and not the mere details connected with the case, which has excited such keen interest.[22]

The judge's statement raises a number of issues central to the formation of scandal. It points to the ways in which public interest in "immo-rality" is felt to be reprehensible, especially when this public requires moral guidance. Even though the judge presents himself as neutral on this question, the public airing of private indiscretions cannot but serve to instruct the audience in what is considered corrupting. When he dis-misses concerns over the public's interest in the case by attributing them merely to the conspicuousness of "those who stand in high places," however, he betrays a certain disingenuousness. That the actors in the

---

22. *An Official Report of the Cause Célèbre Mordaunt v. Mordaunt, Cole, and Johnstone* (London: Evans, Oliver, 1870), 114.

trial are famous makes it a public matter, but the sexual content is what gives the case its interest. The popularity of the trial provides the occasion for discussing a host of questions: about aristocrats' sexual habits, about the veracity of a supposed madwoman's confessions (it was the first time the divorce court had to deal with an insanity plea), about postpartum depression (from which Lady Mordaunt seemed to be suffering), about venereal disease, and about the wrongful confinement of women in mental hospitals—not to mention the unmentionable details that surfaced of Lady Mordaunt's hysterical fits, involving everything from smearing herself with fecal matter to threats of suicide and infanticide.[23]

A case with such conspicuous participants and such tantalizing contents sponsors rumors that are in themselves often felt to be menacing. There is, however, an important distinction to be made between scandal and the related phenomenon of gossip. While scandals always generate and frequently originate in gossip, the latter is far less formally structured than scandal. Gossip, as the term is ordinarily used, takes place within a circumscribed community, and its objects tend to be known personally to those engaging in it. The modern scandal, by comparison, is a function of mass media, which rely on an anonymous audience far from the event's dramatis personae.[24] Even more closely related to scandal is sensation—and in some cases they converge—but I differentiate between them because sensation designates a public effect while not, like scandal, necessarily exposing incidents construed as secret by the nature of their commission. By contrast with scandal, which reveals the

23. See Hyde, *Tangled Web*, 98.

24. Max Gluckman, in "Gossip and Scandal," *Current Anthropology* 4 (June 1963): 307–16, does not make a sharp distinction between the two phenomena, largely because the domain of his inquiry is pre-urban and pre-industrial society. Gluckman understands gossip to bind communities together, demarcating insiders from outsiders: "A community . . . is partly held together and maintains its values by gossiping and scandalizing both within cliques and in general. . . . Gossip, and even scandal, have important positive virtues. Clearly they maintain the unity, morals and values of social groups. Beyond this, they enable these groups to control the competing cliques and aspiring individuals of which all groups are composed" (308). Patricia Meyer Spacks, *Gossip* (New York: Alfred A. Knopf, 1985), also considers her subject mostly in the context of self-contained communities. This purview allows Spacks to generalize about gossip's function as a community bonding agent, a subversive mode of discourse for subordinated groups, and a means of social control. Spacks's extensive comments on the affinities between gossip and imaginative literature (in particular, the novel) have bearing on my discussion of scandal's constitutive role in Victorian fiction, but the account of gossip is sometimes so general that it seems capable of serving any social function.

secrets of famous people, the sensation is what makes its subject note-worthy. Gruesome murder cases, for instance, create sensations, but no one can be said to be scandalized by them; they simply represent crimi-nal activity that for various reasons makes tantalizing news. On the other hand, an adultery scandal—though its revelation may be sensational—gains its force by making public a particular person's private life.[25]

Through the information they circulate, scandals propagate new sexual knowledge, and they accomplish this task partly through their representation of the public imagined to receive such material. News-paper battles over how much evidence to report make explicit the fan-tasy of embodied public opinion, and this public comes to be imagined in quite concrete ways.[26] Scandal reports make a vivid spectacle out of gender and class differences—features fundamental to the imagination of the public itself—and contests over sexuality in such accounts throw into confusion the preexisting categories for these stories' public recep-tion. In the light of such cases, the usual nineteenth-century alignment of the bourgeois public/private dichotomy with respective male and female spheres appears to be an ideological fiction—one that feminist historians have shown is both variable and unstable.[27] Despite the usual construction of the public sphere as male, scandal's public is routinely portrayed as female, whether because of its penchant for gossip or its imagined need for paternalistic custody. At the same time, the abject private bodies that scandal puts on public display are by no means ex-

25. Studies of newspaper sensations and the sensation novels of the 1860s tend not to interrogate the relationship between their literary and nonliterary materials beyond gen-eral assertions about a Victorian Zeitgeist that produced both. See Richard Altick, *Evil Encounters: Two Victorian Sensations* (London: John Murray, 1986); Thomas Boyle, *Black Swine in the Sewers of Hampstead: Beneath the Surface of Victorian Sensationalism* (New York: Viking, 1989); and Winifred Hughes, *The Maniac in the Cellar: Sensation Novels of the 1860s* (Princeton: Prince-ton University Press, 1980). Ann Cvetkovich analyzes sensation fiction in relation to nineteenth-century sexual and class ideologies in *Mixed Feelings: Feminism, Mass Culture, and Victorian Sensationalism* (New Brunswick: Rutgers University Press, 1992).
26. On the formation of the concept of public opinion in the nineteenth century, and on J. S. Mill's critical contributions to this effort, see Welsh, *George Eliot*, esp. chap. 4.
27. The chapter on "new social actors" in Walkowitz, *City of Dreadful Delight*, as well as Leonore Davidoff and Catherine Hall, *Family Fortunes: Men and Women of the English Middle Class, 1780–1850* (London: Hutchinson, 1987), suggest how women materially entered the sphere designated public in the nineteenth century; Poovey, *Uneven Developments*, de-constructs the strict public/private alignment with gender division by showing how the very categories mutually inhabit each other. Jürgen Habermas discusses the emergence of the public/private opposition in *The Structural Transformation of the Public Sphere: An Inquiry into a Category of Bourgeois Society*, trans. Thomas Burger (Cambridge, Mass.: MIT Press, 1991).

clusively female, as cases of deviant masculinity demonstrate decisively.

Scandal stories thus have important ramifications for the public sphere against which they differentiate privacy. The distinction between the terms *scandal* and *scandalize* condenses the difference between these private and public effects. The subject of *scandal* is the public person whose private life is exposed; but those who are *scandalized* form the drama's audience, the public that makes a revelation scandalous by feeling it to be so. Feeling is indeed crucial to the process, for scandal trades on emotions: it does its work less by extinguishing unorthodox or illegitimate behavior than by generating powerfully affecting narratives, which elicit horror, pleasure, shame, and enthrallment in its audience.[28] By dint of the reactions scandal arouses, and the terror of humiliation it instills, its audience members learn to feel what behavior is normative, what is deviant, and who is privileged to adjudicate between them. While it may terrify, scandal is also—as its endless popularity testifies—an undeniable source of pleasure to its consumers. The ways in which readers respond to such pleasure is itself telling. A refined audience, which esteems such enjoyment prurience, finds itself embarrassed by its own interest in this sort of news, and frequently disavows the scandalized response by attributing it to others. Yet even readers who frankly admit to the pleasure of witnessing someone else troubled, disgraced, or exposed—readers therefore designated vulgar—will, if they *are* truly scandalized, end up getting more than their fascination had bargained for.

As a public drama about the sins of private life, scandal generates news whose ideological compulsions are all the more powerful for being experienced as popular entertainment. Occupying the borderline between news and amusement, between hard facts and speculative fictions, scandal—its reputation for vulgar, plebeian appeal notwithstanding—discloses affinities with more decorous forms of fictional narrative, to which I now want to turn.[29]

While it ought to be obvious, it has not been remarked that scandal, often sex scandal, structures the usual plot of the realist novel in the Vic-

28. William Ian Miller, *Humiliation and Other Essays on Honor, Social Discomfort, and Violence* (Ithaca: Cornell University Press, 1993), supplies a thoughtful discussion of the affective dimension of social life.

29. In addition to the works cited in notes above, the following contain accounts of other scandals in the nineteenth century: J. B. Atlay, *Famous Trials of the Century* (London:

torian period. The typical story of the Victorian novel involves the loss and eventual recovery of a fortune, benefactor, parent, child, sibling, or spouse. The course of recovery necessitates disclosure of a secret, which has been hidden because it is in some way immoral or illegal; most often, it involves adultery or illegitimacy. The plot of the novel unfolds by threatening and finally effecting the exposure of this secret to the community, and once this revelation has occurred, the goods (property, family) are redistributed, now more justly, among those who survive. The novelistic plot, distilled in this way, is analogous to the form of the scandal. Let us take the well-known example of Charles Dickens's *Bleak House* (1852–53), although other equally canonical works—Charlotte Brontë's *Jane Eyre* (1847) or George Eliot's *Middlemarch* (1871–72), for instance—would do just as well. The plot of *Bleak House* is driven by the impulse to disclose Lady Dedlock's premarital sexual liaison, which issued in the novel's protagonist, the illegitimate Esther. As is usual in Dickens, the narrative works to avoid the sexual revelation, and fear of exposure alone is enough to destroy several characters. It is also usual for Dickens to invoke a sex scandal in order to move the plot forward, but then to displace its full efflorescence onto a legal or financial scandal (in this case, the chancery suit of Jarndyce and Jarndyce). In the way that I have

---

Grant Richards, 1899); Madeline Bingham, Baroness Clenmorris, *Earls and Girls* (London: Hamish Hamilton, 1980); Henry Blyth, *The High Tide of Pleasure: Seven English Rakes* (London: Weidenfeld and Nicolson, 1970); Tom Cullen, *The Empress Brown: The Story of a Royal Friendship* (London: The Bodley Head, 1969); Richard Dellamora, *Masculine Desire: The Sexual Politics of Victorian Aestheticism* (Chapel Hill: University of North Carolina Press, 1990); Lillian Faderman, *Scotch Verdict* (New York: Quill, 1983); H. Montgomery Hyde, *The Love That Dared Not Speak Its Name* (Boston: Little, Brown, 1970); Christine Keeler and Robert Meadley, *Sex Scandals* (London: Xanadu, 1985); Charles Kingston, *Society Sensations* (London: Stanley Paul & Co., 1922); Thomas Laqueur, "The Queen Caroline Affair: Politics as Art in the Reign of George IV," *Journal of Modern History* 54 (September 1982): 417–66; Steven Marcus, *The Other Victorians: A Study of Sexuality and Pornography in Mid-Nineteenth Century England*, 2d ed. (New York: New American Library, 1974); Iain McCalman, *Radical Underworld: Prophets, Revolutionaries and Pornographers in London, 1795–1840* (Cambridge: Cambridge University Press, 1988); Michael Roe, *Kenealy and the Tichborne Cause: A Study in Mid-Victorian Populism* (Melbourne: Melbourne University Press, 1974); William Roughead, *Bad Companions* (Edinburgh: W. Green & Son, 1930); Roughead, *Malice Domestic* (Edinburgh: W. Green & Son, 1928); James D. Steakley, "Iconography of a Scandal: Political Cartoons and the Eulenburg Affair in Wilhelmin Germany," in *Hidden from History: Reclaiming the Gay and Lesbian Past*, ed. Martin Bauml Duberman, Martha Vicinus, and George Chauncey, Jr. (New York: New American Library, 1989), 233–63; and Janet Street-Porter, *Scandal!* (London: Allen Lane, 1981).

suggested is typical of scandals, a search for truth impels the story (particularly, in Bleak House, through the vehicle of the detective), but disclosure of the truth finally proves so unremarkable that it seems unequal to the energy expended in anticipating it. The fact of Lady Dedlock's sexual indiscretion and Esther's illegitimacy, that is to say, ultimately seems to be of little consequence. Like the scandals trumpeted in newsprint, the one threatened in the novel is sustained by deferral and protraction.

The connections between novels and newspaper scandal stories are not only structural, though; they arise from the deeply intertwined histories of the two forms, as the work of recent literary critics has made clear. Scandal and the novel derive, according to these accounts, from a common ancestor, and the history of the novel has involved a series of efforts actively to dissociate itself from the taint of scandal. Drawing in part on Lennard Davis's notion of an originally undifferentiated "news/novel matrix," as well as on Michael McKeon's account of how the novel came to privilege verisimilitude over accuracy, Catherine Gallagher has argued that the unique feature of novels—their fictionality (or explicit nonreferentiality)—arises in eighteenth-century England in reaction against earlier types of writing, which used fiction as an alibi for political scandal stories that encoded real-world referents.[30] Gallagher links this fictionality to fundamental literary conceptions then emerging: authorial property and originality, sympathetic characterization, and the conventions of realism. By the mid-nineteenth century, this constellation of literary features was so sturdily in place that the danger of novels being taken for stories about real people had virtually evaporated (except in the relatively anomalous case of the roman à clef). Victorian novelists betray little of their eighteenth-century forebears' characteristic anxiety about the representation of fiction rather than fact, and when they do express such concerns—for instance, in debates over realism— they are preoccupied more with aesthetic or philosophical than with moral questions, which are now cast in merely conventional terms. For all that novel-reading was still felt to endanger ingenuous readers, by the middle 1800s the genre could assert its triumph over charges of making scandal by appropriating scandal as its subject matter.[31]

30. Lennard Davis, Factual Fictions: The Origins of the English Novel (New York: Columbia University Press, 1983); Michael McKeon, The Origins of the English Novel, 1600–1740 (Baltimore: Johns Hopkins University Press, 1987); Catherine Gallagher, Nobody's Story: The Vanishing Acts of Women Writers in the Marketplace, 1670–1820 (Berkeley: University of California Press, 1994), esp. chap. 4.

31. The best source on the mid-Victorian legacy of efforts to sanitize the novel is Richard

Yet even the strongest form of the literary-historical argument—that novels and newspaper scandals share a parent—does not, in itself, account for the pervasiveness of scandal as the prototypical story of the novel in the nineteenth century. The scandal plot is so persistent, I suggest, because it provides a way of working out the novel's own double duty: the duty of telling stories composed centrally of incidents from private life and, simultaneously, of using these stories to teach widely applicable public lessons. Scandal motivates a type of moral pedagogy in the novel, generating exemplary narratives that both school readers in acceptable behavior and enable them to experience vicariously the violation of norms. Novels toe the orthodox line in castigating sexual transgression by the same means that they occasion its pleasurable consumption. Through the critique of scandal's procedures in which they frequently engage, moreover, literary works provide readers the thrill of following a scandal while exempting them from the discomfort of being scandalized.

The novel accomplishes this complex mediation by distinguishing its readership from scandal's own exalted or anathematized subjects. For just as scandals participate in the formation of a general public, lending that body an imaginary coherence and ascribing to it certain values, so the novel in the second half of the nineteenth century takes as one of its principal tasks to imagine an appropriate audience for itself, capable of reading and understanding it in the proper ways—particularly when it is in the hands of writers like George Eliot and Henry James, who strive to distinguish their highbrow work from its demotic origins. While scandals in the popular press rely on the invisibility of their audience to their victims, readers of Victorian novels know that fictional scandal stories, by contrast, are frequently set within circumscribed communities, in which gossip poses more of a threat than do newspapers. This difference can be explained in part by the nineteenth-century novel's propensity for nostalgia and its tendency to set the action back a generation or two. More importantly, fiction's evocation of this outdated gossip model of scandal, in which victims are personally known to their audience, serves as a screen for the identical conditions of anonymity and distance upon which the novel itself, as a mass cultural form, depends. As the product of imaginative labor, novels frequently seek to mystify the process of

---

Stang, *The Theory of the Novel in England, 1850–1870* (New York: Columbia University Press, 1959). Stang's evidence shows that the moral questions raised by novels in this period concern sexual explicitness in individual works, not the genre's ontological status.

their own manufacture for the marketplace, obscuring the contemporary conditions of the market through the anachronism of their setting.

A further connection between scandal and fiction bears directly on the lives of the authors here under consideration. It is no accident that many of the most prominent writers in an age in which respectability was paramount found themselves at odds with that ideology. If these authors were simply unusual in experiencing that tension, then their distance from the ethical standard might have supplied them the means of speaking powerfully to it; but their alienation from convention may itself have been more representative than is often acknowledged. The norm, that is to say, is rarely a lived reality, and deviance from it is probably more regular, not to say normal, than orthodoxy itself. Three of the fiction writers I treat—Dickens, Eliot, and Wilde—were themselves the subjects of sex scandals. For all of these writers, literature compensates for or recasts the problems of their scandalous lives. Charles Dickens's largely unobjectionable work—the definition of family reading—counterbalanced rumors of his clandestine infidelity and the public breakup of his marriage, while the literary productions of George Eliot challenged pious reactions to the open and ongoing scandal of her adulterous relationship with George Henry Lewes. The moral defensiveness of Dickens's fiction, as well as Eliot's high-handed efforts at discrediting scandalized responses, may have been two (among the many) models Oscar Wilde had in mind when he sought to justify his scandalous sex life with a literary alibi. The other major literary figure I consider, Anthony Trollope, led a relatively conventional private life, and his lack of sexual transgressivity may explain the sense that he among these authors appears to collude most closely with the scandal audience represented in fiction.

For a number of reasons, this study does not devote much attention to the literary genre most frequently identified with scandal: sensation fiction. While sensation novels typically turn on scandals, they tend to be concerned more with vividly representing the commission of scandalous acts than with commenting upon them and their reception. Such standards of the genre as Wilkie Collins's *The Woman in White* (1859–60) and Mary E. Braddon's *Lady Audley's Secret* (1862) aim to insinuate the reader into the scene of scandalous revelation and to eliminate any critical distance from the events they narrate, rather than to exploit that distance. These works were considered so notoriously corrupting in their own day less because they contain material unrepresented in other fiction than because they seem indifferent to the ethical questions that their scandalous plots raise. Writers of such work self-consciously exploited the outrageousness of their stories to render *themselves* scandalous and thereby to enhance their market value; whatever moral suspicion still adheres to the novel in the nineteenth century reaches its height with attacks on sensation fiction. This book focuses on scandal in the mainstream of the novel tradition rather than in its subgenres. The obvious pertinence to sensation fiction of scandal makes it relatively less interesting in such a context than in its appearance under the respectable heading of realism.

This effort is in keeping with my desire throughout this study to consider the appearance of deviant sexuality at the center of orthodox cultural formations, not just at the margins. I pursue this aim by locating a cannily erotic aspect of the Victorian imagination within the period's classic fiction. Such fiction frequently draws upon perversity, and not simply as the demon it conjures up to cast out; deviance is the cud that normative sexual ideology must constantly chew, swallowing and regurgitating it in order to derive its sustaining nutrients. As the most explicit form of sexual expression, however, illicit fiction—pornography—also illuminates conventional narratives. It functions both as a relative of the newspaper scandal story (as in chapter 3, where I discuss an explicitly pornographic rewriting of a scandal) and as the unacknowledged twin to respectable fiction (as in chapter 6, where I consider a pornographic text as the complement to Wilde's literary project). If in one sense pornography is continuous with more legitimate kinds of scandal stories, it also throws into relief the circumscription upon which both newspapers and novels rely. By virtue of being illicit, pornography claims to be capable of expressing anything, and this explicitness lays bare the coded language elsewhere requisite to conveying unspeakable content. Pornography demonstrates how self-regulating censorship subtends the full spectrum of scandal rhetoric, as it extends from courts of law to newspapers to novels. This censorship does not merely prohibit discourse, but serves as one of its enabling conditions.

If pornography marks the most explicitly sexual end of this continuum, on the other end, representing the most self-consciously literary form of expression, is the proper name. Proper names are a persistent point of interest in the chapters that follow—several of these readings turn on a name—and this focus is not coincidental. According to various critical accounts, proper names function as the very sign of the literary, and they operate by a logic analogous to that of sexual signification—

the unnameable—insofar as they too convey meanings by connotation.[32] The homology between proper names and sexual discourses is one of the crucial junctures of indeterminacy that enables the erotic and the literary mutually to generate each other. The names of characters, not to mention those of authors, are loaded with provocative suggestion, and in some cases they overlap with sexual meanings. While the effort to unveil its meanings sometimes seems to make too much of a name, not to expose them—like the refusal to acknowledge sexual signification simply because it is sexual—is to fall prey to the discretion upon which names (like sex) insist. Dickens's resourcefulness with characters' names has often been remarked, and Trollope and Wilde, I will argue, both strategically circulate the common meanings of their own names; the pseudonymity upon which Eliot's work depends may explain its less pronounced mobilization of names. In addition, the overdetermined names that appear in nonfiction cases exemplify the protoliterary qualities of scandal itself: it would be easy to label "ironic" the appearance of a Mr. Straight and a Mr. Flowers in the Boulton and Park homosexual scandal, or the involvement of young men named Newlove and Thickbroome in the Cleveland Street male prostitution case, but that would simply deny the literary potential of the world beyond the bindings of a novel. Scandal in fact always hangs upon a name, since reputation itself is about maintaining a good name, and keeping one's name out of the mouths of others is the principal goal of avoiding scandal.

Neither a phenomenology of scandal nor an encyclopedia of cases, this study strives to consider some of scandal's local effects on sexual ideology in nineteenth-century Britain. Interpreting literary works requires a different set of tools and methods than does analyzing nonfiction texts in a historical frame, and readers will detect corresponding differences in my approach to the various subjects I treat. I have allowed the material in each chapter to guide me by what seem to be its pertinent features and proclivities, yet regardless of the divergences among them, these readings are all indebted to deconstruction and psychoanalysis, even beyond the work of Foucault that shapes the project as a whole. While

32. Joel Fineman discusses how proper names indicate literary language in "The Significance of Literature: *The Importance of Being Earnest*," *October* 15 (Winter 1980): 79–90. In *Nobody's Story*, Gallagher suggests that proper names are the marker of fiction's defining nonreferentiality: "The most radical and least explored distinction between prenovelistic and novelistic narratives is that the former often claim particular extra-textual reference for their proper names and the latter normally do not" (165).

poststructuralist theory inflects the interpretations, however, the means I employ for unbinding the sexual possibilities within texts are at least as Victorian as they are Derridean. The logic of sexual unspeakability, that is to say, and the interpretive resources it necessitates, arise out of, as much as they are applied to, the nineteenth-century works I consider.

This work constitutes a project in gay studies not only because of its historical materials but also because of the historical moment in which it is written. The most sophisticated tools available for gaining leverage on the issues that interest me—privacy and publicity, conventional and aberrant sexualities and genders, the cultures of literary writing and sensational reporting—are those of gay-identified criticism. Such scholarship, and the larger cultural milieux it inhabits, have made evident the power relations that structure all sexuality, not only non-normative practices and identities, and have in turn made clear the effects on other forms of power that sexuality itself exerts. The persistence of sex scandal down to the present day, and the occasions it supplies for both castigating and vindicating deviancy, make critical the project of locating the conventions of this form of cultural exercise.

The next two chapters maintain a division in material between scandal and fiction. Chapter 2 argues that in *Great Expectations*, Dickens generates a type of linguistic expression continuous with a form of sexuality—male masturbation—perfectly suited to the secret and solipsistic imaginative work of the novel in general and of the male *Bildungsroman* in particular. In showing how literary language functions simultaneously to connote and to obscure sexual meanings, this chapter deliberately defers a consideration of scandal. By locating the collection of rhetorical techniques through which a sexual pulse can be felt beating subcutaneously in a novel that does not overtly represent sex, I identify a specifically literary form of sexual unspeakability in advance of the nonfiction public mode exemplified by scandal. A central concern of this argument, and one that recurs throughout my discussion of literary texts, is with the contradiction between the story that a novel tells and the language it uses to do the telling—or between what it professes in moments of metanarrative commentary and what its overdetermined language demonstrably accomplishes. In *Great Expectations*, this tension amounts to a contest between the overtly heterosexual (though largely abstemious) tale that is told and the frenzied non-normative sexual thematics inscribed in the narrative voice. The balance the novel thus achieves between discretion and expression serves effectively to hold scandal at bay.

By contrast with the Dickens novel, where we recognize the centrality of sex to private subjectivity only in its reticence, scandal performs the valuation of privacy in its very exposure of sexual secrets for public consumption. Examining journalistic, legal, medical, and pornographic accounts of the men accused of buggery in the Boulton and Park scandal, I analyze the costs exacted by scandal through this constitution of the private subject *as* a sexual subject in the third chapter. In the newspaper and the courtroom, moreover, discussions of sexuality serve as much to formulate the attributes of the public sphere—as an inviolate, decorporealized female body—as to imagine the private life of the anathematized subject in the perverse male body. While each account of the defendants conforms to the conventions of its own narrative genre, literature is a relatively minor player in this chapter. I explore the procedures of scandal in all the complexity of a single remarkable case from the archive, and suspend until the last section of the chapter consideration of its implications for literature.

The two lines of inquiry converge in the second half of the book, through a discussion of novels that explicitly take scandal as their plot and of a sex scandal demonstrably motivated by literary issues. My focus in the fourth and fifth chapters, on works by George Eliot and Anthony Trollope, pursues the discussion begun in chapter 3 of scandal's dual capacity to imagine a public audience for itself and to render sex a topic not to be talked about. The two novels I consider exemplify two principal means of responding to scandal. Eliot portrays an audience that frankly derives pleasure from scandal, and in condemning this public for its vulgarity, she differentiates it from her own readership. In the process, Eliot demonstrates how wide a gulf separates obtuse public opinion from the private struggles of scandal's victims. To effect these distinctions, The Mill on the Floss relies upon a contradiction, like that of Great Expectations, between plot and narrative: in the plot, Eliot criticizes those who generalize on the basis of partial knowledge of particulars, while her narrator's rhetoric depends upon precisely such generalizing methods to establish its authority and to solicit the audience. Eliot acutely describes the public reception of news about sex, and it is consequently in this portion of the book that I address the affective dimension of scandal response.

While Eliot condemns the hypocrisy of sexual unspeakability, and does so with particular attention to gender, she nonetheless contributes to this ideology the prestige of her own commanding narrative voice. Trollope uses the purchase of sexual implication as well—as, in the case of The Eustace Diamonds, the connotations of female sexuality flagrantly attaching to the jewels of the novel's title. But Trollope takes an invidious narrative pleasure in aligning his novelistic craft with the talents of his sexually unscrupulous heroine. Like the other novelists, Trollope relies on a type of narrative contradiction: here the conflict is between a narrated tale in which the market clearly determines value and, by contrast, a narrative language that rejects the market in favor of absolute standards. The pose that Trollope adopts of urbane sophistication, which can count on sexual meanings to be understood while dismissing the necessity to parse them, functions, alongside Eliot's anti-philistine ethics, as yet another in our compendium of tactics for designating sex the unspeakable subject. Both novelists also use stories of sexual exposure to meditate upon their own fiction-making and audience-producing work.

The final chapter turns to the figure upon whom scandal and the literary converge most obviously and inexorably at the end of the century, Oscar Wilde. Wilde's career and his trials represent the horizon for Victorian scandal not only in the ways they put sex into language but in the use they make of, and the ramifications they have for, literature. I focus on *The Portrait of Mr. W. H.*, both a novella and a work of homoerotic literary criticism, for this text theorizes the relation of sexual to self-consciously literary discourse. Wilde presents the limit case of strategies for encoding sexual meanings, because in his work the emphasis on indeterminacy is palpably deliberate. The system of connotative possibilities that we witness in other writers solidifies with Wilde into denotative certainty, and so collapses: once sexual thematics become too legible, they can be prosecuted. In Wilde's scandal, therefore, the dangers of the literary itself go on trial. Alone among the authors I consider, Wilde was not a writer of long realist novels, and this fact dramatizes the sense in which his career and his scandal mark the end of that high Victorian moment when the restrictions on sexual expression could generate fertile literary opportunities. The erotic/aesthetic system that Wilde fashioned, in which sexual and literary meanings explicitly stand in one for the other, ceases to find the multivolume realist novel a congenial form. This is to say not that such works ceased being written after Wilde, but that it was the literary genre at which he felt no need to try his hand. In the final pages of chapter 6, I turn to an author who did continue productively drawing on codes of sexual unspeakability in commodious works of fiction, Henry James. In his tales that theorize the literary, James stakes out a path strikingly antithetical to Wilde's, repudiating sexual possibilities as deliberately as Wilde embraces them. Finally, the book's afterword offers some brief speculations on what the Victorians have to teach us about the contemporary culture of sex scandal.

TWO

MANUAL CONDUCT IN

GREAT EXPECTATIONS

If one were writing the masturbator's guide to the English novel, certain correspondences would soon become evident. Like the novel, the discourse that constitutes masturbation (as a medical condition, a moral sin, a personal identity, a psychological stage) first arose early in the eighteenth century; like the novel, too, it achieved full cultural currency by the Victorian period and began its decline early in the present century.[1] By the middle of the nineteenth century, both masturbatory practice and novel-reading were firmly installed in popular imagination and culture. With the cultural designation of these practices as significant, anxieties about an unregulated, excessively productive imagination arose, impelling both anti-onanist doctrine and anti-novel

---

1. On the history of masturbation, see E. H. Hare, "Masturbatory Insanity: The History of an Idea," *Journal of Mental Science* 108, no. 452 (January 1962): 2–25; R. P. Neuman, "Masturbation, Madness, and the Modern Concepts of Childhood and Adolescence," *Journal of Social History* 8, no. 3 (Spring 1975): 1–27; Robert R. Hazelwood et al., *Autoerotic Fatalities* (Lexington, Mass.: D. C. Heath, 1983). The most widely available Victorian medical materials on masturbation are: William Acton, *The Functions and Disorders of the Reproductive Organs* (1857; 6th ed., London: Churchill, 1875); Joseph W. Howe, *Excessive Venery, Masturbation and Continence* (1887; rpt. New York: Arno, 1974); and *The Secret Vice Exposed! Some Arguments Against Masturbation* (New York: Arno, 1974), which reprints five works from 1723 to 1858, including the famous founding text of masturbation, *Onania; or, the Heinous Sin of Self-Pollution* (10th ed., 1724), and S. A. Tissot, *Treatise on the Diseases Produced by Onanism* (1832 ed.).

invective.[2] Through famously repressive techniques, medical authorities sought to control the onanistic vice that, as we now suppose, they thereby invented; the novel, meanwhile, so perilously implicated in encouraging kindred forms of imaginative self-abuse, had to find ways of managing the erotic reveries it was accused of arousing in its readers.

Having been stigmatized for its association with fantasy, the novel eventually internalized and accommodated that charge. By the mid-nineteenth century, fictional narratives were seeking to exonerate themselves from incrimination in readers' imaginations. Even as the novel strove to redirect its readers *away* from masturbatory vice, however, this now-dominant form of imaginative literature could hardly cease its sexual provocations. The novel increasingly learned how to perform this simultaneously regulatory and arousing function while having (perhaps until Hardy) ever *less* to say about sex overtly. Through specifiable narrative techniques, the Victorian novel at once encrypted representations of sexuality and demonstrated a frantic need for managing and redeeming sexual practices.

In the masturbator's guide to the English novel, at least under the heading "men's bodies," Charles Dickens would doubtless merit a good deal of attention. Charley Bates, a character in *Oliver Twist* (1837–39), first alerts us to the valence of the term in Dickens's corpus. When, as sometimes happens, he is called "Master Bates," we are assured of not being able to lose sight of the pun; yet when, more usually, he is referred to as "Master Charles Bates," we are guaranteed to continue imagining it — like the onanist, always fantasizing about what is not at hand in order to keep aroused what is. The volatility of Charley's name might in itself make us suspicious, for in the mouth of the narrator it constantly shifts toward and away from the little joke. When he first appears, for instance, he is described as "a very sprightly young friend . . . who was now formally introduced to [Oliver] as Charley Bates." Farther down on the

<hr />

2. I take the links between the novel and masturbation that concern stimulating and regulating the imagination from Thomas W. Laqueur, "Onanism, Sociability, and the Imagination" (unpublished essay), which traces the historical dimensions of this conjunction fully. See also G. J. Barker-Benfield, *The Horrors of the Half-Known Life: Male Attitudes Toward Women and Sexuality in Nineteenth-Century America* (New York: Harper & Row, 1976), chaps. 14–15; and Walter Kendrick, *The Secret Museum: Pornography in Modern Culture* (New York: Viking, 1987), 88–92. On the charges of wastefulness and immorality that punctuated the early history of the novel, see John Tinnon Taylor, *Early Opposition to the English Novel* (New York: King's Crown, 1943).

page, he is referred to as "Mr. Charles Bates." Finally, he delivers the gear for cleaning up whatever mess his name might imply: " 'Wipes,' replied Master Bates; at the same time producing four pocket-handkerchiefs." [3]

The peculiar attention to the young scoundrel's name is dramatically amplified by the following exchange:

> [The Dodger] looked down on Oliver, with a thoughtful counte-nance, for a brief space; and then, raising his head, and heaving a gentle sigh, said, half in abstraction, and half to *Master Bates:*
>
> "What a pity it is he isn't a prig!"
>
> "Ah," said *Master Charles Bates;* "he don't know what's good for him."
>
> The Dodger sighed again, and resumed his pipe: as did *Charley Bates.* They both smoked, for some seconds, in silence.
>
> "I suppose you don't even know what a prig is?" said the Dodger mournfully.
>
> "I think I know that," replied Oliver, looking up. "It's a th——; you're one, are you not?" inquired Oliver, checking himself.
>
> "I am," replied the Dodger. "I'd scorn to be anything else." Mr. Dawkins gave his hat a ferocious cock, after delivering this sentiment, and looked at *Master Bates,* as if to denote that he would feel obliged by his saying anything to the contrary. (181; empha-sis added)

Through this, one of the many scenes depicting Oliver's initiation into the secret community of male adolescence, the term prig floats with as much instability as that of "Master Bates." The gloss on prig that Oliver is incapable of uttering is presumably "thief," yet the persistence with which the term goes undenoted throws us deliberately back upon the signifier—where, with the alacrity of any English schoolboy, we might take Grimm's usual phonemic detour from a bilabial to a fricative and detect a frig (Victorian slang for manual stimulation of the genitals). If the revelation that Master Bates himself is a prig merely establishes a relation of synonymity, the Dodger nonetheless asserts superiority over the smaller boys with his "ferocious cock."

Dickens's linguistic attention to the male body and male eroticism compels all his Bildungsromane to trace not only their heroes' social, emo-

---

3. Charles Dickens, *Oliver Twist* (London: Penguin, 1966), 109; further references will be made parenthetically to this edition.

tional, and intellectual development, but their sexual maturation as well. While *Oliver Twist* confines its fantasies about boys' budding bodies to closeted puns, *Great Expectations* (1860–61) refers those same sexual feelings back onto the bodies of its characters. In so doing, however, the later novel relegates sexual sensations to parts of the body different from those in which they are usually imagined to originate; *Great Expectations*, on this reading, manages to anatomize whole species of erotic dispositions without ever mentioning sex.

The novel generates these erotic meanings not only in the absence of explicit representations of sexuality, but also without broaching an overt scandal story. It may seem curious that this study, which proposes a consideration of scandal and Victorian fiction, should begin with a work whose plot does not center in an obvious way on a scandal. I intentionally postpone a discussion of scandal here, however, in an effort to lay the groundwork for the chapters that follow. In the process of becoming the unspeakable subject, sexuality is represented in complex, subtle, and convoluted ways, *even in the absence* of the pressure from the narrative form of scandal. Certainly the masturbatory thematic that pervades the novel, were it explicitly revealed within the story, would be scandalous: it would expose the sexual dependencies of fiction's subject-making enterprise. The very implicitness and diffusion of the novel's account of autoeroticism, however, acts as a shield against the scandal of its exposure. This chapter thus concerns the conceptual antecedents to the sex scandals, both fictional and not, that I take up elsewhere in this book. Prior to exploring the paradoxical situation presented by scandal, where public discourses converge upon topics to which their language is inadequate, I want to illustrate the force of the sexual domain as both unspeakable and conditioning of the literary.

Let us therefore look at a scene in *Great Expectations* thematically paralleling the one I have discussed in *Oliver Twist*, in which Dickens raises the issue of masturbation by referring to it in such a way as to announce the impossibility of articulating it as such. The scene that probably constitutes Dickens's most vivid account of the pleasures and anxieties of autoeroticism occurs just when one would expect it in the maturation of the novel's prepubescent hero. Soon after the primal scene of his encounter with Magwitch in the graveyard,[4] still stunned by the fear of it,

---

4. Peter Brooks designates the "scene" as such; *Reading for the Plot: Design and Intention in Narrative* (New York: Alfred A. Knopf, 1984), 110.

and a long way from knowing what it means, Pip lifts a slice of bread and butter from his sister's table and hides it for later delivery to the convict. Pip, the Dodger might say, thus becomes a prig. Like Oliver's truncated definition of *prig*, which in refusing the signified turns us back upon the phoneme (thus stimulating, as Roland Barthes would suggest, the desire to eroticize—if not to frig—the sign), Pip's language also abjures denotation: "Conscience is a dreadful thing," he states, "when it accuses man or boy; but when, in the case of a boy, that secret burden co-operates with another secret burden down the leg of his trousers, it is (as I can testify) a great punishment."[5] Pip carefully avoids a definition of that "secret burden"; his ambiguity, now semantic instead of phonemic, allows the bread and butter to function as an alibi for the arousal that he is—as anyone familiar with the perturbations of male adolescence can attest—at such pains to conceal.

Having secreted the morsel down his pants leg, Pip continues to be harassed by his "wicked secret" (55) through the novel's early scenes. When he undertakes the chore of stirring the Christmas pudding, he finds himself altogether discomfited: "I tried it with the load upon my leg (and that made me think afresh of the man with the load on his leg), and found the tendency of exercise to bring the bread-and-butter out at my ankle, quite unmanageable. Happily, I slipped away, and deposited that part of my conscience in my garret bedroom" (45). Stealing the meager repast does not merely coincide ("co-operate") with the primary arousal ("another secret burden down the leg of his trousers"): it literalizes the economic metaphor, by which masturbation is classically imagined, of counterproductive labor. Likewise, while the load of which Pip relieves himself surreptitiously in his bedroom signals the irresistible culmination of such titillation, it also completes the analogy between masturbation and theft through a common charge of wastefulness. The trail of butter down his leg points further toward that scene in which, on his first night in London, a now-idle gentleman-Pip claims to detect in his bed "much of [a boiled fowl's] parsley and butter in a state of congelation when I retired for the night" (202).[6] Whether through

---

5. Charles Dickens, *Great Expectations* (London: Penguin, 1965), 44; further references will be made parenthetically to this edition.

6. In still another instance, Pip and his friends display a nearly postcoital serenity at being smeared with the butter from their tea and toast: "The Aged prepared such a haystack of buttered toast, that I could scarcely see him over it. . . . We ate the whole of the toast, and drank tea in proportion, and it was delightful to see how warm and greasy

the profligacy of moneyed leisure or the degeneracy of desperate theft, autoeroticism is figured as wasteful sexual energy.

If the discovery of these suspiciously buttery emissions in Pip's bedrooms suggests an excessively lubricious reading strategy, disavowal of this discovery would itself partake of the very paranoia that structures Pip's response. For in the scene we have been examining, Pip is quick to identify himself with the criminal. First, through corporeal metonymy (that oedipal limp) he links himself to the shackled Magwitch. Further, in abetting the convict, Pip fears he may *become* a convict, by virtue of the paranoiac imagination that affiliates his crime (and his body) with an illegality whose discipline is materialized almost immediately in the soldiers on the doorstep. Victorian proscriptions of self-abuse and the concomitant vigilance in preventing their infringement notoriously inspired among habituated onanists the kind of guilt this passage bespeaks.[7] Not least in an effort to resist the continuing allure of the prohibitions against a practice otherwise made thoroughly banal today, this reading will insist that *Great Expectations* is imbued with lessons about the erotic dispositions of bodies. Rather than recapitulate the protagonist's phobic recoiling against sexual possibilities, I will, in what follows, propose to locate at the very heart of the Victorian literary canon a deeply saturated perversity. One of the nineteenth-century novel's principal accomplishments is to formulate a literary language that expresses eroticism even as it designates sexuality the supremely unmentionable subject. While the regulatory, often punitive dimension of these articulations cannot be overestimated, there is a comparable danger in recognizing nothing other than their prohibitive aspect, thereby merely relocating the

---

we all got after it. The Aged especially, might have passed for some clean old chief of a savage tribe, just oiled" (315).

7. Robert Newsom, "The Hero's Shame," *Dickens Studies Annual* 11 (New York: AMS, 1983): 1–24, convincingly charts the dynamics of guilt and shame in Dickens's writing using a psychoanalytic model. As if to validate those pathologies, however, Newsom preempts a full treatment of sexual thematics: "It is easy to feel in reading this novel [*Oliver Twist*] a real streak of perversity or at least sense of perversity in it, but just because it is so easy to interpret these scenes, one may leave it to the imagination to determine exactly what activities pocket-picking, oyster-eating, and so on, may represent" (16). Also relevant is Elliot L. Gilbert, " 'In Primal Sympathy': *Great Expectations* and the Secret Life" (ibid., 89–113), which argues that the "secret vice" under scrutiny in the novel is selfishness; the latter might reasonably serve as a figure for masturbation if one excised all considerations of sexuality and the body.

critical institutions that have traditionally prevented readers from identifying erotic pleasures—call them perversions—within so respectable a text as Great Expectations. The novel both arouses and coerces its readers' desires; tracing the productive interplay of pleasure and power allows not only a reconception of this work but a charting of Victorian sexual ideology's formidable operations.[8]

Thanks to the Victorian novel's renowned loquaciousness, the subjects it cannot utter generate particularly nagging silences. How can we make these silences speak? Precisely through attention to the rhetoric of unspeakability: such tropes as periphrasis, euphemism, and indirection give rise to signifying practices that fill in these enforced absences.[9] The novel, we will see, encrypts sexuality not in its plot or in its announced intentions, but in its margins, at the seemingly incidental moments of its figurative language, where, paradoxically, it is so starkly obvious as to be invisible. The novel directs our attention to its visibly invisible surface with its manifest interest in the materiality of the sign; it offers a model for such reading in, for instance, young Pip's assumption that "the shape of the letters" (35) on the tombstones conveys the physical appearance of his parents, or in the silenced Mrs. Joe's ideogram for Orlick—the hammer—which everyone misreads as a letter (150–51).[10] If the very letters that constitute its matter bear meanings beyond the literal, then by analogy we can detect other sorts of hidden information in aspects of the novel's surface usually considered so conspicuous as to

8. This is to argue along with Michel Foucault, who writes in The History of Sexuality, vol. 1, trans. Robert Hurley (New York: Vintage, 1978): "Pleasure spread to the power that harried it; power anchored the pleasure it uncovered. . . . The power that lets itself be invaded by the pleasure it is pursuing; and opposite it, power asserting itself in the pleasure of showing off, scandalizing, or resisting. . . . These attractions, these evasions, these circular incitements have traced around bodies and sexes, not boundaries not to be crossed, but perpetual spirals of power and pleasure" (45; emphasis in original).

9. On the enticements and concomitant hazards of reading connotation generally, and homosexual meanings in particular, I am indebted to D. A. Miller, "Anal Rope," Representations 32 (Fall 1990): 114–33.

10. The assumption that the materiality of writing bears some organic relation to its semantic content is hardly unique to Great Expectations. The notion of a writing that holds the key to the hand (and by extension, the personality) which inscribed it was reinvigorated in 1872 by Abbé Hypolite Michon's Le mystère de l'écriture (which invented the term graphology) and by the numerous derivative guides to interpreting penmanship. Exemplary among these is Edward Lumley, The Art of Judging the Character of Individuals from Their Handwriting and Style (London: John Russell Smith, 1875), and Don Felix de Salamanca [John H. Ingram], The Philosophy of Handwriting (London: Chatto & Windus, 1879).

be undeserving of comment. The arena of the unnoticeable (or what it comes down to, the unnoteworthy) shelters what can hardly be thought, much less articulated, in the novel.

The placement of hand on genitals remains a secret in the Victorian novel, but like all secrets it wants to be told. The scene with which we have been concerned, of masturbation's near exposure, is only the most explicit instance of a pattern that runs throughout *Great Expectations*, a pattern that figures the sexual caress not in the genitals being handled but in the hands doing the touching. From this early point, at which the boy's bulge virtually speaks its own name, the narrative quickly relegates such unutterable instances of provocation and arousal to the commonplace, benign, and unblushing representation of characters' hands. In a genre that forbids direct observation of genitals in action, this manual code gives voice to what otherwise cannot be spoken.

Why hands? An account of their place in Victorian culture would consider its wealth of tracts on chirology, palmistry, and graphology, as well as such anatomo-spiritual works as Sir Charles Bell's popular treatise *The Hand: Its Mechanism and Vital Endowments, as Evincing Design*.[11] The fact is not simply that the hand was paid a great deal of attention, but that—given the extent of Victorian self-regulation, both literary and sartorial—it was one of the few anatomical parts regularly available for attention: the usual costume of middle-class English adults in the nineteenth century covered all of the body but the head and the hands. Much has been made of the head, both in literary representation and in those famous Victorian pseudo-sciences, phrenology and physiognomy. But critics have had little to say about the other part of the body that could be examined—the hand.[12] Nineteenth-century observers believed the hand

11. Fourth in the Bridgewater series on "the power, wisdom and goodness of God, as manifested in the creation" (first published in 1833 and reprinted throughout the century). For histories of chiromancy and chirology including but not limited to the rage for such work in the nineteenth century, see N. Vaschide, *Essai sur la psychologie de la main* (Paris: Rivière, 1909); Géza Révész, *The Human Hand: A Psychological Study*, trans. John Cohen (London: Routledge, 1958); and Walter Sorell, *The Story of the Human Hand* (Indianapolis: Bobbs-Merrill, 1967).

12. Notable exceptions include "Class and Gender in Victorian England: The Diaries of Arthur J. Munby and Hannah Cullwick," *Feminist Studies* 5 (Spring 1979): 86–141, in which Leonore Davidoff discusses Munby's eroticization of Cullwick's hands as a class crossing that reverses gender roles (111–13); and Christopher Craft, *Another Kind of Love: Male Homosexual Desire in English Discourse, 1850–1920* (Berkeley: University of California Press, 1994), who suggests the specifically homoerotic aspect of hands in Victorian culture (56–

to be fully saturated with information about its possessor's character; a book entitled *The Hand Phrenologically Considered: Being a Glimpse at the Relation of the Mind with the Organisation of the Body* (1848) exemplifies the Victorian investment in readings of the hand, the technical discourse of the work enabling it to sidestep the dubiety of palmistry:

> The hand not only affords us characters by which the age and sex may be determined, it is likewise an index of the general habit of body, of the kind of temperament, and of the mental tendency and disposition. . . . A soft, thick hand, loaded with fat, denotes little energy of character, and a soft, yielding, inactive disposition; while, on the contrary, a thin, bony, or muscular hand indicates a rough, active, energetic nature.[13]

Whether through its physiology, the lines that mark it, or the writing with which it is synonymous, the hand is so freighted with significance as to reveal all the vital information about the body and mind behind it.

For the Victorian reader, the hand would immediately be available both as a site of sexual signification and as a dangerous sexual implement. Hands are particularly important to any rendering of masturbation, as the putative etymology of the word suggests: *manus* (hand) + *stuprare* (to defile).[14] Preferring a Greek derivation, urologist William Acton suggests *chiromania* as a synonym for onanism, which he states, in

---

57). Craft's parenthetical proposal—"imagine, for instance, counting the handshakes in Dickens"—exercised an earlier generation of critics. Most thorough of these is Charles R. Forker, whose "The Language of Hands in *Great Expectations*," *Texas Studies in Language and Literature* 3 (Summer 1961): 280–93, substantially catalogues a "*leitmotif* of plot and theme—a kind of unifying symbol or natural metaphor for the book's complex of human interrelationships and the values and attitudes that motivate them" (281). In the same spirit, of seeking to prove through the representation of hands what the novel's plot and characterization have already made clear, see: M. H. Levine, "Hands and Hearts in *Great Expectations*," *Ball State University Forum* 6 (Autumn 1965): 22–24; Jack B. Moore, "Hearts and Hands in *Great Expectations*," *Dickensian* 61 (Winter 1965): 52–56; and Bert G. Hornback, *Great Expectations: A Novel of Friendship* (Boston: Twayne, 1987), 83–93.

13. Anonymous (London: Chapman and Hall, 1848), 56–58.

14. Although the word's origins remain obscure, the supposition that the etymology of *masturbation* collapses ideas about hands with those about sex is all the more telling if invented to fit the apparent facts. According to the OED, the source is either *mazdo-* (virile member) + *turba* (disturbance), or *manus* (hand) + *stuprare* (to defile). Seventeenth- and eighteenth-century writers tend to rely on the latter etymology: from *manual stupration* to *manustupration* to *mastupration*; see Hare, "Masturbatory Insanity," 20, n. 5.

The Functions and Disorders of the Reproductive Organs (1857), "can be properly applied, in the case of males, only to emission or ejaculation induced by titillation and friction of the virile member with the hand." In his account of the usual symptomatology of the onanist, Joseph W. Howe argues in *Excessive Venery, Masturbation and Continence* (1887) that hands deserve the special attention of "the experienced eye": "The superficial veins of the integument covering the hands and feet on the dorsal aspect, are very much enlarged or dilated. . . . The hands are often moist and clammy. While the patient is sitting, his shoulders stoop, and both hands are generally placed on the inside of the thighs." [15] Despite anti-onanists' attempts to constrain hands, their resistance to being covered (one can manage, as Miss Skiffins demonstrates, only so far with gloves on) marks their importance: the hand is the only exposed site of sexual communication below the neck. [16]

I cite Victorian manual and medical authorities not to establish any specific resonance with *Great Expectations* but instead to demonstrate the kinds of attention that the hand received in the period. We need not show that, say, Dickens was familiar with *Onania* to prove Pip a masturbator; we hardly want to, in fact, for the novel nowhere delivers the

---

15. Acton, *Functions and Disorders*, 38; Howe, *Excessive Venery*, 72–73. For instances of binding the hands to prevent self-abuse, see Neuman, "Masturbation, Madness," citing cases in which muffles and straitjackets are used to prevent the vice (12); see also Acton (52) and Howe (209). By the advent of psychoanalysis, such manual discipline is taken to hypostatize the threat of castration attendant upon the little boy's discovery of the genital orientation of his eroticism. Freud writes in "The Dissolution of the Oedipus Complex" (1924), in *The Standard Edition of the Complete Psychological Works of Sigmund Freud*, ed. James Strachey, 24 vols. (London: Hogarth Press, 1953–74):

> When the (male) child's interest turns to his genitals he betrays the fact by manipulating them frequently; and he then finds that the adults do not approve of this behaviour. More or less plainly, more or less brutally, a threat is pronounced that this part of him which he values so highly will be taken away from him. . . . [Adults] mitigate the threat in a symbolic manner by telling the child that what is to be removed is not his genital, which actually plays a passive part, but his hand, which is the active culprit. (19:174–75)

16. While the hand arguably bears a less organic metonymic relation to female than to male masturbation, its utility as a sign for autoeroticism derives from its lack of gender designation. It is worth noting that *digitate* is a nineteenth-century term for specifically female masturbation; John S. Farmer, *A Dictionary of Slang*, 7 vols. in 2 (1890; rpt. Ware, Hertfordshire: Wordsworth, 1987), s.v. *frig*, 3:73–74. Nineteenth-century anti-onanist literature fully treats both male and female cases, making progressively greater distinctions between the two.

reified identity of the onanist. The history of masturbation is both institutional *and* private (however oblique our access to the latter), and its story is one of both proscription and excitation. Given the novel's implication in both efforts—warning against and encouraging solitary vice—my interest here is in tracing the enfolding of that erotic practice in particular literary structures, specifically in linguistic formations of codification, connotation, and euphemism. These rhetorical modes, it must be emphasized, are not intentional reactions to sexual prohibitions (the result of repression or censorship) but generative possibilities for sexual meanings that cannot yet recognize themselves: within a constellation of broader, including nonliterary, discursive systems, such strategies contribute to the *production* of sexuality as the very category of the unspeakable. Rather than take the novel as a document in the institutional history of masturbation, then, my concern is to consider masturbation as a figure in the history of the novel.

When hands take on a specifically sexual meaning, I have suggested, they speak of masturbation; but their sexual qualities are also *generalizable*. The metonymic association of hands with autoeroticism functions as a conduit between representation and sexuality, but it does not restrict manual signification to a solitary sexual act. *Great Expectations* constructs its sexual taxonomy through its representation of hands, and while its master trope is therefore masturbation, the novel oversees a remarkably wide range of what will come—not least through the genre's own efforts at discriminating types—to be known as sexualities. I will consider the links between the overt representation of the manual, on one side, and the mystification of sexuality, on the other, first through the novel's thematics of male masturbation. I will then proceed to broaden the affiliation of the manual and the erotic and to examine the hand's capacity to signify nonsolitary sexuality, specifically through its potential for both inciting and regulating male homoeroticism. Finally, I will assess the novel's efforts at representing and managing women's sexuality through increasingly phantasmatic conjurations of the female hand. As exemplar, the novel trains the bodies of its characters—as instructor, those of its readers—in exceedingly particular lessons; it becomes, in this peculiar sense, a novel of manners.

Like many avid masturbators, Pip is deeply ashamed, and, just short of growing hair on his palms, he transfers his generalized sense of guilt onto the hands themselves. Pip is sorely touched by Estella's disdainful remark upon their first meeting: " 'And what coarse hands he has!' " He responds, "I had never thought of being ashamed of my hands before; but I began to consider them a very indifferent pair. Her contempt for me was so strong, that it became infectious, and I caught it" (90). Pip's hands focus and localize the virulent shame that, articulated here in the register of social class, bears with it all the marks of a sexual embarrassment. What he learns from Estella, that is to say, is that embodied signs of labor are distasteful; the way in which he learns it, though, is through the shaming of a physical exposure, having his vulgar, vulnerable members seen by a girl. The disgrace that attaches to the hand would, to Dickens and his audience, as surely be coded for that other subject routinely repressed—work—as it would be for sex. Humiliation over the laboring (productive) hand converges on shame over the autoerotic (wasteful) one.[17]

Pip's rough appendages perennially trouble him, and the novel meticulously traces the coalescence between the laboring hand and the masturbatory one under the sign of embarrassment. When he tells his family tall tales of his first visit to Satis House—his initial step out of the working class—he strikes the pose of the guilt-ridden onanist: "They both stared at me, and I, with an obtrusive show of artlessness on my countenance, stared at them, and plaited the right leg of my trousers with my right hand" (98). Once he comes into his expectations, Pip's newfound riches—or is it his newly bulging body?—plague him with another kind of awkwardness: "I went circuitously to Miss Havisham's by all the back ways, and rang at the bell constrainedly, on account of the stiff long fingers of my gloves" (183). This manual erection coincides with Pip's rising expectations, as overt anxiety about class again takes the narrative form of a sexualized humiliation. The process of Pip's Bil-

---

17. Though it might be argued that labor is as ineffable as sex, the former's unspeakability can at any rate be explicitly denominated: after Estella's initial rejection, Pip designates his class shame "the smart without a name" (92). Even if only as "nameless," class can be denoted; sex, by contrast, signifies through connotation. In "Work and the Body in Hardy and Other Nineteenth-Century Novelists," *Representations* 3 (Summer 1983): 90–123, Elaine Scarry writes: "As in the literature of desire the genitals become the spoken or unspoken locus of orientation, so throughout the literature of creation the hands become the most resonant and meaning-laden part of the human anatomy" (110). The difficulty of distinguishing the hand that signifies desire from the one that stands for creation (i.e., work) in *Great Expectations* suggests a distinction less absolute than the one that Scarry's terms propose.

dung is an aggressive repudiation of the labor inscribed on his body: it tells the story of his refusal to *be* a hand.[18] Consequently, he takes the rowing master's compliment that he has "the arm of a blacksmith" (218) as the worst kind of insult.

In the logic of the plot, Pip can finally overcome the blackening of the forge—the shame of the laboring hand—with burns of another sort: after rescuing Miss Havisham, he notes, "When I got up, on the surgeon's coming to her with other aid, I was astonished to see that both my hands were burnt; for, I had no knowledge of it through the sense of feeling" (414). These burns finally serve as a badge of honor, not shame, for Pip, a mark of adult arrival that overwrites his adolescent humiliation. This trial by fire obliterates at once his infantilized relation to Satis House and the calloused hands of his youth: he is required to pass through it in order to locate the appropriate alloerotic, heterosexual object. In this developmental narrative, which the novel overtly endorses, Pip's desires are ultimately as self-regulating as the free market that Adam Smith had envisioned as being—or being ruled by—an invisible hand.

When masturbation and labor are supplemented with a third sense of the hand—writing itself—the manual shame embedded in the narrative discloses its profound effects. Unlike most first-person novels, *Great Expectations* lacks an explicit scene of writing—that scene before the beginning and after the end in which readers are offered an account of the text's genesis.[19] Like the worker, the writer is ashamed of his hand; he insists upon effacing (though perhaps succeeds only in displacing) the signs of his own manual labor at bringing the novel into being. Although we never witness the inscription of the novel itself, the narrative obses-

18. This is the laboring hand whose plight Dickens could alternately decry and idealize. From *Hard Times* (1854; New York: Norton, 1966): "Among the multitude of Coketown, generically called 'the Hands,'—a race who would have found more favour with some people, if Providence had seen fit to make them only hands, or, like the lower creatures of the seashore, only hands and stomachs—lived a certain Stephen Blackpool, forty years of age" (49). From *Bleak House* (1852–53; London: Penguin, 1971): "Some of Rouncewell's hands have just knocked off for dinner-time, and seem to be invading the whole town. They are very sinewy and strong, are Rouncewell's hands—a little sooty too" (902).

19. Dickens's other first-person novels—*The Old Curiosity Shop, David Copperfield, Bleak House*—all do, to a lesser or greater degree, present such explanations. See Brooks, *Reading for the Plot*, on the site of narration: "Repetition speaks in the text of a return which ultimately subverts the very notion of beginning and end, suggesting that the idea of beginning presupposes the end, that the end is a time before the beginning, and hence that the interminable never can be finally bound in a plot" (109).

sively renders the exertions of the writing hand: from Pip's early problems learning to cipher ("getting considerably worried and scratched by every letter" [75]) down to his final scrivening labor for the Firm whose name merely embellishes that of his occupation—"I was clerk to Clarriker and Co." (489)—the hero writes throughout the story.[20] We would expect the writer's hand, like the productive one of the laborer, to exhibit the telltale marks of its toil (callouses, ink stains, cramps)—to bear witness to the work of what Melville dubs "a poor be-inked galley-slave, toiling with the heavy oar of a quill, to gain something wherewithal to stave off the cravings of nature"[21]—but the narrator never displays his laboring hand. Only when he lives as a gentleman does Pip have the leisure to read, and he then does little else; writing is as much a mark of the protagonist's class descent (the economic necessity of writing) as of his rise (the intellectual ability to do so). We are prohibited from seeing Pip write this fiction for reasons both economic and sexual: on one side, the writing of this life is itself the signal of a fall in class terms, which must be occluded;[22] on the other, any exposure of himself in the act of imagining his life would violate the autoerotic scene with which the solitary reverie, accompanied by manual manipulation, has already been aligned. Writing, like masturbation, cannot be narrated outright—yet it also *need not* be, for it has already left its mark (spilled its ink) everywhere; it too is made shameful, so chastened by that interior conduct manual, the conscience, that it is evident only in its traces.[23] Whether it covers

20. On Pip's writing, see Robert Tracy, "Reading Dickens's Writing," *Dickens Studies Annual* 11: 37–59. The classic deconstructive account of the affinity between writing and masturbation is Jacques Derrida, " '. . . That Dangerous Supplement . . . ,' " in *Of Grammatology*, trans. Gayatri Chakravorty Spivak (Baltimore: Johns Hopkins University Press, 1976), 141–64. The most sophisticated grammatological study of the hand is Jonathan Goldberg, *Writing Matter: From the Hands of the English Renaissance* (Stanford: Stanford University Press, 1990).

21. Herman Melville, *Pierre; or, the Ambiguities* (1852; New York: Grove Press, 1957), 362.

22. At its end, the novel generates the usual Dickensian mystification of social class, with Pip vacillating between claims for his poverty and those for his wealth—as if, in the aggregate, we will simply feel him to occupy that ambiguous middle: "I must not leave it to be supposed that we were ever a great House, or that we made mints of money. We were not in a grand way of business, but we had a good name, and worked for our profits, and did very well" (489).

23. The false hands of the forge and the forger ultimately converge in Orlick: an indolent laborer in Joe's smithy, he also joins forces with Compeyson, the counterfeiter. " 'I've took up with new companions, and new masters. Some of 'em writes my letters when I wants 'em wrote—do you mind?—writes my letters, wolf! They writes fifty hands;

work, writing, or sex, the coy hand seems to signal displacement itself.

The young Pip conforms most nearly to the identity of the onanist not because, as in some historical narrative, he evinces characteristics typical of the contemporary pathology, but because in his case hands take over the expression of emotions such as shame, self-assurance, arousal, or dejection more usually affiliated with sexuality.[24] If Pip's hands encode certain features of autoeroticism, we might inquire how they became so accomplished. The narrative offers an initial, ontogenetic explanation: from the first, Pip avers that his sister "had established a great reputation with herself and the neighbours because she had brought me up 'by hand,'" and that he knows "her to have a hard and heavy hand, and to be much in the habit of laying it upon her husband as well as upon me" (39). Here is one source, then, for so total a cathexis of the hand: it is both the punished and the punisher, the organ that sins and the one that disciplines. By taking literally the euphemism "brought up by hand" (conventionally used in reference to a child who is not breast-fed), Pip suggests how, in substituting for the maternal breast, the hand comes to be sexually charged. While Pip's hands designate him a masturbator, Mrs. Joe's serve unambiguously to phallicize her (particularly through their tool, Tickler)—at least until her penchant for dealing blows is dealt a stronger one and she is silenced "by some unknown hand" (147), which unsurprisingly turns out to be Orlick's "murderous hand" (438).

To the muscular femininity of his surrogate mother's bad cop, Pip's father-figure correspondingly exhibits the sentimental masculinity of a good one:

> Joe laid his hand upon my shoulder with the touch of a woman. . . .
> O dear good Joe, whom I was so ready to leave and so unthankful to, I see you again, with your muscular blacksmith's arm before

---

they're not like sneaking you, as writes but one'" (438). As the opposite of Pip's manual formulation—where writing and labor collapse into shame—Orlick's is the negative moment, where deceptive writing and resistance to work are linked through anger, with Orlick's sexual violence as the correlate to Pip's guilty masturbation. See Eve Kosofsky Sedgwick, *Between Men: English Literature and Male Homosocial Desire* (New York: Columbia University Press, 1985), 132. Mary Poovey, *Uneven Developments: The Ideological Work of Gender in Mid-Victorian England* (Chicago: University of Chicago Press, 1988), describes the ways in which Dickens represents literary work as unalienated and thereby distinguishes it from degrading forms of manual labor (100–101, 122).

24. For an argument that does, by contrast, discover the pathological "erotic identity" of the onanist in a nineteenth-century novel, see Eve Kosofsky Sedgwick, "Jane Austen and the Masturbating Girl," in *Tendencies* (Durham: Duke University Press, 1993), 109–29.

your eyes, and your broad chest heaving, and your voice dying away. O dear good faithful tender Joe, I feel the loving tremble of your hand upon my arm, as solemnly this day as if it had been the rustle of an angel's wing! (168)

The portrayal of Joe is in keeping with the usual representation of male sentimentality; the class signification of bodily attributes provides that the "muscular blacksmith's arm," which could so humiliate Pip on the Thames crew team, functions in the forge from which it derives as the sign of an unimpeachably wholesome and regenerate masculinity. The antithesis of his wife's hand, the "woman's touch" that characterizes Joe's paradoxically serves to fortify, not to destabilize, the edifice of his virility, even as it threatens Pip, the precarious arriviste, whose feminized masculinity has an entirely different class valence. Where Mrs. Joe's hand trains Pip's through violence and terror, Joe's works more subtly, as a nostalgic—but for all that, no less thoroughly repudiated—negative exemplar. The child is always in danger of being slapped by "Mother" for touching himself; the gentleman is always in danger of becoming as manly as "Father," and thus losing his class standing, or seeming as womanly as he, and thus losing his manhood.

Although Pip's body is schooled in a gender curriculum whose first instructors are, by virtue of their class status, comically reversed, the simplicity of this role reversal ensures that the inculcation will do its work all the same. It might be imagined that in such a scheme, Pip's early assimilation to a masturbatory erotics functions in keeping with a developmental narrative, so that his discovery of an interest in Estella can sweep over the adolescent vice and mature heterosexuality install itself. In fact, the presence in the novel of several other immature male characters with a predilection for self-abuse suggests the very normality of Pip's habit, if not of its persistence in his story. Instances of what teenage boys still term pocket pool abound: young Pip "religiously entertained" the belief that his deceased "five little brothers . . . had all been born on their backs with their hands in their trousers-pockets, and had never taken them out in this state of existence" (35); Orlick typically "would come slouching from his hermitage, with his hands in his pockets" (140); and Bentley Drummle "sat laughing in our faces, with his hands in his pockets" (238). The model of normative development we will wish to call seriously into question, but for now we shall consider the challenge offered by the fact that the behavior of at least one adult character in the novel is equally, though in different ways, coded for autoeroticism.

The characteristics we associate most with the body of Pip's guardian, Jaggers, are those of touching himself—his trademark "biting the side of his great forefinger"—and otherwise drawing attention to his unaccountably large hands (Pip notes the solicitor has "an exceedingly large head and a corresponding large hand" [111–12]). His classic pose: "The strange gentleman . . . with a manner expressive of knowing something secret about every one of us . . . remained standing: his left hand in his pocket, and he biting the forefinger of his right" (163). Even if we overlooked the finger he keeps in his mouth, we could hardly avoid noticing the one stashed in his pocket—for Pip's is not the only pants leg found bulging with secret burdens. Jaggers "pushed Miss Havisham in her chair before him, with one of his large hands, and put the other in his trousers-pocket as if the pocket were full of secrets" (262). Jaggers's case is somewhat more profound than that of the boys who pocket their hands, both because he is the only adult to do so and because the secrets in his pockets connote the other reason for keeping one's hands there: to lay hold of money. Both Pip (309) and Drummle (238) keep their wealth so concealed, and, as Pip executes the pun on the family name, he relies on our knowledge that while money is kept in pockets, it is not in the Pockets: "Both Mr. and Mrs. Pocket had such a noticeable air of being in somebody else's hands, that I wondered who really was in possession of the house and let them live there, until I found this unknown power to be the servants" (213). Jaggers is famous for ensuring that, as he says, "the secret was still a secret" (425),[25] and it is his skill at keeping secrets in his pocket that makes him so adept at getting money (even if not spending) there as well. Through Jaggers, the novel lends vivid materiality to the familiar Victorian analogy between male sexuality and a money economy. According to this formulation—condensed in the theory of spermatic economy—a man must jealously conserve his fixed capital of bodily energy, not squander it in unproductive forms of sexual release.[26]

25. Pip and Estella asseverate Jaggers's propensity for keeping secrets: " 'Mr. Jaggers,' said I . . . 'has the reputation of being more in the secrets of that dismal place [Newgate] than any man in London.' 'He is more in the secrets of every place, I think,' said Estella, in a low voice" (289).

26. On spermatic economy, see Barker-Benfield, *Horrors*, chap. 15. Laqueur, "Onanism, Sociability," argues against scarcity theories of sexuality, claiming that masturbation is, on the contrary, perceived to be threatening because of its seeming *limitlessness*. Whether masturbation is imagined as unproductive or excessively productive, however, its association with the hand would in any case set it in a conflicting relation to genuinely productive manual labor.

If Jaggers's version of autoeroticism functions in one sense as that which is sublimated by his acquisitiveness and in another as, say, the bodily inscription of his propensity for taking charge of others' secrets, in a third sense it registers the consistent pattern of his solipsistic withdrawal from scenes of potential erotic engagement. Again taking hands as our clue, we first recognize his distaste for human contact in his Pilate-like hygiene mania:

> I embrace this opportunity of remarking that he washed his clients off, as if he were a surgeon or a dentist. He had a closet in his room, fitted up for the purpose, which smelt of the scented soap like a perfumer's shop. It had an unusually large jack-towel on a roller inside the door, and he would wash his hands, and wipe them and dry them all over this towel, whenever he came in from a police-court or dismissed a client from his room. (233)

Pip figuratively lays his hands on ("embraces") this account of Jaggers's revulsion at literally being handled; as if to establish a redolent armor against such cuddling, Jaggers often signals his approach with the advance guard of his scented soap (112, 261). Jaggers's attention to others' hands amounts to no less a form of self-involvement than his fastidiousness about his own. In one instance, he takes a peculiar interest in Bentley Drummle: before the dinner party he throws for Pip and his "intimate associates" (227), Jaggers remarks, upon first laying eyes on Drummle's form, " 'I like the look of that fellow' " (234); " 'I like the fellow, Pip; he is one of the true sort' " (239), he repeats after dinner. In an effort to get a better look at the body of "the Spider," Jaggers stages a competition among the boys by provoking Pip's future rival to demonstrate the strength of his arm:

> [Drummle] informed our host . . . that as to skill he was more than our master, and that as to strength he could scatter us like chaff. By some invisible agency, my guardian wound him up to a pitch little short of ferocity about this trifle; and he fell to baring and spanning his arm to show how muscular it was, and we all fell to baring and spanning our arms in a ridiculous manner. (236)

Like the comparison of equipment common among adolescent boys, this scene belies the pretense of romantic rivalry (it predates Bentley's interest in Estella) with its own gleeful erotics. Yet for all the zeal of his "invisible agency," Jaggers's taste for Drummle—and, in particular, for his arm—is "quite inexplicable" (236). The plot never sufficiently rationalizes it, except through some vague notions of the solicitor's perverse contrariety. Likewise, the occasion that this arm-wrestling provides for showing off Molly's superior strength—" 'Very few men have the power of wrist that this woman has' " (237)—remains largely unexplained, as does the sadomasochistic dramatization of this master/servant relationship. Wemmick's later explanation—" 'She went into his service immediately after her acquittal, tamed as she is now' " (406)—merely asserts its own insufficiency; surely if all Jaggers wanted was a domestic servant he need not have taken in "a wild beast tamed" (224). Although they work according to the novel's usual manual semiotics, these sites of Jaggers's prospective erotic interest rapidly lose their motivation; the plot abandons them as false leads, and Jaggers seems finally more interested in keeping his hands to himself than in pursuing others'.

If the lawyer appears to suffer from an unaccountable withholding, he can at least be said to have made professional use of this attribute, as Pip testifies in describing one of his most effective litigious techniques:

> He always carried (I have not yet mentioned it, I think) a pocket-handkerchief of rich silk and of imposing proportions, which was of great value to him in his profession. I have seen him so terrify a client or a witness by ceremoniously unfolding this pocket-handkerchief as if he were immediately going to blow his nose, and then pausing, as if he knew he should not have time to do it before such client or witness committed himself, that the self-committal has followed directly, quite as a matter of course. (261–62)

Jaggers's handkerchief trick gives objective form to the particular erotic disposition we have identified with him: autoeroticism as a mode of refusal. Not unlike the flirtation between "prig" and "Master Bates" in Oliver Twist, this spectacle—in the context of Jaggers's finger-biting and pocketed secrets—encodes the sexualization of refusal that it cannot name. While Pip's frigs result in sticky messes (butter down the pants leg, butter in the bed), Jaggers turns refusal—here, to allow the phlegm to come—into ars erotica. Through the representation of an adult character coded for onanistic behavior, Dickens gives literary form not so much to a Victorian pathology or sexual identity as to a particular perverse sexual practice. Although Pip and Jaggers both bespeak autoeroticism, they personify two very different modalities of it, neither in an especially proximate relation to the classic onanist of Tissot or Acton: Pip's practice is guilty, excessive, uncontrolled, a sexualized strategy for repudiating the manual labor he abhors; Jaggers's is manipulative, parsimonious, recoiling, a performance and extension of his economic motivations. To insist upon the conformity of literary characters to the genuinely repressive models of medical authorities may itself be to fall victim to a coercively normalizing sexuality; instead, without obliging ourselves to abandon the postulate that all sexuality is shot through with ideology, can we imagine that the novel engages sexualities unaccounted for by official pathologies?

The solitary hands we have observed so far in *Great Expectations* are marked, via a metonymic connection, for male masturbation: when hand and genital organ touch, the former (speakable) can connote the latter (unspeakable). The novel's erotic investment in hands is so general, however, as to allow for metaphoric links as well, so that sexual practices less directly managed by the hand may nonetheless be imagined as manual. I now want to shift my attention from singular hands to redoubled ones in order to read sexuality: the moments at which two men's hands are engaged arise first, in the most highly socialized form of male handholding, the handshake, and then in the other shape they principally assume in the novel, pugilism. Returning to Jaggers, we again find his mode of refusal striking. While he is frequently "throwing his finger at [one] sideways" (165), and is quick to lay a hand on Pip's shoulder or arm (163, 190–91, 424), he rarely takes the young man in hand. Indeed, Jaggers is all but unwilling to extend his hand—and the largeness of his endowment makes the fact of his withholding all the more disappointing:

> It was November, and my guardian was standing before his fire leaning his back against the chimney-piece, with his hands under his coat-tails.
> "Well, Pip," said he, "I must call you Mr. Pip to-day. Congratulations, Mr. Pip."
> We shook hands—he was always a remarkably short shaker—and I thanked him. (305)

A man who has so massive a hand and yet is such a "remarkably short shaker" will always fail to satisfy.[27] As Pip comes to learn, however,

27. Jaggers offers a hand in one other place (352). When it fails to issue its olfactory warning, this appendage is capable of inciting Pip's paranoiac delusions through an approach from the rear: "I had strolled up into Cheapside, and was strolling along it, surely the

handshaking in the world of this novel has a curiously negative valence in any case.

The handshake is the one social ritual by which men — especially those who are strangers — routinely touch each other. It functions to draw people together by holding them apart: it interposes hands between other body parts as a safe form of contact. Why, then, this shortness on the part of Jaggers's shaker? Why, even more pertinently, the castigation of this ritual in the form of Pumblechook's unctuous insistence on it? After learning that Pip has come into his expectations, the seedsman clings to the boy with an obsequiousness as oppressive as the proverbial cheap suit that Pip has just come from being fitted for by Trabb:

> "But do I," said Mr. Pumblechook, getting up again the moment after he had sat down, "see afore me, him as I ever sported with in his times of happy infancy? And may I — may I — ?"
>
> This May I, meant might he shake hands? I consented, and he was fervent, and then sat down again.
>
> "Here is wine," said Mr. Pumblechook. "Let us drink, Thanks to Fortune, and may she ever pick out her favourites with equal judgment! And yet I cannot," said Mr. Pumblechook, getting up again, "see afore me One — and likewise drink to One — without again expressing — May I — may I — ?" (180)

Pumblechook's sycophancy is insatiable, at least so long as Pip stays in the money; once Pip is "brought low," however, the hand is extended "with a magnificently forgiving air," and Pip notes "the wonderful difference between the servile manner in which he had offered his hand in my new prosperity, saying, 'May I?' and the ostentatious clemency with which he had just now exhibited the same fat five fingers" (483). Here is the novel's signal instance of a hand freighted with meaning, yet what it bespeaks is not the efficacy of gestural communication. Instead, at the moment the novel raises the possibility that in the most familiar code of manual conduct — the handshake — something might supervene upon the literal, the narrative can be nothing but derisive (as if to confirm that hands are evocative only where they are not, in the novel's

---

most unsettled person in all the busy concourse, when a large hand was laid upon my shoulder, by some one overtaking me. It was Mr. Jaggers's hand, and he passed it through my arm" (400). The "large hand" that claps Pip on the shoulder gives fleshy form to the fantasies that so often "unsettle" him.

conscious terms, meant to be so). At the point where connotations of the manual—including but not limited to the erotic—seem most likely to proliferate, the mode of parodic excess preempts all meanings but the most repugnant hypocrisy.[28]

Pip's hand remains insufficiently chafed by Pumblechook's grip, for in the progressive tale of his body's schooling it has to receive a final chastening lesson. Jaggers's second, Wemmick, is noted for comically representing the schizophrenic divide between the office persona of the bureaucratic modern man and his home life (" 'the office is one thing, and private life is another' " [231]). While on the job, Wemmick faithfully emulates the withholding posture of his employer: "Something of the state of Mr. Jaggers hung about him too, forbidding approach beyond certain limits" (281). Like Jaggers also, Wemmick finds distasteful Pip's provincial penchant for handshaking:

> "As I keep the cash," Mr. Wemmick observed, "we shall most likely meet pretty often. Good day."
>
> "Good day."
>
> I put out my hand, and Mr. Wemmick at first looked at it as if he thought I wanted something. Then he looked at me, and said, correcting himself,
>
> "To be sure! Yes. You're in the habit of shaking hands?"
>
> I was rather confused, thinking it must be out of the London fashion, but said yes.
>
> "I have got so out of it!" said Mr. Wemmick—"except at last. Very glad, I'm sure, to make your acquaintance. Good day!" (197)

28. Dickens exploits the handshake's erotic possibilities in, for instance, the following reunion in *The Mystery of Edwin Drood* (1870; London: Mandarin, 1991): "The two shook hands with the greatest heartiness, and then went the wonderful length—for Englishmen—of laying their hands each on the other's shoulders, and looking joyfully each into the other's face. 'My old fag!' said Mr. Crisparkle. 'My old master!' said Mr. Tartar" (242–43). In "The Pursuit of Homosexuality in the Eighteenth Century: 'Utterly Confused Category' and/or Rich Repository?" in *'Tis Nature's Fault: Unauthorized Sexuality During the Enlightenment*, ed. Robert Purks Maccubbin (Cambridge: Cambridge University Press, 1987), 132–68, G. S. Rousseau suggests that, at least in the mid-eighteenth century, handshaking was felt to provoke (rather than to sublimate) closer erotic encounters between men. He cites a 1749 tract: "Tho many Gentlemen of Worth, are oftentimes, out of pure good *Manners*, obliged to give into it [squeezing of the hand]; yet the Land [England] will never be purged of its *Abominations*, till this *Unmanly, Unnatural* Usage be totally abolish'd: For it is the first Inlet to the detestable Sin of *Sodomy*" (150).

The perplexity that Wemmick evinces at Pip's quaint amiability here is only elucidated later. For the man of business, handshaking is shown to have practical purposes: besides the exhibition of the "portable property" (224) he has acquired from condemned prisoners ("he wore at least four mourning rings" [195]), he reserves demonstrative use of his hands for its utility *as* a sign. As he leads Pip on a tour of Newgate prison, the narrator notes: "He turned to me and said, 'Notice the man I shall shake hands with.' I should have done so, without the preparation, as he had shaken hands with no one yet." After the brief conversation between Wemmick and the designated man, "They shook hands again, and as we walked away Wemmick said to me, 'A Coiner, a very good workman. The Recorder's report is made to-day, and he is sure to be executed on Monday'" (281–82). Wemmick hopes to land a bit of portable property from the condemned man, and reserves his embrace to satisfy this materialistic impulse. His handshake, like Pumblechook's, foregrounds its own function as coded behavior; divested of any erotic significance, Wemmick's secret handshake holds no secret (except so far as the unwitting Coiner is concerned) because its code is transparent. No wonder he is so reluctant to take up Pip's hand when they first meet: to do so would, in Wemmick's bodily lexicon, be tantamount to marking him for the gallows.

While the handshake routinizes and sublates manual contact among characters, the other context in which hands regularly meet—fisticuffs—tends in a rather different direction. If the text loads handshaking with a significance so ostentatious that it paradoxically empties itself out, the novel's most fully embodied moments of physical violence are either so curiously undermotivated or so thoroughly overdetermined as to proliferate the meanings available to a manual semiotics. Although in the logic of the novel's plot, fights interpose at junctures of fierce romantic rivalry, the *narration* of the battles consistently provides the occasion for the playing out of erotic contact, both homo- and heterosexual, between combatants.[29] Insofar as this precipitate collapse of the pugilistic into the erotic becomes a problem for Victorian masculinity, we might take John Sholto Douglas, Marquess of Queensberry, as the figure effectively to drive a wedge between them. By dint of historical accident, the

---

29. Sedgwick writes persuasively of the murderous anal erotics that pervade male-male combat—"male rape"—in late Dickens novels (*Between Men*, chaps. 9–10). Sedgwick may, however, overestimate the reliance of the Magwitch/Compeyson and Pip/Orlick violence on even the minimal alibi of heterosexual motives.

very man who, in 1867, codified the rules of fair play in boxing—thereby regulating and legitimating the procedures for homosocial sparring—was destined to initiate the century's most notorious legal proceedings for homoerotic touching—thereby taking the lead in the fin-de-siècle anathematization of homosexuals.[30]

At Pip's first encounter with Herbert Pocket, for instance, the relationship is one of immediate and unmediated physical aggression: " 'Come and fight,' said the pale young gentleman." As Herbert's provocation appears wholly unmotivated, he soon supplies the incitement it is felt to require: " 'I ought to give you a reason for fighting, too. There it is!' In a most irritating manner he instantly slapped his hands against one another, daintily flung one of his legs up behind him, pulled my hair, slapped his hands again, dipped his head, and butted it into my stomach" (119). To such ungentlemanly conduct the gentleman's reaction—that is, the bellicosity Herbert desires—itself must be reconfigured, albeit in hindsight, as a form of chivalrous combat for feminine affections. Pip's payoff for sparring with Herbert is the opportunity to kiss Estella, the scene's unseen observer. Yet even if this putative erotic aim were capable of sustaining a state of arousal, it would nonetheless function only retrospectively and defensively as the alibi for the more provoking touches elaborated in the battle with Herbert. In fact, Pip feels as a result that he has prostituted himself, "that the kiss was given to the coarse common boy as a piece of money might have been, and that it was worth nothing" (121). In compensation for the tussle's lack of motivation, then, the text supplies a series of rationales—ranging from insult to romance to monetary recompense—whose insufficiency is demonstrated by the very rapidity of their deployment.

However persuasive the pretext for pugnacity in the novel may be (in this case, hardly at all), it functions primarily as the occasion for physical contact between adversaries—contact whose cathexes evince a logic

---

30. Dennis Brailsford, *Bareknuckles: A Social History of Prize-Fighting* (Cambridge: Lutterworth Press, 1988), explains how, by the middle of the nineteenth century, barefisted pugilism in England had come to be considered vulgar, excessively violent, and insufficiently regulated; it was associated with the lower classes, with the United States and Australia, and with black men. Long before he provoked Oscar Wilde to sue him for libel, Queensberry initiated the effort to rehabilitate pugilism's declining popularity among the respectable classes by limiting the length and number of rounds and by introducing boxing gloves. In Queensberry, then, the new regulatory system for boxing dovetails with other efforts at disciplining male-male touching; in all instances, hitting below the belt is clearly forbidden.

quite different from the plot's. While the sensory modality of the novel's eroticism is primarily tactile, there is a peculiarly embodied form of the visual—an assaultive kind of looking—which also partakes of these haptic significations. In the present scene, the bout between Herbert and Pip is preceded by both narrator-Pip's account of Herbert's awkward frame (he later discreetly terms it "a little ungainly" [201]) and Herbert's somewhat more suspect examination of Pip's physique. In a remarkable description of his adversary's seminudity, Pip recounts:

> [Herbert] fell to pulling off, not only his jacket and waistcoat, but his shirt too, in a manner at once light-hearted, businesslike, and bloodthirsty.
>
> Although he did not look very healthy—having pimples on his face, and a breaking out at his mouth—these dreadful preparations quite appalled me. . . . He was a young gentleman in a grey suit (when not denuded for battle), with his elbows, knees, wrists, and heels, considerably in advance of the rest of him as to development.
>
> My heart failed me when I saw him squaring at me with every demonstration of mechanical nicety, and eyeing my anatomy as if he were minutely choosing his bone. (120)

The investment of Pip's narration in looking at and rendering the repulsive particulars of his antagonist's body is strangely at odds with the character's professed distaste for the figure that Herbert cuts.[31] At the moment that Pip, almost despite himself, catalogues the corners of the pale young gentleman's frame, Herbert returns the gaze. The fight then proceeds from this curiously cruising scrutiny; from sizing up to feeling up, we will see, the novel's pattern is here established.

The striptease that Pip witnesses at his introduction to Herbert enacts a form of male-male perusal not uncommon in Dickens's work. Such an androphilic once-over is most fully elaborated in the following passage in The Old Curiosity Shop (1840–41):

---

31. This is not the only instance of Pip's noticing—and then blanching at having noticed—another man's all-too-visible body under the banner of revulsion. At the theater one night he notes, "I found a virtuous boatswain in his Majesty's service—a most excellent man, though I could have wished his trousers not quite so tight in some places and not quite so loose in others" (396). When Pip meets with the "secret-looking man . . . with an invisible gun," who seems inexplicably to be making a pass at him, he notes: "The strange man, after glancing at Joe, and seeing that his attention was otherwise engaged, nodded to me again when I had taken my seat, and then rubbed his leg—in a very odd way, as it struck me" (103–4). In each case, the euphemism is so startling as to beg decoding.

Mr. Swiveller looked with a supercilious smile at Mr. Cheggs's toes, then raised his eyes from them to his ankle, from that to his shin, from that to his knee, and so on very gradually, keeping up his right leg, until he reached his waistcoat, when he raised his eyes from button to button until he reached his chin, and travelling straight up the middle of his nose came at last to his eyes, when he said abruptly, "No, sir, I didn't." [32]

The point at which one man can no longer anatomize another's body —"and so on very gradually"—is always telling. But as if to redress Herbert's enticing literalization of that familiar gaze ("he undressed me with his eyes"), the revelation moves in the opposite direction when the two meet again, now grown up. As Pip first espies the mature Herbert mounting the stairs, he reverses the striptease both by clothing his friend and by moving this time from the head downward: "Gradually there arose before me the hat, head, neckcloth, waistcoat, trousers, boots, of a member of society of about my own standing" (198). Here the progressive dressing (of a nude ascending a staircase) ensures their rivalry is at an end; proleptically asserting a Freudian developmental mythology, it insists that a more happily socialized and sublimated relation will ensue. [33]

The relationship most thoroughly structured around hand-to-hand combat, of course, is not finally Pip's friendship with Herbert but his enmity with Orlick. This conflict too originates in an aggressive looking: "I had leisure to entertain the retort in my mind, while [Orlick] slowly lifted his heavy glance from the pavement, up my legs and arms, to my face" (254). Even in the midst of Orlick's climactic attack on Pip, he pauses for a leisurely gander at his victim—a glance that can afford to be less furtive than earlier: "'Now,' said he, when we had surveyed one another for some time, 'I've got you.' . . . 'Now, wolf,' said he, 'afore

32. Charles Dickens, *The Old Curiosity Shop* (London: Penguin, 1972), 115–16.

33. Other intermale relationships mediated by erotically charged fights could be adduced here as well: the two scenes of Magwitch and Compeyson fighting, as well as Pip's confrontations with Drummle. Besides the arm-wrestling cited above, the following scene exemplifies the high-voltage wire that delineates hostile looking from tantalizing touching:

> I had to put my hands behind [Drummle's] legs for the poker. . . . Here Mr. Drummle looked at his boots, and I looked at mine, and then Mr. Drummle looked at my boots, and I looked at his. . . . I felt here, through a tingling in my blood, that if Mr. Drummle's shoulder had claimed another hair's breadth of room, I should have jerked him into the window; equally, that if my own shoulder had urged a similar claim, Mr. Drummle would have jerked me into the nearest box. (369–70)

I kill you like any other beast—which is wot I mean to do and wot I have tied you up for—I'll have a good look at you and a good goad at you. Oh, you enemy!' . . . Then, he took up the candle, and shading it with his murderous hand so as to throw its light on me, stood before me, looking at me and enjoying the sight" (435–38).

Violence is visualized before it is actualized; but Orlick's is of a specially ferocious variety, requiring not only specular conjuration but verbal confirmation as well. For however violating this staring-down may be, its narration is always coy in the elision of certain body parts. The linguistic analogue to the so-far-and-no-farther gaze is a device (comparable to the "prig" from *Oliver Twist*, the "secret burden" from Pip's childhood) by which the novel evokes, while still refusing to denote, terms for male sexuality around Orlick. "He pretended that his christian name was Dolge—a clear impossibility—but he was a fellow of that obstinate disposition that I believe him to have been the prey of no delusion in this particular, but wilfully to have imposed that name upon the village as an affront to its understanding" (139–40). With no other objection than this—that in its inscrutability the name simply *feels* obscene—Pip implies that a lack of definition itself signifies a transgression against propriety. Pip's assertion of this name's "impossibility" aims to bolster the straightness and clarity of his own narrative, a species purportedly remote from the obscenity of Orlick's indirection; yet the proximate impossibility of his own name belies this effort, as the novel's opening words attest: "My father's family name being Pirrip, and my christian name Philip, my infant tongue could make of both names nothing longer or more explicit than Pip. So, I called myself Pip, and came to be called Pip" (35). The case for the perversity of connotation becomes unequivocal in the next instance:

> "Well then," said [Orlick], "I'm jiggered if I don't see you home!"
> This penalty of being jiggered was a favourite supposititious case of his. He attached no definite meaning to the word that I am aware of, but used it, like his own pretended christian name, to affront mankind, and convey an idea of something savagely damaging. When I was younger, I had had a general belief that if he had jiggered me personally, he would have done it with a sharp and twisted hook. (158)

Here the insistent nonmeaning of the word redounds upon the victimized body with a sexual signification that cannot otherwise be uttered.

The denotative refusal entailed in the "supposititious case" functions as a place-holder for sexual meanings, not simply by obliterating some other, straightforward language (as in this example, by eliding the term *buggered*), but by producing those meanings *as* inarticulable.

Orlick's visual and verbal pugnacity toward Pip issues in the inevitable corporal confrontation between them, at the sluice-house by the limekiln at novel's end. In returning to characters' bodies, the scene naturally refers us, through its usual synecdochal route, to their hands. Throughout the final chapters Pip is sorely disabled by the burns his arms received at Satis House; Orlick's attack is so effective in part because it exacerbates Pip's condition. As the lights go down Pip finds himself pinned to the wall:

> Not only were my arms pulled close to my sides, but the pressure on my bad arm caused me exquisite pain. Sometimes, a strong man's hand, sometimes a strong man's breast, was set against my mouth to deaden my cries, and with a hot breath always close to me, I struggled ineffectually in the dark, while I was fastened tight to the wall. "And now," said the suppressed voice with another oath, "call out again, and I'll make short work of you!"
>
> Faint and sick with the pain of my injured arm, bewildered by the surprise, and yet conscious how easily this threat could be put in execution, I desisted, and tried to ease my arm were it ever so little. But, it was bound too tight for that. I felt as if, having been burnt before, it were now being boiled. (434)

If the hand of Pip's that touches his own body is regularly subject to rebuke, the one that feels (and is felt by) other men is even more thoroughly penalized. Yet here the brutal ferocity of "a strong man's hand" and its arousing caress are absolutely coterminous. Fearsomely violent as this assault is, its erotic sensations are manifest: the "strong man's breast" set against Pip's mouth, and, in return, the attacker's own "hot breath" against him, serve to literalize the lickerish "kiss" inhering in Orlick's surname.[34] As if to draw on Pip's youthful training matches with Herbert and Bentley—as if to dramatize the tantalizing prospect of being "jiggered"—this serious adult business with Orlick enacts all the erotic potential of murderous male combat. The particular correspondence that the novel has established between the manual and the genital

---

34. To "lick" the "or": Latin *os, ora,* mouth; thus, "I could only see his lips" (434).

only barely prepares us for the scene's concatenation of terror and tenderness, of the one hand that savors to inflict pain and the other that anguishes to endure it.[35]

At this point we can identify—although, as I will suggest, only prematurely—what might be termed the novel's homophobia. On the one hand, it denies the handshake any of the erotic valence we might well expect to attend this ritual: either because of the refusal of others (Jaggers or Wemmick) or because of Pip's own repulsion (at Pumblechook), this manual contact is insufficient to bring men together. On the other hand, Pip's pugilistics with Herbert, Drummle, and Orlick (as well as Magwitch's with Compeyson) represent a form of contact too close for comfort: however ecstatically and erotically charged one may suspect these passages of being, the form they take—of increasingly savage violence—must sit uneasily with any cheerfully homotropic reading. If, that is to say, the cost of men touching men is that one of them be pummeled, we must recognize a certain ideological resistance in the text to such an erotics. To this apparent dead end, however, the novel proposes several alternate routes. Thanks largely to the fluidity with which *Great Expectations* structures the thematic of hands, we are left not with an antithesis between homophobic and homophilic, but rather with an apparatus that ultimately brings these two terms—not to mention their hetero counterparts—into a relatively stable and consolatory relation of mutually reinforcing regulation.

For instance, let us, in pursuing our investigation of pugilism, witness the novel's strenuous effort to redeem it for normative heterosexuality. Earlier I ascribed Wemmick's refusal to shake Pip's hand as much to the single-mindedness of his economic motives in the workaday world as to any phobic pathology. When turning to his erotic interests at home, however, we find Wemmick himself must overcome another's refusal, in the resistance of his fiancée, Miss Skiffins, to yield to his hands. Upon

---

35. We learn the following precise details about the placement of the men's hands—phrases which, strung together, relate the plot of the scene in brief: "I quickened my pace, and knocked at the door with my hand"; "I tried the latch. It rose under my hand"; "I could see his hands"; "He sat with his arms folded on the table"; "He put his hand into the corner at his side"; "He leaned forward staring at me, slowly unclenched his hand and drew it across his mouth as if his mouth watered for me"; "'I know'd you at Gargery's when you was so small a wolf that I could have took your weazen betwixt this finger and thumb'"; "His hands hanging loose and heavy at his sides . . ."; "The last few drops of liquor he poured into the palm of his hand, and licked up"; "'I have no hurt but in this throbbing arm'" (433–41).

meeting her, Pip "might have pronounced her gown a little too decidedly orange, and her gloves a little too intensely green"; he notes further that "Miss Skiffins . . . retained her green gloves during the evening as an outward and visible sign that there was company" (313). Like her suitor, Miss Skiffins knows full well the hand's capability to signify. These gloves ensure her genteel incapacity for domestic labor as much as they conceal her dishpan hands: she "washed up the tea-things, in a trifling lady-like amateur manner that compromised none of us. Then, she put on her gloves again" (315). But while the gloves afford Miss Skiffins an "outward and visible sign" of *class* propriety, their verdancy promises a *sexual* steaminess as surely as her unwillingness to remove them withholds it.

The elaborate charade by which Wemmick makes a pass at his inamorata confirms this dynamic; it is his hands now that her gloves must peel off:

> As Wemmick and Miss Skiffins sat side by side, and as I sat in a shadowy corner, I observed a slow and gradual elongation of Mr. Wemmick's mouth, powerfully suggestive of his slowly and gradually stealing his arm round Miss Skiffins's waist. In course of time I saw his hand appear on the other side of Miss Skiffins; but at that moment Miss Skiffins neatly stopped him with the green glove, unwound his arm again as if it were an article of dress, and with the greatest deliberation laid it on the table before her. Miss Skiffins's composure while she did this was one of the most remarkable sights I have ever seen, and if I could have thought the act consistent with abstraction of mind, I should have deemed that Miss Skiffins performed it mechanically.
>
> By-and-by, I noticed Wemmick's arm beginning to disappear again, and gradually fading out of view. Shortly afterwards, his mouth began to widen again. After an interval of suspense on my part that was quite enthralling and almost painful, I saw his hand appear on the other side of Miss Skiffins. Instantly, Miss Skiffins stopped it with the neatness of a placid boxer, took off that girdle or cestus as before, and laid it on the table. (316)

By contrast with the performances of sexual excitation we have previously observed, this one can afford to be frankly erotic. Yet even as this pantomime of heterosexual courtship struggles to establish a relation to the normative, it repeatedly collapses into the realm of proscribed sexuality. Even—perhaps especially—when the flavor of eroticism is most vanilla (heterosexual, monogamous, genital), its pungency does not diminish against the palate; through the very nearness of its *exposure* in the narration, the representation of sexuality here continues to sting the readerly tongue. The "slow and gradual elongation of Mr. Wemmick's mouth" and the collateral distention of his arm, for example, only barely keep under wraps the other turgidity to which they give rise. The "mechanical" procedure of Miss Skiffins's resistance itself is metaphorized as *déshabillement* (she "unwound his arm again as if it were an article of dress, and . . . took off that girdle"), as though to confirm that so hot a refusal functions as an enticement to arousal. Furthermore, however superficially normative this passage's sexual thematics may be, the *mise en scène* returns us to a spectacle of sexual impropriety: in a manner unusual in the novel, Pip is here positioned as observer of others' erotic play, and his "interval of suspense . . . that was quite enthralling and almost painful" bespeaks a more-than-passive relation to the scene. Indeed, the pas de deux between Wemmick's arm and Miss Skiffins's gloves titillates Pip into a state of voyeuristic autoeroticism no different from that which novels themselves had been accused of arousing.

Finally, the contest between "his hand" and her "green glove" drifts irresistibly toward an allegory of fisticuffs. The narrative alignment of the modest maiden to "a placid boxer" installs the scene among those of intermasculine, androphilic pugilism; at its most explicit moment of heterosexual pursuit, then, the novel's erotic language modulates into the definitionally male and homosocial. For all that Miss Skiffins boxes with kid gloves on, it seems to say, she throws her punches with determination. Yet if in one sense the current of fistic homoeroticism unsettles the characters most preoccupied with bourgeois propriety, the Wemmick-Skiffins match, as we shall see, also works in the other direction (not unlike the Marquess of Queensberry) toward the reform and sanitization of boxing and its attendant sexual connotations.

The novel works arduously to redirect the erotic divagations set loose here. Lest the state of premarital arousal prove unsustainable, Miss Skiffins eventually removes her green gloves (still fully cognizant of their utility as signifiers) as a means of marking a new order of conjugally sanctioned eroticism. Arriving at church with Wemmick, Pip observes: "That discreet damsel was attired as usual, except that she was now engaged in substituting for her green kid gloves, a pair of white" (463).[36]

---

36. On the wedding day, the narrative's cathexis of gloves is curiously transferred from Miss Skiffins—de-eroticized the moment she steps up to the altar—to a comic attack on

Refusal having been abandoned as an erotic mode, domesticity triumphs in the Castle at Walworth: "It was pleasant to observe that Mrs. Wemmick no longer unwound Wemmick's arm when it adapted itself to her figure, but sat in a high-backed chair against the wall, like a violoncello in its case, and submitted to be embraced as that melodious instrument might have done" (464). The spur to desire is now so fully normalized by the institution of marriage that it loses its edge: although Wemmick evinces no sign of disappointment, one need only set an ungirdled boxer beside an encased cello to determine which woman — Miss Skiffins or Mrs. Wemmick — is the more enticing. In the miniature, mechanical, businesslike form that the Wemmicks lend it, the marriage plot's usual propensity for damage is made starkly evident: characters' bodies are disciplined into conformity, domesticity cancels eros, married life instantly obliterates memories of the prior excitation requisite for having brought it about. Here proven in its punishing aspect is a cardinal rule of the novel genre: that nuptials represent the end, not the beginning, of things.

The fights we have examined illustrate different modes of repression, in varying degrees of punitiveness, for managing and disciplining the play of hands. In each instance, the sexual possibilities generated by hands are expunged from the plot — from the register of articulated representation — by means of violence, only to resurface in the contours of the narrative voice, where they can pass by virtue of going unheard inside the novel. Male homosocial desire is expressed as brutality, while premarital sex is narratable only insofar as it fuels the hegemony of matrimony. But in addition to these transformations of errant manual desire accomplished through battle, the novel manages other, less violently chastening ones. As against the compulsions of the handshake and the fistfight, we will now want to consider the *consensual* modality of male manual regulation in the novel.

Through the shift from denuding to redressing, I have suggested, Herbert's youthful belligerence is rehabilitated as properly sublimated,

---

Wemmick's father: "The old gentleman . . . experienced so much difficulty in getting his gloves on, that Wemmick found it necessary to put him with his back against a pillar, and then to get behind the pillar himself and pull away at them, while I for my part held the old gentleman round the waist, that he might present an equal and safe resistance. By dint of this ingenious scheme, his gloves were got on to perfection" (463). As if to overcome the barriers of decrepitude and infirmity, the two younger men here assault the Aged Parent in a scene less vivid than Orlick's attack on Pip only for being sanctioned by place (the church) and occasion (the wedding).

adult male homosociality. Following his adolescent ineptitude in the boxing ring, moreover, Herbert's mastery of the hand correspondingly matures as well. Although we learn surprisingly little about his grown-up appendages, this lack is more than compensated by the peculiar knack he develops for tending to Pip's hands—a taste initiated, perhaps, in those first moments of "eyeing [Pip's] anatomy as if he were minutely choosing his bone" (120). Herbert's proclivity is confirmed both by his impulse, almost immediately upon becoming reacquainted with Pip, to christen him "Handel" and by his own surname, Pocket, the usual receptacle for hands in the novel. At their first dinner in town, Herbert interlards his conversation with a course in table manners for the newly arrived Pip, instructing him in the proper handling of utensils and other matters of the body's polite disposition at table (" 'the spoon is not generally used over-hand, but under,' " etc. [203–6]). Herbert interjaculates this manual conduct lesson (as if to literalize a parody of the silver-fork novel) through his recounting of Miss Havisham's history. In the second installment of this tale—when Pip realizes that Magwitch is Estella's father—Herbert is again preoccupied with the condition of his friend's hands, this time changing the bandages that cover Pip's burns (" 'Lay your arm out upon the back of the sofa, my dear boy, and I'll sit down here, and get the bandage off so gradually that you shall not know when it comes' " [416–19]). Through both stories, then, the narrative interpolates information about Pip's hands, as though, at these crucial moments of the protagonist's overt erotic interest, the novel's encrypted sign of that desire need literally be close at hand.

The story that Herbert tells in the midst of his bodywork on Pip is not merely incidental: significantly, this narrative concerns the conspiracy of Miss Havisham's half-brother, Arthur, with her fiancé, Compeyson, to defraud her:

> "It has been supposed that the man to whom she gave her misplaced confidence, acted throughout in concert with her half-brother; that it was a conspiracy between them; and that they shared the profits."
>
> "I wonder he didn't marry her and get all the property," said I.
>
> "He may have been married already, and her cruel mortification may have been a part of her half-brother's scheme," said Herbert. "Mind! I don't know that."
>
> "What became of the two men?" I asked, after again considering the subject.

> "They fell into deeper shame and degradation—if there can be
> deeper—and ruin." (205–6)

The implication of debased criminality in this last line derives its force
from contrast with the scene of its narration. Compeyson's story functions as a cautionary tale about the dangers of excessive intimacy between two young men; conversely, Pip's and Herbert's is the comfortably
homosocialized relation, where eros is sublimated as pugilism, camara-
derie, bachelor-marriage, and eventually marriage brokering. While in
the boys' earlier encounter (the adolescent sparring match) eroticism
was registered only as a "supposititious case," their newfound intimacy
(the now far gentler touching) can be more frankly denoted. In forming the frame of an interpolated tale (which itself has an antithetical
disciplinary moral) the hand-holding dispersed throughout the present
scenes is rendered explicitly—it is the scene of narration—by virtue of
being more highly socialized.

For Magwitch, the other figure given to excessive handling of Pip,
socialization again requires a transposition of eros from narrative discourse to plot, although in his case the change is accomplished through
more radical means. From the first, Magwitch embodies a certain pedo-
philia: the novel's opening, showing his combined aggression and affection for Pip, suggests a species of man-boy love, and it is primarily
through his man-handling of Pip that we come to register such ped-
erastic impulses. At their initial encounter, "The man, after looking at
me for a moment, turned me upside down, and emptied my pockets"
(36); and, "After darkly looking at his leg and me several times, he came
closer . . . took me by both arms, and tilted me back as far as he could
hold me" (37). The recognition scene between patron and protégé later
in the novel stages the climax of the touching here initiated, in the form
of an erotic ballet performed by the hands:

> I saw, with a stupid kind of amazement, that he was holding out
> both his hands to me. . . . He came back to where I stood, and
> again held out both his hands. Not knowing what to do—for, in
> my astonishment I had lost my self-possession—I reluctantly gave
> him my hands. He grasped them heartily, raised them to his lips,
> kissed them, and still held them. . . . At a change in his manner
> as if he were even going to embrace me, I laid a hand upon his
> breast and put him away. . . . I stood, with a hand on the chair-
> back and a hand on my breast, where I seemed to be suffocating—

> I stood so, looking wildly at him, until I grasped at the chair, when
> the room began to surge and turn. He caught me, drew me to the
> sofa, put me up against the cushions, and bent on one knee be-
> fore me: bringing the face that I now well remembered, and that
> I shuddered at, very near to mine. . . . The abhorrence in which I
> held the man, the dread I had of him, the repugnance with which
> I shrank from him, could not have been exceeded if he had been
> some terrible beast. . . . I recoiled from his touch as if he had been
> a snake. . . . Again he took both my hands and put them to his lips,
> while my blood ran cold within me. . . . He laid his hand on my
> shoulder. I shuddered at the thought that for anything I knew, his
> hand might be stained with blood. (332–39)

This narration has a perilously overt sexual charge: one need hardly cite
the bended knee, the kissing of hands, the prostration on the couch, the
insistent caresses, to locate the courtship conventions of which it partakes. Pip's gag reflex serves to bolster, not to diminish, the eroticism of
the episode, for it demonstrates his revulsion to be as highly cathected
as the convict's attraction. The narrative attention to Magwitch's manipulation, in its root sense, empowers his cataclysmic revelation even
as it threatens to run out of control through a homoeroticism we are
made to feel and, through Pip, to feel repulsed by.[37] But like his former
partner, Molly, this "terrible beast" must be tamed as well.

How does the novel recuperate Magwitch's erotic palpation and Pip's
corresponding palpitation? For Pip, the immediate antidote to the fearsome caress of the grizzled convict's "large brown veinous hands" (333)
arrives in the form of his companion's reassuring embrace: "Herbert received me with open arms . . . got up, and linked his arm in mine" (356–
58). Through the developments of the plot, moreover, Pip is capable
of turning Magwitch's lecherous pawing back upon him, lending it a
normalized, moralized signification. On his deathbed, Magwitch again
feels Pip's hands, now silently communicating through a sentimentalized hand-holding. "He had spoken his last words. He smiled, and I
understood his touch to mean that he wished to lift my hand, and lay it
on his breast. I laid it there, and he smiled again, and put both his hands

---

37. By comparison with Pip's relation to Miss Havisham, it might be argued that this
eroticism has more to do with age than gender, but a careful examination of the touches
between Pip and his "fairy godmother" indicates a cathexis far less entailed upon physical contact than his relation with Magwitch.

upon it" (469). Then, as if to repay Magwitch for the earlier episode, Pip makes his own revelation:

> "You had a child once, whom you loved and lost. . . . She is living now. She is a lady and very beautiful. And I love her!"
>
> With a last faint effort, which would have been powerless but for my yielding to it and assisting it, he raised my hand to his lips. Then, he gently let it sink upon his breast again, with his own hands lying on it. (470)

Pip is at last able to translate his benefactor's uncomfortable stroking into heterosexual terms, now giving that touch a proper meaning in the plot: he transposes it onto the heterosexual economy by lending it the valence of the "consent of a beloved's father to a suitor's entreaty." Much as he has had to endure Magwitch's caress, that is to say, the hand he now can own to wanting is Estella's, in marriage. Those earlier, less fully accountable hand-squeezings are now available to him reworked retrospectively as the beneficence of a future father-in-law. Pip can afford to be "yielding" and "assisting" to the old man's supplications by virtue of his knowledge that whatever homoerotic force they might once have had has been de-fused and rewritten—written into the story proper—as straight desire.

Both Magwitch and Herbert partake of a homoerotic handling of Pip, and both must be retrofitted in order to discipline those desires. Whether through visceral repugnance or progressive socialization, the novel attempts to school the men's bodies in normative heterosexual touching. It is not only through other men that Pip learns these lessons, however, for the women in his story must also undergo dramatic transformations in order to rectify the manual problems they present. The two modes of regulating sexuality that we have identified for the men—the violently coercive and the consensual—also structure female eroticism. While Biddy submits to her training for respectable femininity, Molly resists domestication to the utmost; Estella, meanwhile, never has the option of choosing because she never properly has any desires that require management. The novel, moreover, makes a distinction between male and female sexuality broadly conceived, through its phantasmatic construction of the latter, which functions largely in the service of a solitary male dream of its own sexual capacity. In situating erotic subject and object in the same body, autoeroticism, as we have seen, alienates the onanist from himself, thereby paradoxically constituting him *as* a subject.[38] Rarely more than fantasy objects, the female characters buttress the narrative's masturbatory mode, for the novel's sexual architectonics bars them from sustaining a position as desiring subjects.

Biddy and Pip start out as perfect counterparts, their as-yet ungendered identities equally oriented around the manual. "She was an orphan like myself," says Pip; "like me, too, had been brought up by hand" (74). Also like Pip, Biddy exhibits a hand replete with the dirtying signs of both manual labor and onanistic indulgence: "Her hands always wanted washing" (74), Pip notes early on; and at one point, to reassure him, "she put her hand, which was a comfortable hand though roughened by work, upon my hands, one after another" (156). For all their youthful likeness, however, the specter that Biddy presents of female masturbation and of an affirmative female desire is more than Pip can abide. The novel manages the anxiety Biddy inspires by ascribing to her all the dreariness of provincial working-class life, the ignominy of which is routed specifically through the femininity of her touch. The uncleanliness of her hands distresses Pip vividly at the point he repudiates her: while they converse, Biddy is shown "plucking a black-currant leaf," "looking closely at the leaf in her hand," and "having rubbed the leaf to

---

38. In his remarkable study *La main et l'esprit* (Paris: Presses Universitaires de France, 1963), Jean Brun discusses the "reciprocity" entailed in any manual contact, and evokes the closed circuit through which autoeroticism produces its practitioner as simultaneously subject and object of desire:

> Lorsque de sa main l'homme touche, il tente d'émigrer hors de sa corporéité pour aller à la rencontre de l'autre, et cette expérience s'achève par un retour sur lui-même, retour chargé d'affectivité et peut-être de drames dans la mesure où, par le toucher, l'homme est sans cesse renvoyé à son moi. Car le toucher est le seul de nos sens à être chargé de ce que E. Minkowski appelle «un élément de réciprocité», toucher c'est être en même temps touché par ce que l'on touche; l'œil peut voir sans être vu, l'oreille écoute sans être entendue, mais la main ne peut toucher sans être elle-même touchée. . . . Par la main qui touche, le moi va vers l'autre; par sa main touchée il revient vers soi. (102)

> (When man touches with his hand, he tries to move out of his corporeality to encounter the other, and this experience concludes with a return to himself, a return full of emotion and perhaps drama insofar as, by touching, man is unceasingly thrown back upon his ego. For touch is the only one of our senses to be full of what E. Minkowski calls "an element of reciprocity," to touch is at the same time to be touched by what one touches; the eye can see without being seen, the ear hears without being heard, but the hand cannot touch without itself being touched. . . . Through the hand that touches, the ego approaches the other; by the touched hand it returns to itself.)

pieces between her hands—and the smell of a black-currant bush has ever since recalled to me that evening in the little garden by the side of the lane" (175). Like Jaggers's hands, Biddy's generate a characteristic aroma; but where "scented soap" indicates a fastidious mysophobia, the provocative image of Biddy's "black-currant bush" bespeaks an *odor di femina* that sends Pip running. If we did not already suspect this hedge of signaling a demonstrative and menacing female sexuality, two other references would ensure that we do so. One: the alibi that Jaggers provides for Molly's wrist ("much disfigured—deeply scarred and scarred across and across" [236]), the sign of a more fearsome—and therefore more severely chastised—feminine sexuality: "She had struggled through a great lot of brambles which were not as high as her face; but which she could not have got through and kept her hands out of; and bits of those brambles were actually found in her skin and . . . the brambles in question were found on examination to have been broken through, and to have little shreds of her dress and little spots of blood upon them here and there" (406). Two: the image Pip conjures up for his youthful acquiescence to Biddy's guidance through the thicket of language: "By the help of Biddy . . . I struggled through the alphabet as if it had been a bramble-bush; getting considerably worried and scratched by every letter" (75). The women who navigate these pungent, puncturing bushes offer more of an affront to male sexuality and authority than the novel cares to sustain.

If in Pip's imagination Biddy represents a distressing (all too available, all too appropriate) sexual possibility, whatever desires she herself can be said to express finally appear thoroughly managed and manageable. Her feminine pliancy is evident from the first in her concern for others' hands: when they are children, Biddy tutors Pip, remedying his early orthographic troubles; when, with no apparent discomposure, she eventually transfers her affections from nephew to uncle, she also trains Joe's maladroit hand (473–74). Through a disturbing but not unfamiliar bit of Dickensian sleight of hand, the minimal degree of erotic errancy that Biddy has displayed is fully recuperated in the redirection of her interest toward Joe. He, for one, can identify with having dirt under the nails ("'No, don't wipe it off—for God's sake, give me your blackened hand!'" Pip cries to him [304]), though upon moving into the Gargery household, Biddy concomitantly improves her personal hygiene: "I became conscious of a change in Biddy . . . her hands were always clean" (152). Ultimately the new Mrs. Joe exhibits a hand fully accommodated to matrimonial-maternal orthodoxy: "Biddy looked down at her child, and put its little hand to her lips, and then put the good matronly hand with which she had touched it, into mine. There was something in the action and in the light pressure of Biddy's wedding-ring, that had a very pretty eloquence in it" (490). Light though it may be, the wedding ring exerts sufficient pressure to remind Pip of the female trajectory parallel to, but divergent from, his own.

Unlike Miss Skiffins, who requires combat—however figurative—to bring about the bliss of connubial sterility, Biddy accedes willingly to matrimony. Molly, by contrast with both, perpetrates the story's only interfemale bout, and she is consequently subject to an even more violent form of correction. Intervening in the boys' dilettantish display of arm-wrestling aptitude, Jaggers reveals Molly to be the real heavyweight among the novel's prizefighters: "'There's power here,' said Mr. Jaggers, coolly tracing out the sinews with his forefinger. 'Very few men have the power of wrist that this woman has. It's remarkable what mere force of grip there is in these hands. I have had occasion to notice many hands; but I never saw stronger in that respect, man's or woman's, than these'" (237). While the boys' sparring connotes a certain homoeroticism, the sexual provocation of Molly's violence is identifiable only through the extraordinary means requisite to its suppression. Even the titillating gaze we have come to associate with such manual displays is here rendered paralyzing, as the Medusa one cannot but look upon: "We all stopped in our foolish contention. . . . When she held her hands out, she took her eyes from Mr. Jaggers, and turned them watchfully on every one of the rest of us in succession" (236). Seduction here amounts to a rage kept in check by its ritual humiliation. No mere "placid boxer" in drag (unlike Miss Skiffins's, these hands are always available for viewing), Molly exhibits a savagery that the narrative's libidinal economy can barely contain.

Wemmick later comes to narrate Molly's story, explaining the source of those mysterious scars and that "force of grip":

> "[Molly] was tried at the Old Bailey for murder, and was acquitted. . . . The murdered woman—more a match for the man, certainly, in point of years—was found dead in a barn near Hounslow Heath. There had been a violent struggle, perhaps a fight. She was bruised and scratched and torn, and had been held by the throat at last and choked. Now, there was no reasonable evidence to im-

plicate any person but this woman, and, on the improbabilities of her having been able to do it, Mr. Jaggers principally rested his case. You may be sure," said Wemmick, touching me on the sleeve, "that he never dwelt upon the strength of her hands then, though he sometimes does now. . . . [Molly] was so very artfully dressed from the time of her apprehension, that she looked much slighter than she really was; in particular, her sleeves are always remembered to have been so skilfully contrived that her arms had quite a delicate look. She had only a bruise or two about her—nothing for a tramp—but the backs of her hands were lacerated, and the question was, was it with finger-nails?" (405–6)

In form, Molly's battle with her rival differs little from the other bouts of jealousy in the novel; the fact, however, of the players' gender-reversal (here two women fight for the love of a man), as well as the fight's more serious consequences (the death of one combatant, the other's loss of her child), makes a difference. Pugilism, as we have seen, even when heterosexual, relies on intermasculine codes of conduct to generate its eroticism; when two women fight, crossing the border to sexuality is a more perilous prospect. To fight *as a woman*, this narrative suggests, is a deadly undertaking, because it threatens normative femininity so radically: the possibility of an *avant la lettre* lesbian eroticism here is rapidly chastened and expunged, for female sexuality undergoes the most rigorous surveillance.

Instead of demonstrating pure animus, then, Molly represents so high-voltage a current of sexual violence that its erotic charge must be defused through the most repressive means conceivable. The punishment she suffers for her manual conduct is a life sentence of "taming" at Jaggers's hands, but more is at stake in her representation than a wholesale denial of female eroticism: she exemplifies the way in which repression functions as a vigilant and perpetual *management* of eros. Jaggers, as we have noted, exhibits a sadistic pleasure in displaying and exercising the "wild beast tamed" (224) to the cohort of young men he gathers for dinner:

"If you talk of strength," said Mr. Jaggers, "I'll show you a wrist. Molly, let them see your wrist."

Her entrapped hand was on the table, but she had already put her other hand behind her waist. "Master," she said, in a low voice, with her eyes attentively and entreatingly fixed upon him. "Don't."

"I'll show you a wrist," repeated Mr. Jaggers, with an immovable determination to show it. "Molly, let them see your wrist."

"Master," she again murmured. "Please!"

"Molly," said Mr. Jaggers, not looking at her, but obstinately looking at the opposite side of the room, "let them see *both* your wrists. Show them. Come!"

He took his hand from hers, and turned that wrist up on the table. She brought her other hand from behind her, and held the two out side by side. (236)

This sadomasochistic tableau is the taming technique to which Wemmick has alluded—a performance Jaggers clearly must stage with some regularity in order to keep his handmaid in line. The sheer power of Molly's hands requires the sheer coercion of Jaggers's discipline; his delight at showing her off derives not from admiration of her strength but from pride in having controlled it.

In the magnetic field of the novel's eroticism, Molly occupies the negative pole; what, then, ought we to make of the connection between her and Estella, so clearly designated the protagonist's sexual cathode? Pip first suspects their relationship when, shortly after Jaggers's exhibition of Molly, he has an uncanny feeling upon meeting the grown-up Estella:

What *was* it that was borne in upon my mind when she stood still and looked attentively at me? . . . As my eyes followed her white hand, again the same dim suggestion that I could not possibly grasp, crossed me. My involuntary start occasioned her to lay her hand upon my arm. Instantly the ghost passed once more, and was gone.

What *was* it? (259)

Pip regards Estella's pointing finger and, following the novel's usual exchange, his inability literally to "grasp" his feeling is transferred onto, and compensated by, Estella's laying *her* hand on him. At their next meeting, Estella's hand again disturbs him: as he sees "her face at the coach window and her hand waving," he is once more startled by an ineffable likeness: "What *was* the nameless shadow which again in that one instant had passed?" (284). In being designated "nameless," this relation—unlike those other terms ("secret burden," "jiggered") whose namelessness remains implicit—ceases to be so: the novel of course finally can name it, denominating this uncanniness *maternity*. And as soon as namelessness is articulable, it has consequences in the plot.

Pip at last lights upon the "one link of association" (403) that confirms the affiliation he suspects: having witnessed "the action of Estella's fingers as they worked" (373) at knitting, he then finds "a certain action of [Molly's] fingers as she spoke arrested my attention. . . . The action of her fingers was like the action of knitting. . . . Surely, I had seen exactly such eyes and such hands, on a memorable occasion very lately! . . . I had passed by a chance swift from Estella's name to the fingers with their knitting action, and the attentive eyes. And I felt absolutely certain that this woman was Estella's mother" (403). More surprising than the revelation of Molly as Estella's mother is the suggestion that Pip could establish that relationship based on the appearance of their hands—for other than this "action of knitting," they have nothing in common. The very attempt to align these two sets of hands by force of uncanny conjunction only points up the antithesis between them: Molly's are marked while Estella's are blank; Molly's signify (even if what they designate is sexuality held in check) while Estella's do not. For Estella is so insistently the object of erotic denotation that her depiction virtually evacuates the connotative register in which we have located sexuality elsewhere in the novel.

The link to Molly persists in interfering with Estella's appropriateness as Pip's amorous desideratum, but the novel sufficiently manages this taint to keep it from tarnishing the daughter even as it continually condemns the mother. In a rare moment of offering advice, Jaggers discourages Pip from revealing Estella's pedigree, arguing, " 'Add the case that you had loved her, Pip, and had made her the subject of those "poor dreams" ' . . . then I tell you that you had better—and would much sooner when you had thought well of it—chop off that bandaged left hand of yours with your bandaged right hand, and then pass the chopper on to Wemmick there, to cut *that* off, too' " (426). For Pip "to establish her parentage" would be "to drag her back to disgrace," and consequently to annihilate his own "dreams"; in Jaggers's image, it would amount to amputation—or, by the logic of hands in the novel, castration. This exposure would associate Estella with Molly, whose brutally inscribed flesh has always engendered castration anxiety; the Estella whom Jaggers counsels Pip not to reveal is in a true sense Molly's daughter—one with fantastically disabling sexual powers.

Pip of course resists the impulse to disclose Estella's origins, and in so doing he both protects her from "disgrace" and saves himself from the threat of dismemberment. In fact, Estella has never seemed particularly dangerous, for while her mother is continually and actively tamed, Estella is so almost by definition. Her irascible demeanor and the sexual frigidity that accompanies it have less to do with serving her own desires than with her fashioning as a suitably impossible object for the male characters captivated by her looks. To the extent that Estella appears as a desiring subject, she does so as the "mere puppet" (288) of her guardian, Miss Havisham; and as if to ensure that the willfulness evident in her aggressive passivity will be utterly disarmed, she receives a decisive pummeling at the hands of her husband, Drummle (490–91). Unlike those of the other female characters we have considered, Estella's hands are virtually maintenance-free; there is little of interest to say about them, except that little is said of them. Since she signals the overt representation of the subject's desire, Estella's appearances in the narrative obviate the necessity for sex appeal to reside wholly in the linguistic timbre.[39] As if to amplify the silence of her own desire, Estella is shown simply to have a "white hand" (259), and although Pip can fondle it, hers is possibly the least erogenous hand in the book:

> "I am beholden to you as the cause of [Miss Havisham's relatives] being so busy and so mean in vain, and there is my hand upon it."
>
> As she gave it me playfully—for her darker mood had been but momentary—I held it and put it to my lips. "You ridiculous boy," said Estella, "will you never take warning? Or do you kiss my hand in the same spirit in which I once let you kiss my cheek?"
>
> "What spirit was that?" said I.
>
> ". . . A spirit of contempt for the fawners and plotters."
>
> "If I say yes, may I kiss the cheek again?"
>
> "You should have asked before you touched the hand. But, yes, if you like."
>
> I leaned down, and her calm face was like a statue's. (287–88)

Estella succeeds as Pip's proper erotic object by the very thoroughness of her de-eroticization in the narrative. She does not simply represent the refusal ordinarily requisite to provoke desire; she is constitutively phantasmatic. Although we are meant to register Pip's arousal at the alluring

---

39. George Bernard Shaw registers this sentiment in writing, "The notion that [Pip] could ever have been happy with Estella: indeed that anyone could ever have been happy with Estella, is positively unpleasant"; *Critical Essays on Charles Dickens's Great Expectations*, ed. Michael Cotsell (Boston: G. K. Hall, 1990), 41.

sight of her, the narrative voice — otherwise so rich in provocative peri-phrasis — becomes laryngitic around her "beauty," relying on such tropes as "indescribable majesty and . . . indescribable charm" (491). While the novel elsewhere registers eroticism in a combination of denotative re-fusal and connotative titillation, at the points of Pip's greatest official erotic interest, these strategies are reversed: in asserting fortissimo Pip's desire for Estella, the narrative need no longer marshal its battery of sotto voce techniques. At the moment desire's tale can be told, the narrative modulates into abstract diction, abandoning all of its prior engagement with corporeality: "She was so much changed, was so much more beau-tiful, so much more womanly, in all things winning admiration had made such wonderful advance, that I seemed to have made none" (256).[40]

For those who take the singular voicing in the plot of Pip's feelings for Estella to indicate the text's only genuine eroticism, the novel reads as a conventional romance. Such readers, however, are obliged to account for the fact that, even in its famously revised ending, *Great Expectations* resists bringing about the usual novelistic resolution in matrimony. As though to clear the space necessary for sanctioned, sanctified hetero-sexual romance, male homoeroticism is finally repudiated and female subjectivity thoroughly thwarted; yet we are left wondering why, despite these preparations, the romance plot is not more emphatically accom-plished. One might, of course, point to the final version of the novel's ending, where Pip records the sensation of "what [he] had never felt before . . . the friendly touch of the once insensible hand" (491). If the novel does, as Bulwer-Lytton wished, conclude in happy domesticity, then its last sentence — "I took her hand in mine, and we went out of the ruined place . . ." (493) — would provide a coherent resolution for its manual thematics. Yet the suspended animation entailed not only by the preservation of the original ending but also by the ambiguity of the final version itself ("I saw no shadow of another parting from her") makes so smug a termination precarious.[41] Despite critical attestations of the

---

40. The narrative here relies on what Roland Barthes identifies as the trope for beauty, which "cannot assert itself save in the form of a citation": *catachresis*, the "rhetorical figure which fills this blank in the object of comparison whose existence is altogether trans-ferred to the language of the object to which it is compared"; *S/Z*, trans. Richard Miller (New York: Hill and Wang, 1974), 33–34. Catachresis evokes that which *has no name* (still in a denotative register), unlike the tropes for unspeakability (associated with connota-tion), which designate that which *must not be named*.
41. On the ambiguity of the novel's ending, D. A. Miller, *Narrative and Its Discontents: Prob-lems of Closure in the Traditional Novel* (Princeton: Princeton University Press, 1981), writes:

plot's "perfection,"[42] the fact that the story is waylaid *before* the threshold has left readers notoriously unsettled about its ultimate outcome.

Why should a novel with such copious erotic investments finally fail to resolve the most basic romance plot? One answer is that its strategies for regulating the vagaries of sexual desire simply prove *too* effective: they discipline all sexuality, even the most orthodox, quite out of existence. Not only are female domination, male homosexuality, onanism, and sadomasochism eliminated, but genitally oriented, maritally legitimated heterosexual monogamy itself comes to seem impossible.[43] Although the novel entertains a range of sexual designations, exchanges, developments, and diffusions, the sexual hegemony in which it issues becomes so powerful as ultimately to suspend not only that order's own ideal—institutionalized heterosexual monogamy—but anything that exceeds the fantasy of the solitary subject.

Yet despite the apparent elimination of all erotic possibilities, this sole remainder—the solitary imagination—suggests that bodily self-

---

"In both endings, evidence of closure coexists, overlaps, and often coincides undecidably with counterevidence of the narratable" (275). I take undecidability—whether, for instance, Pip drops or hangs onto Estella's hand after the tale is told—to be one of the novel's techniques for sustaining the masturbatory erotics that have impelled it.

42. Shaw, for instance, writes: "Dickens did in fact know that *Great Expectations* was his most compactly perfect book" (34); J. Hillis Miller, *Charles Dickens: The World of His Novels* (Cambridge, Mass.: Harvard University Press, 1958), asserts: "*Great Expectations* is the most unified and concentrated expression of Dickens' abiding sense of the world, and Pip might be called the archetypal Dickens hero. In *Great Expectations* Dickens' particular view of things is expressed with a concreteness and symbolic intensity he never surpassed" (249).

43. One is reminded of Freud's ironic account of the strictures fostered by bourgeois sexual ideology in *Civilization and Its Discontents* (1930; New York: Norton, 1961):

As regards the sexually mature individual, the choice of an object is restricted to the opposite sex, and most extragenital satisfactions are forbidden as perversions. The requirement, demonstrated in these prohibitions, that there shall be a single kind of sexual life for everyone, disregards the dissimilarities, whether innate or acquired, in the sexual constitution of human beings; it cuts off a fair number of them from sexual enjoyment, and so becomes the source of serious injustice. . . . But heterosexual genital love, which has remained exempt from outlawry, is itself restricted by further limitations, in the shape of insistence upon legitimacy and monogamy. Present-day civilization makes it plain that it will only permit sexual relationships on the basis of a solitary, indissoluble bond between one man and one woman, and that it does not like sexuality as a source of pleasure in its own right and is only prepared to tolerate it because there is so far no substitute for it as a means of propagating the human race. (60)

regulation may generate its own rewards. For even as the novel inculcates lessons about sexual continence in its audience, it agitates and incorporates the erotogenic pleasures of solitary reading. Indeed, the very irresolution of the ending offers an alternative to erotic abjuration, one that animates the oscillation between the hegemony of the marriage plot and the violence of its refusal. Rather than resolving all the previous travails of hands through the story, the novel's concluding ambivalence may instead reinscribe the mode of sexual deferral by which it has operated from the first: in the manner of an imaginary object held perpetually at bay by autoerotic reverie, its eroticism can persist precisely by being suspended as undecidable. Just as Estella can never be more to Pip than a "poor dream"—the object of solitary sexual fantasy—so the residuum of the novel's ending demonstrates the sustainability, rather than the complete evacuation, of the masturbatory thematic that has mobilized its eroticism throughout. The ambiguity of the ending thus accomplishes a shift in the location of the novel's erotics that I have already suggested: in its finality it extinguishes the evocative narration through which sexuality has been connoted; but in the irresolution of its plot—its denotative practice—it now preserves those concerns as strictly undecidable. Even as it draws to an end, the novel resituates masturbation—sustains it, that is to say, by refusing closure.[44] The originary sexuality that enables the novel's flood of erotic potentials, masturbation also serves as the remainder left behind when all other possibilities have been forsworn.

The novel's emptying out of all erotic prospects—except for the initial one, which secures solipsistic subject-formation against the erotic intrusions of the other—also functions as a powerful defense against scandal. In cultivating indirection to insinuate sexual meanings, and in

---

44. This is to argue that the oft-discussed problem of the novel's ending be seen as *productive*. It is precisely the resistance to closure that makes *Great Expectations* such a peculiar choice as exemplar for Brooks's discussion of plottedness:

> We have at the end what could appropriately be called a "cure" from plot, in Pip's recognition of the general forfeiture of plotting, his renunciation of any attempt to direct his life. Plot comes to resemble a diseased, fevered state of the organism caught in the machinery of a desire which must eventually be renounced. Plot, we come to understand, was a state of abnormality or deviance. . . . Deviance is the very condition for life to be "narratable": the state of normality is devoid of interest, energy, and the possibility for narration. (*Reading for the Plot*, 138–39)

I understand the reinscription of "deviance" (particularly if we allow the word its sense as sexual deviance) to unsettle the novel's closure, and the attempt to "cure" it—however unsuccessful—as an effect of sexual ideology's "machinery."

demonstrating that such meanings belong to a regimen of the strict-
est privacy, Dickens's literary technique guards against the revelation
of secrecy upon which scandal depends. Having considered how unspeakability arises from both a sexual formation imagined to be utterly
private and a textual form that derives enormous benefit from it—the
realist novel—I will, in the chapters that follow, take up narratives of
public, illegal, and illicit sexuality in the arena of scandal, both fictional
and not. While *Great Expectations* exemplifies a literary mode of holding
scandal in check, it still depends upon the danger of scandal's eruption:
keeping this threat hanging before it enables the novel to shape the constraints on sexual expression into a fecund form of literary possibility.

THREE

PRIVACY AND PUBLICITY

IN THE VICTORIAN

SEX SCANDAL

Dickens's account of sexuality in *Great Expectations* is so thoroughly relegated to the linguistic register of connotation as to exemplify for the reader that the subject simply cannot be discussed openly. The very unwittingness of the representation, which finds its way into that respectable prose without its author seeming to know about it, is testimony to the unspeakability of sexuality in the novel. Imagined as entirely secret, the sexuality that *Great Expectations* conveys is by definition unavailable to public scrutiny; autoeroticism is the form of sexuality historically structured as the most solitary of proscribed acts, and is thus the principal figure for this covert sexuality. Masturbation is the novel's prototypical erotic mode, for it is the species of sexuality most apposite to a narrative of such affirmative repression.

The present chapter shifts its focus away from the novel—though not from narrative—in order to investigate the other site in Victorian Britain most productive of sexuality as the unspeakable subject: the scandal. A good sex scandal—one that grips the imagination with the lavish recounting of scurrilous details—appears at first glance the very inverse of the Dickens novel; but the ideological entailments of the scandal and the novel are very nearly related. For all its talk, that is to say, a scandal sheet also teaches its readers the words they must avoid.

This chapter analyzes an archetypal scandal, the case of Ernest Boulton and Frederick Park, two young men who were arrested in 1870 for dressing as women and subsequently tried for conspiring to commit sodomy. The texts for this reading consist of court transcripts, depositions, and indictments, as well as contemporary accounts of the trial.[1]

1. Information on this case comes largely from material in the Public Record Office, Chancery Lane, London. I am indebted to Jeffrey Weeks for generously guiding me to the archival material. The principal documents relating to the case are: the initial indictments in the Central Criminal Court, from June 6, 1870 (CRIM4/777), which were subsequently dropped; the two indictments in the Queen's Bench, on the indictment roll for Trinity Term, 33rd Vict. (1870) (KB12/99); the index of indictments for the Queen's Bench (INDI/6687/1), which records the issuance of the indictments along with the results in the case; the depositions taken at the police court in Bow Street, April 28–May 30, 1870 (KB6/3, part 1); and the trial transcripts from the Queen's Bench, subsequently filed in the records of the Department of the Public Prosecutor (DPP4/6). The last item, entitled "The Queen v. Boulton and Others, at Westminster Hall in the Queen's Bench, May 9–15, 1871," contains longhand transcriptions produced daily during the trial from shorthand reporters' verbatim notes; each of the trial's six days is numbered individually (day four taking two volumes separately numerated), and the whole is bound together. Parenthetical page references herein indicate day/volume number followed by page number. Punctuation, capitalization, and spelling, which are highly variable in the trial records (depending on the idiosyncracies of each transcriber), have been regularized, presumably not to the detriment of the records, since they report spoken words. Documents that do not transcribe speech (principally the indictments) have been reproduced verbatim. Further contemporary accounts that I have consulted include London newspaper reports from April 29, 1870, to June 7, 1871: the *Times* (daily and Sunday), the *Pall Mall Gazette*, the *Daily News*, the *Daily Telegraph*, the *Standard*, the *Illustrated Police News*, and the *Globe and Traveller*. I also refer to a pamphlet published in May 1870 by George Clarke, first under the title *The Lives of Boulton and Park: Extraordinary Revelations*, and reprinted with some additions as *Men in Petticoats*. The case is reported as well in *The Annual Register: A Review of Public Events at Home and Abroad* for 1871 (London: Rivingtons, 1872), 220–24.

The only published accounts of the case to make use of the trial documents are those of Jeffrey Weeks, in "Inverts, Perverts, and Mary-Annes: Male Prostitution and the Regulation of Homosexuality in England in the Nineteenth and Early Twentieth Centuries," *Journal of Homosexuality* 6, no. 1/2 (Fall/Winter 1980–81): 113–34; and Neil Bartlett, in his evocative account of gay male life in late-nineteenth-century London, *Who Was That Man? A Present for Mr. Oscar Wilde* (London: Serpent's Tail, 1988), 128–43. Weeks also mentions the case in *Coming Out: Homosexual Politics in Britain, from the Nineteenth Century to the Present* (London: Quartet, 1977), 14, 37. H. Montgomery Hyde describes the affair in *The Love That Dared Not Speak Its Name* (Boston: Little, Brown, 1970), 94–98, and reprints this account in *A Tangled Web: Sex Scandals in British Politics and Society* (London: Futura, 1986), 84–88. Hyde relies entirely on the more elaborate and pejorative version, entitled "Pretty Fanny's Way," in William Roughead, *Bad Companions* (Edinburgh: W. Green & Son, 1930), 149–83. Roughead's account, in turn, derives from newspapers (which were largely unable to report the massive medical evidence) and upon a contemporary pamphlet that appears to redact the newspaper version of the events: *The Trial of Boulton and Park, with Hurt and Fiske. A Complete*

This case serves well as a model scandal for several reasons: it was sensational and enormously popular, widely reported in all the major papers of the day; it demonstrably created controversy and roused public feelings of outrage and horror; and its content, sex between men, was felt to be the most execrable and unspeakable of crimes. The arguments adduced in and around the trial were typical of Victorian scandals generally, covering issues that range from the judicial regulation of private life, the relation of the news media to their subjects, and the credibility of scientific authorities, to the English national character, middle-class privilege, and gender prerogatives.

If the most scandalous scandal is unquestionably the sex scandal, then the scandal most sexual is arguably the male homosexual one. In post-Enlightenment Western Europe, the male homosexual has required scandal in order to come into being. Public homosexual identities were formed in large measure through the revelation, via scandal, of private sexual activities between men; unmentionable even according to its ancient legal definition (*crimen inter Christanos non nominandam*), male-male sex has traditionally been the locus for scandals considered so heinous as to be designated utterly unspeakable—and never more so than in the nineteenth century.[2] The Boulton and Park case occurred at the point when the homosexual was first becoming identifiable within a sociomedical sexual taxonomy, but was not yet recognized as a juridical subject.[3] The trial arose in the midst of the shift, which Foucault emphasizes,

---

and Accurate Report of the Proceedings . . . (Manchester: John Heywood, 1871). Peter Ackroyd discusses Boulton and Park briefly, and includes a newspaper illustration of them, in *Dressing Up: Transvestism and Drag, the History of an Obsession* (New York: Simon & Schuster, 1979), 83–85.

2. For accounts of male homosexual scandals in the era prior to the one under consideration here, see Rictor Norton, *Mother Clap's Molly House: The Gay Subculture in England, 1700–1830* (London: GMP, 1992), and Louis Crompton, *Byron and Greek Love: Homophobia in 19th-Century England* (Berkeley: University of California Press, 1985).

3. The institutionalization of homosexuality as illegal is a familiar story: the notorious Labouchère amendment of the 1885 Criminal Law Amendment Act made "any act of gross indecency" between men, whether committed in public or private, punishable with up to two years of hard labor; the act subsumed the narrower injunction against sodomy—anal sex with a man *or* a woman, or bestiality—by virtually criminalizing gay male style itself. See Weeks, *Coming Out*; Hyde, *Love That Dared*; F. B. Smith, "Labouchère's Amendment to the Criminal Law Amendment Bill," *Historical Studies* (Melbourne) 17, no. 67 (October 1976): 165–75; Ed Cohen, *Talk on the Wilde Side: Toward a Genealogy of a Discourse on Male Sexualities* (New York: Routledge, 1993), chap. 4; and Christopher Craft, *Another Kind of Love: Male Homosexual Desire in English Discourse, 1850–1920* (Berkeley: University of California Press, 1994), chap. 1.

from prosecuting specific sexual acts to disciplining the type of person who was likely to commit such acts.[4] Precisely because statutory law lagged behind ideological formations of sexuality, the case demanded a far more explicit elaboration of sexual definitions than trials after the legislative changes of 1885, which could simply enforce the law without inquiring into its rectitude.

My discussion of the case is divided into three broad areas. I first take up the phantasmatic notion of privacy upon which scandal depends, a construction promoted on the one hand by the court, through both the elaborate medical testimony it demands and its own shifting legal architecture, and on the other by the newspapers, which make a show of exhibiting this privacy for public consumption. The second phase of my inquiry considers how disputes over sexuality serve as the occasion for debates about the distribution of power across social axes set in an oblique relation to sex — namely, nation, class, and gender. I examine the configuration of such attributes in the representation of the sex-criminal's antithesis, the so-called general public. In the third section of the chapter, I consider the interdependency of literature and scandal exemplified by this case. Through a discussion of the trial's literary moments — when epistolary evidence arises, when questions of literary culture and interpretation are thematized, and when the case is subsequently written into a pornographic memoir — I analyze the reliance of the whole scandal procedure on hermeneutic maneuvers, from reading bodies to reading texts. Through this progression from privacy to publicity, from individual subjects to social categories, and from abstract to concrete texts, I hope also to adumbrate a move from the relatively overt and demonstrable ideological efforts at enunciating sex through the scandal, to the attenuated, subtle, and anfractuous process through which literary texts put sex into language.

I

The facts — as the detective novel would say — are these. Upon leaving the Strand Theatre on April 28, 1870, Ernest Boulton and Frederick Park, two middle-class Londoners in their early twenties, were arrested on charges of outraging public decency. Boulton, known to his admirers as Stella, wore a cherry-colored silk evening gown trimmed with white

---

4. *The History of Sexuality*, vol. 1, trans. Robert Hurley (New York: Vintage, 1978), 43.

lace, as well as a wig, a braided chignon, and bracelets; "Fanny" Park was arrayed in a low-cut dark green satin dress trimmed with black lace, a matching shawl, blond curls, and white kid gloves. The police had been trailing the two drag debutantes for the preceding year, from their legitimate appearances playing women's parts in amateur theatrical performances to their frequent cross-dressed promenades through public markets and arcades, restaurants, public houses, balls, and theaters. After being arrested for appearing publicly in women's attire, they were taken into the police station at Bow Street where they were detained overnight. They might have been routinely charged and dismissed the next morning with little commotion, as they had been before, had it not happened that the police superintendent ran across a friend of his, the divisional police surgeon, in the street the next morning.

The superintendent invited the doctor, James Paul, into the station and requested that he examine the cross-dressers "for the purpose of ascertaining their sex."[5] Despite the fact that, even according to the officer who arrested them, "they certainly looked . . . more like women than men" (*Times*, April 30, 1870), the superintendent's insistence on obtaining a professional opinion seems intended more to harass the prisoners than to determine their sex — which must have been recognized as the basis for the arrest in the first place. When Paul caught sight of the two effeminate men, a novel idea occurred to him, inspired perhaps by the Continental sexologists whose work he appears to have just been reading.[6] The doctor "wished to ascertain something more" than the prisoners' sex,

5. Police court records (KB6/3, part 1) of May 20, 1870.
6. In "Inverts, Perverts," Weeks gives credence to Paul's testimony that he "had never encountered a similar case in his whole career," and had only read of it once in an ill-remembered volume on medical jurisprudence (116). Paul's testimony, however, was in many places discredited, and he was seriously reprimanded for his examination by the judge, who stated that the doctor had "evidently been studying foreign works upon this subject" and made reference to "the French writers who prompted the inquiry of Mr. Paul" (6:264, 267). We might also note the congruity between Paul's description of his examination and that of sexologist Ambroise Tardieu, in *La Pédérastie* (1857): "Most [suspects] submit without difficulty, and of their own will, in a sense, to the examination. I command [the prisoner] to strip, and very often, without any other formality, he spontaneously adopts the position most favorable to my inspection"; quoted and translated in Sherwood A. Williams, "The Perversion of Representation: Naturalism and Decadence in the Late Nineteenth Century" (Ph.D. diss., University of California, Berkeley, 1990), 85. Nonetheless, Weeks's larger point — that legal and medical authorities were, in the main, ignorant about homosexual subcultures — stands.

and he interpreted the superintendent's request as a "justification for examining them in any way [he] thought proper." He took them into a
dimly lit room at the back of the station house and completed his examination in less than five minutes. Here, as he deposed three weeks later
before the magistrate's court, is what his *recherches* led him to discover:

> I examined Boulton first. He was then dressed as a woman. . . . I
> said, "Unfasten your things and drop them down; please to step
> out of them." . . . The clothes having been removed out of the way,
> I took a desk stool and said to the prisoner, "Put yourself over that
> stool." Without saying a word he did so, in the very way I required
> him. I examined him and found him to be a man. The anus was
> dilated, and more dilatable, and the muscles surrounding the anus
> easily opened and I could see right into the rectum. And the appear-
> ances I saw could be accounted for by the insertion of a foreign
> body, and one insertion could not account for the appearance I saw,
> but the insertion of a foreign body numerous times would account
> for those appearances. Boulton said nothing to me, or I to him.
> I considered the penis and scrotum were of an inordinate length.
> Boulton was then removed and the prisoner Park came behind the
> screen. I said to him the same I had said to Boulton. Park at the time
> was wearing female apparel. He is a man. I noticed that his private
> parts were elongated. I examined the anus: that was very much di-
> lated, and dilatable to a very great extent. The insertion of a foreign
> body numerous times would cause such an appearance. The rectum
> was large and there was some discoloration round the edge of the
> anus, caused probably by sore. I have been in practice sixteen years,
> seven years out of that at the St. Pancras General Dispensary, and I
> have on very many occasions examined the anus of persons. I do
> not in my practice ever remember to have seen such an appearance
> of the anus as those of the two prisoners presented. The insertion
> of a man's person would cause the appearances I have described.[7]

The moment Dr. Paul turned the prisoners around and shifted his
gaze from their genitals to their anuses, a critical transformation took
place: the issue ceased to be the conflict between the drag queens' costumes and their anatomical gender, and became instead a question of
their illicit sexual practice. A penis, in this context, supplies information

7. Police court records (KB6/3, part 1) of May 20, 1870.

about the public ascription of gender, while an anus bespeaks private sexuality. The hidden crime Paul claimed to have revealed—buggery—was, until 1967, punishable with ten years to life imprisonment in England (the death penalty for the crime having been repealed a decade before Boulton and Park's arrest). Largely on the basis of the doctor's evidence, the prisoners were remanded to custody, now no longer for the misdemeanor of public indecency, but on far graver charges that, in the language of the indictment, they "feloniously wickedly and against the order of nature with each other did commit and perpetrate that detestable and abominable crime of buggery not to be named among Christians."[8] Through the course of sensational legal proceedings that lasted more than a year, evidence astonishing for both its quantity and its character was brought to court. The case implicated not only these two divas of the London drag circuit, but several of their paramours as well, including Boulton's so-called husband, Lord Arthur Clinton, M.P., who died (possibly a suicide) before the case came to trial, and other unidentified men of substance.[9] To the relief of most of the trial's par-

---

8. Initial indictments (later rescinded) from the Central Criminal Court, June 6, 1870 (CRIM4/777). To his credit, the chief justice reproved the police surgeon for his conduct, and further chided the treasury department for relying upon evidence obtained in such a ludicrous manner. Recounting Paul's contributions to the case, though with more than a hint of his own pleasure in doing so, the judge admonished:

> He had no more authority to call upon them to undergo this revolting examination than if he had caught a man in the street and asked him to unbutton his breeches and let him see what was behind. And I hope that gentleman in the future will know better than to take upon himself, without the direction of a magistrate and without the direction even of the police, the responsibility of inquiring into such a thing as this. If instead of two effeminate young men he had met with a man having the strength and energy to do it, he would not have escaped summary punishment for proposing so revolting a thing. (6:264–65)

In the same breath that the justice rebukes the doctor he reinforces the essential reasonableness of his actions, given the "effeminate" appearance of the men. It was the same reasoning that led the doctor to his examination in the first place, as he explained: "I should examine any man in the same way if dressed in women's clothes" (KB6/3, part 1).
9. The Pall Mall Gazette editorialized: "That Lord Arthur Clinton must be tried as soon as he is caught is clear from what has already come to light, and it is understood that the evidence in possession of the Government involves at least one person whose title is more than one of courtesy" (June 8, 1870). The class status of the defendants is indicated by a report in the Times: "Boulton is, it appeared, the son of a stockbroker, a young man of about 23 years of age, of no occupation; Park is the son of one of the Masters of the Court of Common Pleas, was educated to the law, and is articled to a respectable firm of attorneys" (May 10, 1871). With respect to their income, which had bearing on the solici-

ticipants and spectators, Boulton and Park were ultimately acquitted of all but the initial charges of outraging public decency.

Beginning with the evidence that presented itself as most objective—the medical testimony—we can see how the scandal promulgated a fantasy of privacy in order to exhibit its violation for public consumption.[10] The medical evidence was crucial to the scandal's establishment of privacy by means of its exposure, for medicine construes personal identity through examination and interpretation of the individual body. But such evidence is far from decisive: once the testimony about the state of Boulton and Park's anuses had catalyzed the felony indictment against them, its accuracy was almost immediately contested. A week after Paul's examination, while the accused were still detained at Bow Street, a second medical inspection took place at the behest of the prisoners' counsel. Several weeks after that, a third examination, made by six of the most prominent physicians and surgeons in the city, was carried out at great length on the young men in Newgate prison. Several doctors contradicted Paul's evidence, such as Frederick Le Gros Clark, vice president of the Royal Medical Society, who testified that the appearance of the prisoners' posteriors "was natural, differing in no respect from hundreds whom I have examined" (Times, May 30, 1870). The assumption behind the examinations was that buggery leaves legible traces upon the body, and that, given a sufficiently penetrating gaze ("I could see right into the rectum"), no criminally sexual act could go undetected by medical science. Doctors on opposing sides of the case disagreed only about what they had seen, not about the supposition that observation could adequately reveal the defendants' sexual practices. If they were sodomites, their bodies should have said so.

---

tation charges, Boulton's mother testified that "her son was a clerk at a bank, and had to leave from ill health. . . . With regard to the expenses of performances, she believed that Lord Arthur received the proceeds of performances in the country and paid all the expenses. The performances were not for the purpose of money, but she believed money was taken. . . . Her son had about 1£ a week pocket money." Park's father was called to give "some evidence as to the resources of his son, and stated that since 1867 he had had about 2,500£. (This was to show he had not been in any want of money)" (May 13, 1871).

10. Jürgen Habermas, in The Structural Transformation of the Public Sphere: An Inquiry into a Category of Bourgeois Society, trans. Thomas Burger (Cambridge, Mass.: MIT Press, 1991), supplies a theory and history for the reciprocal reliance of privacy and public opinion on each other. Habermas writes, for instance: "Subjectivity, as the innermost core of the private, was always already oriented to an audience (Publikum). The opposite of the intimateness whose vehicle was the written word was indiscretion and not publicity as such" (49).

Apparently straightforward medical questions—what was the condition of the defendants' behinds and what did this condition signify?—issued in hopeless irresolution.[11] Such confusion was hardly without merit, though, for it functioned effectively to recast the medical evidence from a realm of neutral observation into a series of polemics capable of generating extraordinary publicity. The physicians' testimony probed what it understood to be the absolute frontier of privacy: in exposing for general consumption the defendants' anuses, it focused unblinkingly on that usually invisible fundament of personal subjectivity whose penetration has long been synonymous with perversion.[12] Lest

11. Contemporary medical treatises bear out the physicians' confusion: they tend to doubt that sodomy can be determined solely on the basis of physical signs, yet they indicate the availability of sexological work from the 1850s that makes such claims. Alfred Swaine Taylor, author of a prominent forensic pathology text, *Medical Jurisprudence*, and a defense witness in the case, treats sodomy (together with bestiality) as a strictly legal question in both the 1850 (third) and 1866 (eighth) editions of his work; likewise, Theodric Romeyn Beck and John B. Beck's influential *Elements of Medical Jurisprudence*, 10th ed. (Albany: Little & Co., 1850), adduces "the effects of a frequent repetition of the crime," but cautions, "No man, however, ought to be condemned on medical proofs solely: The physician should only deliver his opinion in favor or against an accusation already preferred" (199). One American text, Francis Wharton and Moreton Stillé's *Treatise on Medical Jurisprudence* (Philadelphia: Kay & Brother, 1855), assumes that the physical signs of sodomy are widely known but considers them apocryphal:

> It has been customary for authors, in describing the physical results of this vice, to enumerate various local injuries, such as laceration and patulous condition of the sphincter ani, prolapsus of the rectum, and ulcerations, together with constitutional effects, as consumption, dropsy, &c., as the inevitable results by which the commission of it could be ascertained. The observations of Parent Duchatelet and of Casper show, however, that such consequences are far from being even the common effect of this disgusting vice. (350)

Within a decade of Boulton and Park's trial, such medical identifications of sodomites require little apology; *Forensic Medicine and Toxicology* (Philadelphia: Lindsay & Blakiston, 1877), by distinguished English physicians W. Bathurst Woodman and Charles Meymott Tidy, having dismissed bodily evidence as unreliable for detecting the vice, goes on to describe the invert pathology both in terms of character traits ("They are usually of feminine appearance, and strive to appear like women") and physical symptoms ("The parts of generation are generally much relaxed, the scrotum pendulous, the penis elongated"), including as well a reference to Boulton and Park (600–602).

12. In one formulation of the anus as the locus classicus for situating individual, particularly male, subjectivity, Guy Hocquenghem writes: "Whereas the phallus is essentially social, the anus is essentially private. If phallic transcendence and the organisation of society around the great signifier are to be possible, the anus must be privatised in individualised and Oedipalised persons. . . . The functions of this organ are truly private; they are the site of the formation of the person. The anus expresses privatisation itself";

the grounds for fully exposing both defendants' behinds be felt insufficient, the medical witnesses provided evidence for the anal ailments with which both were supposed to be beset. Boulton had suffered from an abscess of uncertain origin, which resulted in a fistula requiring surgical operation, and while the prosecution's medical authorities claimed that this condition derived from the performance of unnatural acts, the defense used it as evidence that such crimes would have been impossible to commit.[13] (It must be borne in mind that the court was considering only the specific "crime against nature" of anal sex, and that the passive position alone was thought to be medically verifiable.) Just as Boulton's fistular history provided the rationale for exhibiting his rear end to public scrutiny, so a possibly invented medical record for Park justified a similar exposure of him. Dr. Richard Barwell, surgeon at Charing Cross Hospital, claimed to have treated Park for ten weeks for syphilitic anal warts (which, had they been proven, would have been incriminating). Yet on the stand he expressed some doubt as to whether the patient he had treated was Park or another man, and the other medical examiners found no trace of the cicatrix that would have been expected from a

---

Homosexual Desire, trans. Daniella Dangoor (Durham: Duke University Press, 1993), 96. In "Divinity: A Dossier, A Performance Piece, A Little-Understood Emotion," in Eve Kosofsky Sedgwick, *Tendencies* (Durham: Duke University Press, 1993), 215–51, Michael Moon and Sedgwick likewise argue: "On the conventional road map of the body that our culture handily provides us, the anus gets represented as always behind and below, well out of sight under most circumstances, its unquestioned stigmatization a fundamental guarantor of one's individual privacy and one's privately privatized individuality" (246–47).

13. The judge was apparently convinced by the defense on this matter, for in his summing up he reiterated the narrative of Boulton's medical history in favorable terms:

> Throughout the whole period of Boulton's sojourn with Lord Arthur Clinton he was suffering from fistula. The abscess which ended in the fistula began in 1868. Boulton went to Scotland and was obliged to come back on account of his health. He was in the hands of Mr. Hughes, the surgeon. The disease became worse and worse in November, and that is just about the period when all this is supposed to have been going on. . . . You are asked to believe that sodomitical abominable intercourse was constantly taking place between these parties, sleeping together and standing to one another in the unnatural relation of sodomite and paramour. The question is whether you can adopt that conclusion. . . . Can you believe—and forgive me for recurring to this odious and disgusting subject, but I must do it as a matter of justice—can you believe these parts immediately to be the subject of the abominable use were in that state which necessarily implies great tenderness, great irritation, and great pain upon pressure which necessarily must be implied from the existence of abscess and fistula within these delicate parts? (6:212–15)

sore requiring such lengthy treatment. Regardless of the implausibility of Barwell's claim, it, like Paul's, provided ample justification for making public information of the various opinions on the defendants' behinds.

The medical portion of the case exhibits the relation between, on the one hand, a body held to be objectively legible as the index of personal identity and, on the other, a procedure for recognizing that identity through publicity mechanisms apparently antithetical to the subject's constitution as private. The judicial structure of the case yields an analogous pattern, and the legal apparatus negotiates the relation between privacy and publicity in discretely articulated stages. In the year between the arrest of the transvestites at the Strand Theatre and the opening of their trial at Westminster on May 9, 1871, the charges against them were progressively altered in such a way as to link their public exhibitions to personal sexual identities. After their arrest and the examination by the police surgeon, Boulton and Park were brought before the magistrate's court at Bow Street for preliminary hearings on the felony charges of buggery. These proceedings lasted for one month, during which numerous witnesses were called to testify. Among them were policemen and managers of theaters, arcades, and restaurants, who recalled expelling the young men for disorderly conduct; landladies and housekeepers, who testified to the frequency of the defendants' appearances in women's clothes, as well as to their general conduct; other young men, both friends of the defendants and the supposed victims of their solicitations; the physicians and surgeons, who related in minute detail the condition of Boulton and Park's bodies; and relatives of the young men, who narrated their personal histories. Also brought in as evidence were scores of frocks and costumes found in the rooms of the prisoners after their arrest, and more than two thousand letters and photographs, said to implicate them in odious crimes. The presiding magistrate, Mr. Flowers, having been persuaded by the evidence against the defendants, refused them bail and had them bound over for trial to the Central Criminal Court.[14]

14. The judge's proleptically Genetian name is hardly the most remarkable in the case; his ruling dismayed, among others, Park's counsel, who had the credentials-confirming appellation Mr. Straight. The first reports of the events state that Boulton initially gave his name as Cecil Graham upon arrest; Park was known to some admirers as Mrs. Fanny Graham. A generation later, Cecil Graham became a favorite name of Oscar Wilde's: he used it for a principal character in *Lady Windermere's Fan* (1892) and altered it to Cyril Graham for the central figure in *The Portrait of Mr. W. H.* (1889). In 1885 Wilde named his

When *The Queen v. Boulton and Others* went to trial in the Queen's Bench a year later, a battery of the nation's most distinguished barristers participated in the six-day spectacle, half a dozen for the prosecution and ten in all for the defendants.[15] Despite the Crown's exertions in the trial—its highest legal representatives, the attorney general and the solicitor general, appeared in court to prosecute—the evidence mounted by the treasury department could not sustain the initial charges of felonious buggery. This crime was provable only by direct evidence of anal penetration (for example, from a firsthand witness), of which there was none in this case; the medical evidence, as we have seen, was too dubious to prove penetration conclusively and thereby confirm the charges. Prior to the 1885 statute that prohibited acts of "gross indecency" between men, the course open to the government in a case such as this one was to put up charges of *conspiracy* to commit sodomy, which relies upon evidence of intention to commit the act. Paradoxically, however, the law mandated that conspiracy charges could hold up only if the conspiracy was substantially proven to have, in fact, been carried out. While inviting all sorts of evidence about the defendants' probable intentions, the muddled conspiracy approach continued to demand proof positive of the sexual act.[16]

---

first son Cyril, and used the name in "The Decay of Lying" (1889) and elsewhere. See chapter 6 for some speculations on the encoding of these names.

15. Legal historian William Roughead writes that "not even the mighty Tichborne case itself, that gigantic litigation, could boast a more brilliant Bar" than the one in this case (*Bad Companions*, 157). In their final form, the indictments charged eight men in all, though only four could be brought to trial—besides Boulton and Park, the other two (fellow-travellers of theirs) being John Fiske, the United States' consular representative at Leith, and Louis Hurt, another Edinburgh resident, employed by the post office in the surveyor's department. After the hearing in the magistrate's court, the case was transferred, at the request of the defense counsel, out of the Central Criminal Court (the Old Bailey) into the Queen's Bench. There, at Westminster Hall, the case was heard by Lord Chief Justice Alexander Cockburn and a special jury—that is, a jury composed of gentlemen. The special jury request may have resulted from the indictment of a nobleman, from the complexity of the evidence, or from the nature of the legal issues at stake.

16. The illogic of this proceeding is a point to which the defense counsel repeatedly adverted; it is the main judicial issue that makes the case noteworthy. Park's attorney, Mr. Serjeant Parry, argued, for instance:

> What does the prosecution propose to put before you? They do not say he has committed the crime excepting in this way [i.e., in having conspired to commit it], because if he had committed the crime it is one of the highest felonies known to the law, and that you are not trying; but they *do* propose to prove to you that the

The language of the indictment for conspiracy is identical to that of the initial one for buggery, but for the crucial addition of the legalistic redundancy "conspire, confederate, combine, and agree together." While the original charge requires evidence only of certain acts, conspiracy entails a collection of thoughts, intentions, and signs. A conspiracy necessitates a community of understanding, with its own language and codes, which allows illicit activity not only to be imagined and desired but to be articulated and to *mean* as well. In addition to enabling the government to introduce a much wider range of evidence (including the letters, costumes, and accounts of public behavior) than the buggery charges would allow, the conspiracy approach also had the utility of charging all of the accused in the same indictment—thus preventing them from testifying on one another's behalf—and ensuring that the conviction of any one defendant would implicate them all.[17]

---

crime has been committed in order to show that it was agreed to be committed and that the parties conspired to commit it. (4:1:121–22)

The judge began his summing up with an expression of displeasure at the conspiracy approach adopted by the prosecution:

Now I must say that this is not a course which appears to me to commend itself to you. I am clearly of the opinion that where the proof intended to be submitted to the jury is a direct proof of the act itself, it is not a proper course to adopt to charge the parties with conspiring to do the act. My reason for saying so is this: that it manifestly operates unjustly, unfairly, and oppressively against the parties concerned, because by a proceeding like this you are enabled to combine in one indictment and one charge a variety of offenses, which, if tried individually, as they ought to be tried, would exclude the possibility of giving evidence in one to prejudice the defendants or the accused in another, and which takes from them the incalculable advantage of being able to call as witnesses the parties who are thus combined with them in one common indictment. (6:127–28)

As Hyde comments upon these remarks, "The lord chief justice's strictures were to go unheeded, and for nearly a century—that is until homosexual offences between consenting adults in private were abolished in 1967—the conspiracy device was used in many homosexual trials in Britain to draw homosexuals into the net of the criminal law" (*Tangled Web*, 87).

17. In addition to its *de jure* importance, the conspiracy tactic in sodomy cases has broader significance as well. While those following Foucault have often taken the 1885 legislation to indicate the precise moment at which state attention shifted from homosexual acts to homosexual actors, the earlier history of "conspiracy to commit" charges suggests that a rather rich cultural imagination of men who have sex with other men was possible well before that date. In *Talk on the Wilde Side*, Cohen writes that, "by organizing the disparate meanings that the [Wilde] trial and its journalistic representations had engendered into

In altering the charges, the prosecutors made a second important legal distinction, for the indictment in its final form supplemented the counts for conspiracy to commit buggery with accusations of a conspiracy to solicit other men to commit the crime. It thereby suggested that the accused were not only transvestites and sodomites, but prostitutes as well. The defendants, this count charged, "unlawfully and wickedly did conspire confederate combine and agree together to solicit induce incite procure and endeavour to persuade divers persons . . . feloniously wickedly and against the order of nature respectively to commit and perpetrate that detestable and abominable crime of buggery not to be named among Christians." As the subject of the sentence (the defendants) moves syntactically further and further from the verb phrase ("commit . . . buggery") so, it seems, does this gap allow of ever greater evidence about public behavior. While the shift from buggery to conspiracy charges requires a movement from pure privacy to collective understanding, solicitation concerns activity carried out largely in the public sphere.

The solicitation charges significantly raised the public stakes in the case for several reasons. First, they required evidence about how the defendants behaved when out in public places: witnesses testified about their mincing gaits, their made-up faces, and their obscene invitations to demonstrate how the young men entreated others to join them. George Smith, for example, who had thrown them out of the Burlington arcade, stated that he had seen Boulton "wink at men and make a noise with his mouth, as women would to entice them," and that Boulton had said to him, "Oh! you sweet little dear" (*Times*, May 14, 1870). Second, the solicitation charges moved the significance of their behavior out of a purely sexual sphere and into a financial one: if it could be proven that the defendants actually made a profession of their sexuality then all of the moral odium attendant upon female prostitutes could be heaped upon them. The attorney general, for instance, argued in his opening

---

a single, well-known, easily identifiable figure, the newspaper accounts effectively constituted Wilde's body as the meaning of the crime. In so doing, they foregrounded the emergence of a mode of understanding sexual acts that had only become possible in the ten years since the Criminal Law Amendment Act had been passed" (207). The historical rupture identified with the legislative change, and the importance ascribed to the unique charge of "posing" in Wilde's trials, may be undue, for the courts and the press clearly thought they could identify the kind of person likely to commit sodomy—and, as this case demonstrates, they expected to see it inscribed on his body—long before 1895.

statement to the jury that their appearance "was of such a character as to lead to the supposition that they were women, for that is a very important element in the case — that the adoption of these dresses was not an occasional frolic or escapade, but . . . [was] the occupation and business of their lives" (1:11). In response, the defense claimed that cross-dressing *was* their occupation, but that the business was acting, not prostitution. Finally, their conspiracy not merely to commit unnatural crimes with each other but to do so with unsuspecting men raised the fear that their victims would be recruited to homosexuality, which might, as a *Times* editorial suggested, thereby go public:

> The most curious part of the story is the influence which these personations had on other young gentlemen of similar tastes. If the prisoners had been more cautious, and abstained from alternating their costumes under the eyes of the same policemen and the same beadles, there is no saying how far things might have gone in a year or two. "Drag" might have become quite an institution, and open carriages might have displayed their disguised occupants without suspicion, except to the initiated. (May 31, 1870)

The final significant point in the legal organization of the case concerns the separation of the indictment for conspiracy and solicitation from the one for outraging public decency. Public indecency, unlike conspiracy, was both a misdemeanor and a common-law offense, and as such could not be considered in the same trial as the graver indictment. The former was, of course, the charge on which Boulton and Park had originally been arrested, and it was ultimately the only cause in which proof was considered adequate (not to say overwhelming).[18] The

---

18. After the jury in the felony case reached a verdict in Westminster, there was no time remaining to try the misdemeanor indictment, and the defendants entered into recognizance to appear at trial for the outstanding charge. A kind of plea bargain was reached, as a note in the *Times* from three weeks later explains:

> This case went before Lord Chief Justice Cockburn, in his private room, on the rising of the Court of Queen's Bench to-day. It will be recollected that after the trial of the defendants before his Lordship, and a verdict of "Not Guilty" being recorded, the two defendants, Boulton and Park, entered into their recognizances to appear and take their trial on the second indictment, which was for appearing in female attire at public places, this being alleged to be an offence against public morals and common decency. Since the trial nothing further had been heard of the case, and some persons thought the trial might come on after the present term, but it has now been brought to a conclusion.

evocative language of the public indecency indictment indicates precisely what kinds of behavior were found to be so offensive, and brings the case unequivocally into the public sphere:

> The Jurors of Our Lady the Queen upon their oath present that [the defendants] unlawfully and wickedly did conspire confederate combine and agree together and with divers other persons whose names are to the said Jurors unknown to disguise themselves as women and being so disguised to frequent and be present at divers places of public resort to wit public streets and highways theatres music halls licensed public houses and other places of public resort and did then and there in public and in the presence and view of members of Her Majesty's Liege Subjects openly and publicly pretend and hold themselves out and appear to be women and did thereby inveigle induce and incite divers of the male subjects of Her Majesty improperly lewdly and indecently to fondle and toy with them as women and thereby openly and scandalously did outrage public decency and offend against public morals and decency to the great scandal and common nuisance of the liege subjects of our Lady the Queen and her laws to the evil example of all others in the like manner offending and against the peace of our Lady the Queen her crown and dignity.[19]

The charge in this indictment has no overt connection to the "detestable and abominable crime of buggery"; it refers instead to disguising, pretending, producing scandal, offending morals, and creating a public nuisance. These are charges of an entirely public nature, which stand in sharp contrast to the explicitly sexual, intimately private accusations resulting from the medical examinations.

The public indecency indictment both insinuates the private motives lurking behind outrageous behavior and produces its own public fallout in the form of scandal. Its charge—that the men "openly and scandal-

---

. . . The result was that the learned Judge allowed the defendants to withdraw their plea of "Not Guilty" to the first count of the indictment, and to enter into their recognizances, each in a sum of 500£, for two years to be of good behaviour.

The recognizance was signed before his Lordship, and will be entered as a record in the Crown Office, so that in the event of any repetition of the alleged offence the defendants can be called upon to receive the judgment of the Court. (June 7, 1871) This is the last that is known of Boulton and Park.

19. All charges from the indictment roll for Trinity Term, 33rd Vict. (1870) (KB12/99).

ously did outrage public decency and offend against public morals and decency to the great scandal and common nuisance of the liege subjects of our Lady the Queen"—declares the past scandal illicit at the same time that it generates a new, legitimate scandal, now available to the public in open court hearings and extensive newspaper reports. That their behavior *was* scandalous becomes a reason for *making* a scandal of it: the publicity that the *Times* justifies because it is "a case presenting novel and extraordinary features . . . sure to be a subject of curiosity to hundreds of thousands" (May 7, 1870) answers to and disciplines the very scandal charged against the defendants. Although the court was not officially to consider the charge of outraging public decency until after the felony indictment had been heard, in fact the bulk of the nonmedical evidence in the conspiracy trial concerned the defendants' public behavior, addressing their sexual activity only by implication. During the trial, the presiding justice continually had to remind the jury to ignore this evidence—even as he was thereby afforded the opportunity to vent his own righteous indignation at the public spectacle the defendants made:

> Now it is impossible to speak in terms of sufficiently strong reprobation of indecent conduct of that description [i.e., cross-dressing]. No one can doubt that it is an outrage not only upon public morals but upon public decency and one which deserves in some shape or other not only reprobation but nearly severe punishment, and that quite irrespective of the suggestion of any ulterior sinister or odious purpose. It is a thing which would offend every right-minded person of either sex. It is a thing which ought not to be tolerated, and in my opinion where it is done even for frolic, even for the amusement of the individual at the expense of public decency, it ought to be the subject of summary and severe punishment. . . . But, gentlemen, that is not what we are now trying, and we must not allow any indignation we may feel at such unmanly and disorderly proceedings to warp our judgment or bias our mind in trying the far more serious accusation against the defendants. (6:160–62)

In making productive use of the confusion between private homosexuality and public transvestism, the court confounded the privacy it insisted upon with a publicity beyond its control. The authorities increasingly relied on interpretations of public presentation in their effort to apprehend and to criminalize the sexual crux of personal identity.

Moreover, the private life at issue was knowable—and had utility for teaching ethical and ideological lessons—only through the drama of its revelation. The volatile exposure of sexual secrets worked to sanctify privacy's inviolability, and the court and the press repaid the defendants for their outrageous public appearances by lending an exposed criminal meaning to their private lives.[20]

The medical and legal determinations of secret activity that we have observed sponsored public fantasies about criminal private life. While the exposure of privacy supplied the fundamental basis for scandal's publicity, other more self-conscious means of generating public notice were also crucial to its career. Central to this reflexive procedure are the occasions on which newspapers reporting the case accounted for their own role in the affair. In the same way that the core of privacy was consolidated at the point of its public disclosure, sexuality was made unspeakable—for the imperative to censor it was recognizable—at the very moment it was advertised. In the form of a double-discourse that tells without saying, that announces the importance of sexual secrets through their ineffability, the newspapers' self-assessments formed a linguistic analogue to the private subject known through its exposure.

One such crisis of journalistic self-evaluation arrived in the shape of an agent from the Society for the Suppression of Vice. In response to the publication of salacious details from the trial in a popular weekly paper, *Reynolds's News*, he urged that the trial be held in *camera*:

> He said that a great many letters had been addressed to the society, and deputations had waited upon him, urging the society to inter-

20. Written with reference to the Victorian novel, the following remarks of D. A. Miller, *The Novel and the Police* (Berkeley: University of California Press, 1988), pertain as aptly to the real-life drama narrated in scandal sheets:

> It is not just that, strictly private subjects, we read about violated, objectified subjects but that, in the very act of reading about them, we contribute largely to constituting them as such. We enjoy our privacy in the act of watching privacy being violated, in the act of watching that is already itself a violation of privacy. . . . It is built into the structure of the Novel that every reader must realize the definitive fantasy of the liberal subject, who imagines himself free from the surveillance that he nonetheless sees operating everywhere around him. (162)

In *Caught in the Act: Theatricality in the Nineteenth-Century English Novel* (Berkeley: University of California Press, 1992), Joseph Litvak supplies a variety of discussions about how public ("theatrical") displays help to constitute privacy, and about how the retention of secrets depends upon a public performance of them.

fere to prevent the publication of any further evidence in this case in the newspapers. It was felt that this inquiry ought to be conducted in secrecy for the sake of public decency, and . . . that the mere subject of the investigation was so revolting that it became the duty of the magistrate to use the discretion which he had the power of exercising, and to hear the case with closed doors. (*Times*, May 30, 1870)

Unlike present-day arguments over the news media's access to sensational trials, the issue here was not preservation of the defendants' rights and reputations, but protection of the reading public from stories that might endanger it. The newspapers were hardly unaware of their own role in promoting the scandalousness of the trial, and a debate sprung up among them over the defensibility of publishing accounts of the case. The proceedings were never closed to the public, and although overtly sexual evidence was prohibited from publication, articles about the trial could refer implicitly to sexual subjects by mentioning their unreportability.[21] While the *Times*, for instance, provided nearly verbatim accounts of the hearings, it abridged the medical reports, simply noting with parenthetical markers that they had been delivered:

(The witness here described the nature of the disease from which the defendant was suffering, the way in which it was communicated, and his mode of treating it.) . . . Some further medical testimony was given by Dr. Barwell, tending to substantiate the gravest imputations against the defendant, but it was of a character wholly unfit for publication. . . . (The witness stated the result of his examination, and expressed his opinion that the criminal offence charged had been committed again and again.) (May 21, 1870)

Even the mention of medical examinations was more than many papers were willing to publish; but the very thematization of unspeakability at moments such as these could not but provoke readers to imagine — in instructing them to avoid imagining — the sexual details of the case.

The newspapers courted the danger of overstepping a delicate line of insinuation and thereby themselves becoming infected by the contagion of scandal. They adopted a range of strategies for shielding their reports

---

21. See Cohen, *Talk on the Wilde Side*, for a discussion of similar ways in which, during Wilde's trials, "newspapers necessarily developed a compensatory set of signifying practices to invoke the unprintable signifier [sodomy] without naming it directly" (144).

from implication in the scandal, always seeking to deflect liability for the outrageous knowledge they imparted while ensuring their capacity to generate ever more discussion of the subject. The *Times* explained its practice of devoting scores of pages to trial testimony as a public service:

> A scandal like this does not affect only the offenders themselves. In the present day it is impossible to prevent such a case from being discussed by the public at large, and particularly by people who unite to a strong appetite for the morbid and the sensational a credulity beyond bounds concerning the malpractices of the classes above them. The extraordinary rumours which arise, and rapidly take form and consistence and become the belief of millions, render it highly inexpedient that any scandal so serious and so public should seem to be hushed up. The thing is never forgotten, and it is ten to one that some absurd romance comes into being which it is thenceforth impossible to refute. (May 7, 1870)[22]

The interests of the respectable classes are felt to require protection from vulgar opinions, this editorial argues, protection that comes in the form of more, not less, coverage of the case. Yet with the same gesture that it disparages the "morbid . . . credulity" of the "public at large," the paper justifies dishing up exactly the fare that will satisfy the lower orders' "strong appetite" for sensational news—not to mention the more refined, if less frankly appetitive, taste of their betters.

Such rationalizations as the papers present appear all the more disingenuous for their unwillingness to acknowledge the sheer sales value of prurience. Not wanting to risk the respectability of their own reputations by owning to the lubricity of their reports, the papers often adopted a pose of cultivated indifference to the validity of the charges. The press could afford this cool disinterest, because postponement of a final truth sustained both the procedures of scandal and its news value. Understanding that Boulton and Park's acquittal on conspiracy charges

---

22. The *Times* here uncannily predicts the government cover-up to protect a nobleman destined to take place with the Cleveland Street scandal twenty years later. In the later case, the government found it impossible to pursue the cause when the nation's most public private family was involved—for Prince Albert Victor, heir presumptive to the throne, was eventually implicated in the male brothel. See Lewis Chester, David Leitch, and Colin Simpson, *The Cleveland Street Affair* (London: Weidenfeld and Nicolson, 1976); H. Montgomery Hyde, *The Cleveland Street Scandal* (New York: Coward, McCann & Geoghegan, 1976); and Theo Aronson, *Prince Eddy and the Homosexual Underworld* (London: John Murray, 1994).

could not exonerate them except in the most technical sense, a member of the defense counsel demonstrated that the truth is useful to scandal only insofar as it is held in abeyance:

> Unfortunately it does appear that with a large majority of the un-thinking public the very charge itself half proves the charge which is so made to be true. I will venture to say that a man who has a charge of this sort made against him never recovers his position. It may be proved to be false, it may be proved to be unfounded, but when he goes into the world he is pointed out as the man who has been charged with it and there are too many who will believe he has been guilty of it. (4:1:13–14)

One consequence of sexual unspeakability is a generalized taint of scandal. Reporting the story had the negative effect for the newspapers that they were themselves open to the accusation of making scandal, but a countervailing positive benefit of lending credibility to reports that could be tossed off with apparent nonchalance.

Even the papers that refused this hypocrisy—of reporting a story they nonetheless decried as foul and offensive—were not denied the oppor-tunity to fulminate against threats to public morality and to expound upon the responsibilities of publicity instruments. The *Pall Mall Gazette*, for example, staunchly opposed publication of any but the most abbre-viated accounts of the case. At the close of the preliminary hearings, the *Gazette* attacked the attempt in the *Times* to disavow blame for publishing reports of the case: "If the prosecution can hasten its further inquiries and compress its evidence," the *Times* had stated, "it will be doing a real public service" (May 31, 1870). The *Gazette* retorted:

> The *Times* has a peculiar responsibility in this matter, because it alone, among London morning papers, could have properly com-pressed its account of this case without great pecuniary loss. . . . The practice of reporting trials of this kind, except in the briefest possible form, is governed by considerations strictly personal to the newspapers which admit them into their pages. The interests of justice are not promoted by it, the interests of public morality are simply injured by it. The prosecution and the defence do not rely on publicity for the means of getting together their evidence, and the deterrent effect of conviction depends on the fact that such crimes are not beyond the reach of detection, and that when de-

tected they bring inevitable punishment in their train. Neither of these ends is in the least secured by newspaper help, and if the imaginary necessity for reporting sensational cases at full length is to be urged as a reason for cutting short the proceedings themselves, both will eventually suffer from the intervention of these self-constituted assistants. (May 31, 1870)

This tendentious reasoning belies the fact that scandal teaches its chastening lessons irrespective of a judicial result. The more aggressive their reporting of the case, the more the papers could claim to be tending to "the interests of public morality." In fact, the defendants' acquittal on the felony charges was eventually seen to vindicate the papers that had extensively covered the trial, which could now demonstrate the salutary effects of their accounts. The *Daily Telegraph*, which had also been attacked for its reporting, despite a self-proclaimed "resolution to exclude all matters from [its] columns which are unfitted for public perusal," could fully justify itself at the end of the proceedings:

> For many a long day to come we shall see no more youths flaunting about the streets of London, or frequenting places of public resort, in women's clothes. . . . The most effeminate and foolish lad will hesitate before, even in joke, he puts his signature to amatory effusions addressed to some one of his companions. That this should be so is a marked benefit; and to what agency, we may fairly ask, is the benefit to be assigned? The answer to the question is obvious. We owe the suppression of a most dangerous and pernicious abuse, the trampling out of a folly which might easily have grown into a crime, not so much to the investigation set on foot by the police as to the publicity given to that investigation. (May 16, 1871)

Publicity, the *Daily Telegraph* demonstrates, functions like the term *scandal* itself: it constitutes both the transgression and the punishment.[23]

23. In a polemical defense of the press for its very capacity to expose lurid details, the article continues:
> What, we ask, in the name of common sense, is the real punishment to which these "men in women's clothes" and their associates have been subjected? It is not their arrest, their examinations before a police magistrate, their trial at the Court of Queen's Bench. It is the fact that the follies they committed, the letters they wrote, the equivocal positions in which they voluntarily placed themselves, have been made public throughout the length and breadth of the country. . . . Supposing ill-advised counsels had been listened to, and that the PARK and BOULTON case had been tried

From a different point of view, this continuity between criminal and journalistic publicity suggests the scandal's counterhegemonic potential: protogay men and would-be transvestites, otherwise ignorant of their brethren's existence, might discover in the news reports positive lessons about the coded language the defendants used, the places they consorted, and the ways they behaved. Inadvertently distributing a travelogue of London's gay underground, the papers potentially sabotage the punitive logic that guides their reporting.[24] Not simply vindictive or censorious, the newspapers, in their incapacity to specify sexual subjects, proliferate meanings out of control. The excess that rushes to fill the void left by unspoken sexual practices supplies a current of *avant la lettre* gay signification at the same time that it announces the humiliation of having such behavior exposed.

The debates among the newspapers profitably sustain the drama of transforming private criminal behavior into public spectacle. Yet while it is easy to villainize the media in such cases, it has to be recognized that the press serves as the agent, not as the cause, of scandal; we must look instead to the culture that valorizes private life only in seeing it violated, and affirms normalizing standards by making a spectacle of deviance. The battles over publication and censorship ought to be read not as a negative consequence of the reporting (as the papers themselves

---

with closed doors, or had not been reported, the very aim and object of the investigation would have been set at nought. To the defendants themselves a gross injustice would have been done. It would infallibly have been believed by the public, that their acquittal had been due to private influences; or that the whole truth had not been elicited. What is more important still, the very silence of the Press would have afforded positive encouragement to profligates capable of such offences as those of which the defendants in the trial just concluded have been pronounced innocent. The one thing of which offenders against laws sanctioned by the verdict of mankind stand in terror, is the possibility that their malpractices should be made public; and yet, on the plea of decency, it is proposed to let offenders against the laws of nature be released from the dread of publicity. Happily, justice has been done—a terrible abuse has been cut short in the bud; and that such has been the result is mainly due to the careful discharge of a most painful and unpleasant duty by the press of England.

24. In *History of Sexuality*, vol. 1, Foucault suggests the possibility of resistance within official sexual definitions: "Silence and secrecy are a shelter for power, anchoring its prohibitions; but they also loosen its holds and provide for relatively obscure areas of tolerance. . . . [Regulatory discourse] also made possible the formation of a 'reverse' discourse: homosexuality began to speak in its own behalf . . . often in the same vocabulary, using the same categories by which it was medically disqualified" (101).

portray it), but as a positive strategy for maintaining public interest in the case. Neither cynical refusal nor self-righteous defensiveness is antithetical to scandal; rather, both positions routinely serve to disseminate and perpetuate scandal.

I have emphasized the role of publicity in the case partly in order to avoid evaluating it solely in terms of its judicial outcome. When scandal is considered as a phenomenon, the verdict is the last thing known about it: up to that moment, its meanings are in dispute. Neil Bartlett has proposed that the ruling in the Boulton and Park trial indicates the court's aggressive denial of an increasingly visible subculture, and he is right to take the fact of the acquittal not as a vindication of the defendants, nor as evidence of liberal tolerance for their conduct, but rather as a refusal to recognize it for what it was.[25] The verdict's consequences have no bearing, however, on the effects of the scandal up until that point. The court may finally have declared the drag queens nonexistent, but the trial itself provided the public an opportunity to consider and debate their behavior, however onerous (or in this case, relatively innocuous) its end result. While the verdict resulted from the Crown's failure to establish a persuasive link between public persona and private criminality, the scandal functioned to the extent that plausible explanations—provisional fictions—could be sustained and proliferated.

25. In *Who Was That Man?*, Bartlett writes:
> For the jury to accuse them, to announce that it saw them as sodomites, the jury would have to admit that they understood the letters, that they recognized the significance of the frocks. Such admission would suggest a dangerous proximity to the object of their scrutiny. . . . The evidence of [Boulton and Park's] visibility was converted into proof that they didn't exist. . . . Only by silencing, not punishing, the sodomites, could the court breathe a sigh of relief. When Boulton and Park were dismissed, declared improbable if not impossible, the existence of a homosexual culture in London was effectively denied. (141–42)

Weeks's interpretation of the verdict in "Inverts, Perverts" is less conspiratorial, suggesting that it resulted from the authorities' insufficient knowledge: "as late as 1871 concepts both of homosexuality and of male prostitution were extremely undeveloped in the Metropolitan Police and in high medical and legal circles" (117). Alan Sinfield synthesizes the two views, pointing out that different knowledges can coexist and overlap: "The interpretations of Weeks and Bartlett could both be correct. Some people involved in bringing the prosecution may have been aware of a same-sex subculture and reluctant to press the case strongly, whilst members of the jury might have been unaware and uncomprehending. . . . Some people heard same-sex passion loud and clear, whereas others could not conceive of it"; *The Wilde Century: Oscar Wilde, Effeminacy and the Queer Moment* (New York: Columbia University Press, 1994), 8.

II

Having considered how scandal works to determine the private subject through its sexual exposure, we can now turn to that subject's ubiquitously invoked diacritical term: the general public. Ambiguously embodied in both legal arguments and newspaper reports, the public—a phantasmatic entity that collapses into one the courtroom audience, the reading public, and an amorphous notion of public opinion—is a figure whose characterization provides an index of the ideological contests in the case. The constituent national, class, and gender components of this representation point to the ways in which the topic officially at issue— sex between men—both propels and impedes the circulation of power in domains other than the strictly sexual.

At their most expansive and imperious, arguments in the case rely on the emotional rhetoric of national character. The attorney general flings down the gauntlet in this matter when, in his opening remarks, he comments upon his "public duty" to expose the crimes, however unpleasant the task may be, and entreats the jurymen to "do what in you lies to stop this plague, which, if allowed to spread without check, might lead to a serious contamination of our national morals" (1:86). The government's representative is elliptical here about the ways in which "national morals" are at stake in the trial, but Boulton's counsel takes up the challenge and elevates the rhetoric:

> My friend the attorney general in the course of his eloquent peroration asked you to perform your high office, and no doubt he produced an effect upon you at the time when he said he invited you to stop this plague. Gentlemen, I call upon you to perform a higher, a kinder, and a more patriotic office; I call upon you to do something which will be of greater utility, and that is to pronounce by your verdict that they libel the morality and character of this country who say that that plague exists. . . . I trust your verdict will establish that the moral atmosphere of England is not yet tainted with the impurities of Continental cities and that, free as we are from our island position, we are insulated from the crimes to which you have had allusion made, and you will pronounce by your verdict on this case at all events with regard to these facts that London is not cursed with the sins of Sodom, or Westminster tainted with the vices of Gomorrah. (3:323–25)

At issue in the case is not merely individual guilt or innocence, but a whole nation's moral character: to do other than vindicate the young men would be unpatriotic, for it would cast a spell of disease and perversity over the entire country. This inflated imperialist polemic is utterly conventional, and it functions more to incite than to persuade; but its readiness-to-hand in a trial ostensibly concerned only to determine the sexual practices of a few effeminate men suggests just how far-reaching the case is felt to be for English self-definition.

Although questions of national character appear to lie at a vast distance from scrupulously personal evidence about the state of a man's rectum, the other strain of imagery that pervades these discussions—of miasma and pestilence—serves to link overarching national concerns with the individual medical ones rather directly. For both the impending "plague" of sodomy and the medical technology used to detect it are taken as signs of Continental perversion. Just as the attorneys argue that English youth is "not yet tainted," so the medical authorities must be seen as inviolate with regard to contaminating Continental knowledge. The exception that proves this rule is the vicious Paul, and in his summing up, the chief justice rebukes the police surgeon:

> The French writers who prompted the inquiry of Mr. Paul we have not before us. We have, however, the evidence of two very important witnesses, persons whose names are familiar to all of us: we have Dr. Taylor and we have Mr. Gibson. Dr. Taylor says that he has had very little experience in this particular form of alteration of the structure—happily that is the case with all of the medical gentlemen. Therefore that vice has not yet tainted the habits of the men of this country—for that thank heaven. Therefore the medical men here cannot give you as the result of their experience what perhaps medical practitioners in other and less happy countries in that respect could give. (6:267–68)

However *medically* bogus the work of "the French writers" may be, this xenophobia based on *moral* grounds is what generates the court's and the doctors' refusal of putative scientific knowledge, and it explains in part the hopeless confusion over the physiology of anal sex. Moreover, it demonstrates the evidence imagined as most invasive (and thereby constitutive) of privacy to be embroiled within a public discourse of nationalism.

Both sides of the pseudo-debate claim the high moral ground of defending English values. The difference is simply that the defense presents

Boulton and Park as representative citizens whose behavior is "mere folly," while the prosecution excoriates them as aberrations. With his closing statement, Park's lawyer provokes the court on this topic:

> I do hope, gentlemen, you will find that all these defendants have not after all been guilty of the loathsome crime that has been charged against them. Such a verdict in its effect—I do not say would leave a stain upon the national character—God forbid that I should think so!—but perhaps in the press of Europe and of America, if such a verdict were found, it might be and no doubt would be treated with some criticism and reproach; it might even be said to be a part of the manners of the English people in the nineteenth century. But, gentlemen, I believe you will be able to relieve the public mind from the oppression which would be caused by an adverse verdict in this cause. (5:320–21)

Disclaiming the supposition that a conviction would put a "stain upon the national character" even as he advances it, the barrister expresses a fear not that Englishmen will act like the perverts on the Continent but that they will be thought to do so by others. By portraying the defendants in a proximate relation to the normative values ascribed to the public, the defense counsel attempts to forge an identification between the individual subjects under scrutiny and the public at large.

The prosecution, for its part, strives to effect a disidentification between public and prisoner, and to show the public its own values grotesquely inverted in the defendants.

> You expect such proof as reasonable men ought to act upon, and if that proof satisfies you of the prisoners' guilt, to be deterred from expressing your opinion by any apprehension of a stain being inflicted upon the honor of this country in the eyes of foreign nations would be sheer moral cowardice. Gentlemen, no stain is inflicted upon the honor of this country by such offenses being committed by a comparatively few persons—for let us hope that they are few —but our national character might be stained if such offenses when detected and proved were suffered to go unpunished. (6:125–26)

The prosecution's ultimate inability to make out its case may well have resulted from an insufficient mustering of patriotic rhetoric: the jury was unwilling to convict middle-class Englishmen of crimes smacking of foreign depravity.

Such nationalist polemicizing arises in tandem with arguments that secure middle-class moral hegemony, itself fully identified with the management of "manners." These particular (although, as is usual, universalized) class values are threatened because the defendants came from the class whose ideological ascendancy was grounded in its sexual respectability. A *Times* editorial appearing at the conclusion of the preliminary hearings demarcates the range of possible identities to which sodomy could safely be ascribed:

> For a whole month the public curiosity has been fed, though probably not satiated, by the details of the most extraordinary case we can remember to have occurred in our time. The "revelations" came to an end yesterday, and the two prisoners, BOULTON and PARK, were committed for trial at the Central Criminal Court, bail being refused. The existence of such a scandal is a social misfortune. The charges made by the prosecution are such as are seldom advanced in this country, except against the lowest, the most ignorant, and the most degraded. That there should be in English society an association of young men, with ramifications not yet defined, some of the members of which are accused of the most hateful immorality, while the relations of most of them to each other are supposed to have been familiar and indelicate beyond expression, is a thing of which we cannot help being ashamed. We have been accustomed to associate such offences with the sensuous civilization of antiquity, and with the barbarism or demoralization of certain races in our own day. But we were not prepared to find even the suspicion of them attaching to youths of respectable family and position. (May 31, 1870)

The scandal Boulton and Park produced is crystallized here: it reeks of difference from the general public whose "curiosity" engages it, either for its class debasement or for its national or racial foreignness in the social imagination. The third source for sodomy proposed here—"the sensuous civilization of antiquity"—comes to be associated with a decadent aristocratic aesthetic, which I consider in the third section of this chapter.

Insofar as the case redounds to the quality of Englishness, these nationalist concerns and class antagonisms work in concert. Much is made of the defendants' middle-class status, which denies them on the one hand the alibi of working-class brutishness (no scandal comes of the poor being exposed as perverts) and on the other the protection afforded the gentry (such as the unnamed noblemen implicated in the case). While the prosecution finds it useful to raise the specter of an English public endangered by the repulsive behavior of the transvestites, the defense needs to anathematize some other race of creatures as true sodomites. Park's representative describes in evocative terms both what is thought to constitute normal behavior and what the life of real sodomites is imagined to be:

> If these young men were out for the purpose of exciting themselves, is it not a monstrous proposition that it is an overt act of this conspiracy that men engaged in the exchange of wicked and accursed embraces would put on dresses of women for the purpose of going to the theater and public places and do that for the purpose of exciting each other to the commission of this outrageous crime? Gentlemen, the very absurdity of the suggestion is its own refutation. You would expect a different kind of conduct, a secret hiding from the sight of men and of women, in fact conduct anything but that which has been proved by the witnesses for the prosecution—conduct such as one's common experience or one's natural instincts and feelings would expect on the part of persons capable of this crime. (5:195–96)

The barrister's reliance here on "one's natural instincts and feelings" has the clear ring of bourgeois ideology in the process of being generated. He counts on his auditors to have some ideas about the "conduct . . . of persons capable of this crime," yet he does not say what this conduct is, other than "a secret hiding from the sight of men and of women"—which is merely to say what it is not. It is in this way—precisely of not saying—that tacit precepts of the normative accrete authority. The imagery of darkness and barbarism that pervades the descriptions of sodomites tends to associate them with the slums; in one editorial, the *Gazette* refers to "vices which in modern times, at any rate, have been conveniently assumed to be only found in combination with the most degraded and brutal ruffianism" (June 8, 1870). Although the prisoners' extravagant style can still work in *defense* of their questionable behavior in 1871, it will unequivocally become the sign of depravity in the famous homosexual scandals later in the century. Wilde's attempt to use the same strategy in 1895 would prove a catastrophic miscalculation, and claims for artistic or aristocratic prerogatives were doomed to condemn rather than to redeem him. After intervening cases such as the Dublin Castle affair (1884) and the Cleveland Street scandal (1889–90), elite privilege could no longer provide an alibi, let alone impunity, for gay male sexuality.

The scandal that Boulton and Park ignited could not be extinguished by proof of their middle-class respectability in private life, largely because the public component of the case—cross-dressing—repeatedly ruptured attempts to vindicate them from the buggery allegations. Identification of the private subject, synonymous with the truth of sex, locates itself in a palpable male body; yet given the publicly unmentionable status of anal eroticism, cross-dressing serves as its public face. This collapse of homosexuality into transvestism does more than provide a manageable surrogate through which to castigate the defendants, however: it sends the whole structure of the scandal's reception into disarray, since the cross-dressing charge critically implicates the aspect of the general public most complexly intertwined with the scandal's content—its gender. This spectacular drama, I want to propose, is directed at a public audience most powerfully incarnated in female form. This is not to say that those who read about and participated in the scandal were exclusively feminine; it is, however, to submit that, when the public is threatened by reports of gender transgression, it comes to be imagined as female.

For one example of this fantasy, we can look again to the *Pall Mall Gazette*. Information about the case was sufficiently hazardous that some authorities urged the government to abandon the action altogether. While the editors of the *Gazette* did not go quite so far, they promoted a paternalistic policy (even as they bemoaned its necessity) of shielding ingenuous readers from dangerous knowledge:

> It is quite possible that many fathers who dislike being obliged to keep their morning paper under lock and key will be disposed to . . . argue that the crimes charged against these men are at all events not committed in open day, whereas, unfortunately, the evidence adduced in support of the charge is invested with all the publicity that can be given it by a conspicuous place in the columns of the *Times* and *Telegraph*. Is it not better, they will say, that the guilty should be left in the enjoyment of virtual impunity than that the innocent should be exposed to the chance of having their minds polluted by half-understood hints of vices of which they had previously no conception. (June 8, 1870)

The population put at risk by knowledge of public transvestism is consistently constructed as the innocent female, as another editorial in the *Gazette* makes explicit:

The reports of the late proceedings have in one respect been far more offensive than many which are avowedly excluded from every respectable paper. Most cases of this sort bear their character marked on their foreheads. No woman can be in any danger of reading about them unless she does so intentionally. But the heading "Men in Women's Clothes" need not in the first instance have served as an adequate warning of what was to follow; and a lady may have been left to make out the underlying filth for herself, or have had to be warned of its existence by some male relative. (May 31, 1870)

The problem these editorials detect is that the publicity afforded the case by news reports themselves will endanger credulous readers. Ironically, the very discretion demanded of the media—that reports of a buggery trial be printed under misleading headlines about transvestism—makes unsuspecting readers vulnerable.

Imagination of the general public depends on a gendered hierarchy of knowledge, whereby authority, personified as male, seeks to protect an innocent female readership from contaminating information. Though novel-readers had long been imagined as vulnerable (if voracious) women, the mid-Victorian period saw standards of respectability extended to all printed matter, using as its measure what Dickens's Podsnap would term "a blush in the cheek of the young person." The personification of the reading public in a hypothetical schoolgirl bears on the case at hand most immediately through the agency of the judge presiding in the Queen's Bench, Lord Chief Justice Alexander Cockburn. Cockburn was the authority who had ruled three years earlier in the renowned Hicklin case and established the severest obscenity test in English law, one that was to hold for nearly a century. The so-called Hicklin standard evaluated printed material on the basis of whether it had a tendency to corrupt innocent—that is to say, young and female—readers.[26]

26. The chief justice's crucial opinion in the Hicklin case (1868) reads: "I think the test of obscenity is this, whether the tendency of the matter charged as obscenity is to deprave and corrupt those whose minds are open to such immoral influences, and into whose hands a publication of this sort may fall"; cited in H. Montgomery Hyde, *A History of Pornography* (London: Heinemann, 1964), 171. For a fuller account of the so-called young person, see Richard Stang, *The Theory of the Novel in England, 1850–1870* (New York: Columbia University Press, 1959), esp. 191–224; Walter Kendrick, *The Secret Museum: Pornography in Modern Culture* (New York: Viking, 1987); Kate Flint, *The Woman Reader, 1837–1914* (Oxford: Clarendon Press, 1993), esp. 142–47; and Ruth Bernard Yeazell, "Podsnappery, Sexuality,

The clamor over transvestite men confronting vulnerable women emerges in another, more vitriolic attack on Boulton and Park's cross-dressed follies. A pamphlet published after adjournment of the preliminary hearings denounces them for impersonating and affronting true femininity, reserving its harshest judgment for the odious insult entailed in

> the entrance of Park into the retiring room, which is set apart for ladies at the Strand Theatre, who had the unblushing impudence to apply to the female attendant to fasten up the gathers of his skirt, which he alleged had come unfastened.
>
> This act, simple as it appears upon paper, is sufficient in itself to arouse the just indignation of every true Englishman. We can now ask, and with a just cause too, what protection have those who are dearest to our hearts and hearths: those loved ones whom we recognise by the endearing titles of mother, sister, wife or daughter.
>
> Is it right, moral, or just, that their most sacred privacy should thus be ruthlessly violated.
>
> If every debauched *roué* can by assuming feminine garb enforce his way with impunity into the chambers set apart for our country-women, then we call upon law and justice to aid us in exposing these outrages upon decency.

The offense registered here is Park's having made *too* convincing a woman, and the resulting dangers are of two kinds: first, that gullible men will find themselves entrapped by perverts; and second, that the rights and privileges of genuine femininity will be grotesquely intruded

---

and the English Novel," *Critical Inquiry* 9 (December 1982): 339–57. Writing in 1888, Henry James rails against the prudishness that such standards inspire in novelists:

> I should . . . say not that the English novel has a purpose, but that it has a diffidence. To what degree a purpose in a work of art is a source of corruption I shall not attempt to inquire; the one that seems to me least dangerous is the purpose of making a perfect work. As for our novel, I may say lastly on this score that as we find it in England to-day it strikes me as addressed in a large degree to "young people," and that this in itself constitutes a presumption that it will be rather shy. There are certain things which it is generally agreed not to discuss, not even to mention, before young people. That is very well, but the absence of discussion is not a symptom of the moral passion. The purpose of the English novel . . . strikes me therefore as rather negative.

"The Art of Fiction," in *The Art of Fiction and Other Essays* (New York: Oxford University Press, 1948), 21. I am grateful to Barbara Leckie for informative discussion on this topic.

upon. The imbroglio excited by the incursion of cross-dressed men into that sacred chamber—the ladies' room—derives not only from the physical threat they present to "retiring" women, but from the challenge they pose to the whole basis for difference. If gender is contingent and mutable, how can its traditional categories of response function?

This confusion is at the heart of the scandal, and the accused clearly encouraged it. The manager of the Alhambra music hall, who had seen Boulton and Park numerous times over the course of three years, could testify to the trouble they made:

> I told them they must leave directly, for the public believed they were men, and they did so. . . . They walked about in an effeminate way, and people gathered round them, saying they were two women dressed in men's clothes. . . . I could never quite make up my mind about them. Sometimes I thought they were men and sometimes that they were women. Whenever they appeared in male costume their faces were painted. (*Times*, May 14, 1870)

While the transvestites drew upon the fungibility of gender markers in their playful self-presentation, they also used their highly cultivated performance skills in their own defense. In preparation for their days in court, Boulton and Park sought to augment their masculinity by donning men's clothes and sprouting mustaches, following the advice one of their companions, Louis Hurt, had earlier given Boulton in a letter preparing him to meet his mother:

> I am rather sorry to hear of your going about in "drag" so much, partly, I confess, for a selfish reason. I know the moustache has no chance while this sort of thing goes on. You have now less than a month to grow it, for my mother has arranged to stay at Boulogne until the 21st, so as to meet me. . . . I thought it well to tell her that you are very effeminate, but I hope that you will do your best to appear as manly as you can, at any rate in face. I, therefore, again beg of you to let your moustache grow at once. (*Times*, May 16, 1870)

Try as he might, Hurt suggests, Boulton can barely cover the truth of his foppery, even with that addition destined to become so conspicuous and yet so equivocal in gay male culture, the mustache.[27] Conventional mas-

---

27. Roughead notes, "The absence of whiskers was, for the bearded virtuous of the Seventies, in itself suspicious, being regarded as presumptive evidence of naughtiness" (*Bad Companions*, 161n.). In the seventies of our own century, it was instead the presence of

culinity itself is exposed to be as much a mask upon this body as female drag—and not a moment too soon, for the instant the "not guilty" verdict was announced, Stella fainted in the dock.[28]

The case so destabilizes the order of gender that opinion-makers seek to find ways of reimposing familiar dividers. A *Times* editorial endorses a virile response to the persuasive charade: "We find it was the practice of several members of this epicene college to appear in public dressed with such care and success that it was almost impossible to recognize their sex. Should any one of them intrude himself among decent people again, it would be pardonable for any gentleman present to take the law into his own hands, and inflict on the offender a suitable castigation at once" (May 31, 1870). The *Pall Mall Gazette*, for its part, pairs Boulton and Park with the brazen "prophetesses" who spoke out against the Contagious Diseases Acts, for both are felt to undermine the rigid gender basis of Victorian social organization:

> We should be sorry to believe society grows daily more shameless, and yet it is very hard to resist the conclusion. We degrade ourselves systematically on the purest principles. Duty and conscience chaperon shamelessness, and introduce her in her naked meretriciousness to our family circles. She is brought in as a warning, to be sure, not as an example; but perverted human nature, or ingenuous innocence, is just as likely to mistake the intention and reverse the moral. Scandals we have always with us; but the present condition of our atmosphere breeds fouler specimens than we ever recollect. Instinct and reason alike suggest swift and silent suppression as the surest remedy for the inevitable, but an increasing school of moralists feel bound, in the interest of themselves and their fellow-creatures, to give them the widest publicity, and advertise them with an elaboration of detail that shall bring them within the comprehension of the dullest. We may be, as we are told we are, purists and masculine prudes, and the victims of old-fashioned prejudices. But when we see bestial depravity regarded with the amused toleration with which a Grammont might have listened to a tale of intrigue; when we hear social scandals of the most revolting type handled by unsexed females with the very wantonness of sensual

whiskers—upon the upper lip of the gay clone at any rate—that constituted "presumptive evidence of naughtiness."

28. *Daily News*, May 16, 1871.

and technical licence, we are more grieved than surprised at the
steady lowering of tone and morality among us. (June 3, 1870)

The figure of the prostitute [29] affords a neat collapse of the feminist political activist with the female impersonator. Even without mention of the
pending solicitation charge, the transvestite garners the reprobation due
any prostitute, for throughout the trial, the defendants' critics tactically
accede to their femininity for just long enough to condemn them as
actresses, thereby bringing them into proximity with the whore—with
whose taint the feminist is also stained, thanks to her efforts on behalf
of prostitutes. All the more despicable, however, are such crimes when
committed by those who lack even the routine alibi of genuine female
anatomy. The case's gender disruptions now affect even its detractors:
personified "shamelessness" is the whore who contaminates the "ingenuous innocence"—equally feminized—of "our family circles." (The
necessity for the modifier "masculine" indicates the usual femininity of
the family's moral sentinel, the "prude.") The female character overtly
attributed to the vulnerable public must square off against imposter and
impossible women, yoked together through a parallelism between the
"bestial depravity" of drag queens and the political agitation of "unsexed
females."[30] In all its ideological nakedness, the editorial demonstrates
that the breakdown of gender categories within the scandal raises the
specter of an analogous—but more general, more devastating—collapse
in the social structure of its reception. The female public is subject to
offense by the transvestites not least because the latter are in imminent
danger of being taken for the former.

The case suggests a reversal of the traditional formulation, whereby
the public sphere is strictly designated male and the private one female.
This formula, which the Victorians promulgated and which contemporary critics have largely been willing to accept, can now be complicated:
in this scandal at any rate, the male body—particularly at the moment
of its sexual abjection—is the locus for private subjectivity, while femininity represents a generalized, endangered social world. Such a propo-
sition does not require a wholesale rejection of the usual gendering
of public and private spheres, although it suggests that at moments of

29. "Naked meretriciousness" refers to prostitution both in the noun's current sense and
in its etymology (from Latin meretrix, a woman who earns pay).
30. On the latter, see Judith Walkowitz, Prostitution and Victorian Society: Women, Class, and the
State (Cambridge: Cambridge University Press, 1980).

histrionic *embodiment* this division may be just the reverse of what is expected.[31] Alarmed by the gender illegibility of the transvestites, the public sphere itself dresses up as female. In confusing straight men who would take the drag queen to be a real woman (and therefore a sexual object), moreover, cross-dressing also puts heterosexuality itself at risk. The image of the imperiled feminine audience that requires chivalrous male protection allows the press strategically to reinstall heterosexual paradigms in the face of the spectacle of sex between men.

Whether revered as the embodiment of an endangered public or obscenely paraded in the form of the prostitute impersonator, femininity seems in this cultural imagination to mask a fundamental maleness. Yet while the Crown and self-righteous newspaper editors employ representations of women in order to animadvert on the "epicene college," the tactical use of femininity is not strictly limited to the prosecution—nor does it function exclusively as a surface phenomenon. For at one crucial moment that shows how deeply sexual knowledges depend upon representations of gender, the young men's counsel reinstalls femininity at the very basis of the defense: the state of the defendants' anuses. Unlike the prosecution's effort at blurring gender boundaries in the public evidence—of appearance, fashion, gesture, language—the defense transposes this confusion to the core of the somatic question about sodomy. One of the medical witnesses for the defense, Henry James Johnson, fellow of the Royal College of Surgeons and lecturer at St. George's Hospital, delivers this extraordinary testimony:

> Q. There is a question I would ask you: looking to the size of his parts and the structure of Boulton, was it a delicate and small structure?
>
> A. Yes, unusually so—in fact, more like that of a female than a male of his age. I was astonished in fact at seeing what it was because I expected something totally different.
>
> Q. You expected something totally different even in a healthy subject of his age?

---

31. Feminization of the domestic sphere, increasingly identified with privacy, produces the impression of a female private subject. In *Desire and Domestic Fiction: A Political History of the Novel* (New York: Oxford University Press, 1987), Nancy Armstrong renders the starkest formulation of this notion: "the modern individual was first and foremost a female" (66). Publicity itself is subsumed by the domestic realm through the nineteenth century, as news comes to be consumed and experienced at home.

A. Not totally, but under the circumstances of which I had heard,
I expected something different. But it was smaller than the average,
and I [was] of course expecting quite the reverse. (5:82)[32]

The staggering irony of this position—that an apparently feminine pos-
terior is irrefutable evidence of the defendant's unblemished masculinity—seems not to have occurred to the trial's participants, for the
chief justice himself adverts to the statement as fact in his summing
up: "There was a total absence of all the appearance of dilation, but
on the contrary an unusual degree of contraction of the part, so much
so that it appeared rather to be the part of a female than of a male"
(6:266-67). For a man to have his private parts feminized is not compromising—only when this femininity is worn on his sleeve does it
cause problems; indeed, a female anus is a man's surest proof that he
has not behaved sexually in a woman's position. This evidence presumes
the heterosexism it seeks to ratify, for it implies that a woman's anus
remains "delicate and small" because she already has available a legitimate genital orifice through which to accommodate male sexual desire.
By the same logic, it bizarrely homosexualizes normative masculinity
in suggesting that "even in a healthy [male] subject of [Boulton's] age"
one could reasonably expect the anus to appear rather loose and less
than delicate. Like the virtual institutionalization of homosexual practices in boarding schools during this period, this testimony implies that
a dose of buggery in the proper measure can be normalizing. And despite the avidity with which its importance is so often denied, size *is*
everything here—particularly when, against the exculpatorily diminu-
tive proportions of Boulton's anus, one recalls Paul's insinuation that the
"inordinate length" of the defendant's genitals, rather than buttressing
his manhood, bespeaks its renunciation. Not unlike their ultra-butch
descendants of a century later, the 1870s queens are suspect for being
rather too well endowed in signally masculine attributes.

Just at the moment when a man's feminine public presentation can
no longer be justified, then, femininity is transferred back onto the

32. Johnson claims that Park's body testifies equally to his innocence: in response to the
question "Were there any traces of any kind about this young man (Park) indicating that
he had been addicted to these unnatural practices?" Johnson replies, "None whatever,
but the contrary—if possible more so even than in Boulton. The internal sphincter was
as tight or tighter than the external—it was as contracted; and the internal longitudinal
folds were particularly marked" (5:85).

foundational site of his private subjectivity. Femininity signifies innocence even when attributed to the abject body of the drag queen—and
yet appearing feminine is the crime at issue.[33] This fantasy of femininity
seems to arise automatically before the specter of the penetrable male
body, a specter that can be countered only by recourse to the female
ear—which requires that it be silent—or to the feminine anus—which
nullifies its deviancy. The femininity mobilized across this range of materials ultimately suggests the difficulty for the Victorian imagination of
conceiving of sexual intercourse—of sexuality itself—as anything other
than heterosexual. A culture that acknowledges only one, impoverished
script for sex attributes the phantasmatic power of femininity at once to
the icon of state authority and to its debased anathema—to both parties
in this trial, that is to say, Queen Victoria and the Victorian queens.

III

We have seen how the privacy constitutive of the Victorian subject is
structured in and through the public sphere against which it positions
itself. If we account for the formation of the individual subject in either
psychical or social terms—that is, according to either of its two most influential interpreters, psychoanalytic or materialist criticism—we must

33. The Boulton and Park scandal exemplifies the unstable relation between homosexuality and transvestism, whose histories mutually haunt each other. For a demonstration
of the vicissitudes in accounts of this relation, one might consider Marjorie Garber's suggestion (corresponding loosely to the argument of the defense in the Boulton and Park
case), in Vested Interests: Cross-Dressing & Cultural Anxiety (New York: Routledge, 1992), that
transvestism cannot consistently or coherently be equated with homosexuality (she cautions against "the confusion between—or conflation of—transvestism and gay identity
[which] becomes evident virtually whenever transvestism becomes a topic for public
debate" [129]); and, by contrast, Sedgwick and Moon's argument in "Divinity" (which
roughly lines up with the prosecution in the case) that a position such as Garber's is
itself disingenuous since it does not sufficiently interrogate the historically and psycho-
logically felt affinities between the two phenomena. Female drag, they aver, in what
might be read as a redemptive updating of nineteenth-century sexological wisdom, "is
inscribed not just in dress and its associated gender codes but in the body itself. . . . [It
is] a way of inhabiting the body with defiant effeminacy" (220). In an effort to avoid the
disavowals of the first position and the conflations of the second, we might instead see
the relation as one of historically variable vacillation between them. As the case at hand
illustrates, neither an equation between drag and gayness, on the one hand, nor a radical distinction between them, on the other, guarantees a determinate link to progressive
(or punitive) attitudes toward either.

posit that subjectivity upon the articulation of a self/other opposition. The scandal surprisingly suggests that in transposing this fundamental self/other divide onto a public/private axis, the valorized and normalized terms (of, for instance, class and nation) are identified with the imagined public, not the private subject. The public sphere is the locus for value, while the privacy of an execrated other (here, the sodomite) is determined through its violation. This amounts to a relatively coherent and self-sustaining structure (one could imagine its applicability, for example, to racial or ethnic alterity). A crisis arises around sexual difference, however, for gender is itself already mapped onto the same public/private axis upon which the scandal of buggery—and its public representation as transvestism—is articulated.

In enunciating this relation between the general public and the private subject, scandal makes sexual ideology palatable in narrative form. In so doing, it betrays a variety of allegiances to dominant nineteenth-century literary concepts. Literary questions first arise explicitly when hundreds of letters, which the police had confiscated from the defendants, have to be interpreted, and references to sex between men in antiquity elicit discussion of high literary culture. In the climate of debates over English national culture, the invocation of classical Greek texts was frequently used in this period both to justify homoeroticism and to condemn it. Such allusion itself raises the more fundamental question of how words that bear the increasingly recognizable attributes of literary style—verbal complexity, meaning in an oblique relation to representation, as well as certain markers of social privilege—can be distinguished from sexually suggestive language. This literary question in turn manifests the consternation over interpretive matters that permeates the trial. Finally, we will see, the rewriting of the case to conform to the customs of another powerful genre—pornography—highlights the ways in which the scandal as a whole partakes of the conventions of familiar narrative forms.

The epistolary evidence proved critical both to the conspiracy charges and to the popular entertainment value of the case, for it was supposed to indicate the premeditation and execution of unnatural crimes, doing so in an amusingly—to some, dangerously—literary style.[34] In review-

34. Indicating the degree of popular fascination with the correspondence, the Times states in its report of the preliminary hearings:

> During the reading of the letters the audience in the body of the court appeared to be exceedingly amused, and the prisoners themselves smiled occasionally. Cer-

ing this material, the Crown made much of the risqué references, in one letter from Fiske to Boulton, to prostitutes from antiquity, the legendary Greek courtesan Lais and Hadrian's catamite Antinous:

> My darling Ernie,
>
> I had a letter last night from Louis [Hurt] which was charming in every respect except the information it bore that he is to be kept a week or so longer in the North. He tells me you are living in drag. What a wonderful child it is! I have three minds to come to London and see your magnificence with my own eyes. Would you welcome me? Probably it is better I should stay at home and dream of you. But the thought of you—Lais and Antinous in one—is ravishing.
>
> Let me ask your advice. A young lady, whose family are friends of mine, is coming here. She is a charmingly dressed beautiful fool with £30,000 a year. I have reason to believe that if I go in for her I can marry her. You know I never should care for her; but is the bait tempting enough for me to make this further sacrifice to respectability? Of course, after we were married I could do pretty much as I pleased. People don't mind what one does on £30,000 a year, and the lady wouldn't much mind, as she hasn't brains enough to trouble herself about much beyond her dresses, her carriage, etc. What shall I do?
>
> You see I keep on writing to you and expect some day an answer to some of my letters. In any case, with all the love in my heart,
>
> > I am yours, etc.,
> > JOHN
> > (6:97–98)

The letter was suggestive enough to provoke the scandal, but it did not, to the prosecution's dismay, contain anything directly inculpating either sender or recipient in a "conspiracy to commit a felony." The best the attorney general could do was to exploit the letter's implications—"Is

---

tain expressions of endearment addressed by one man to another, caused such an outburst of laughter that Mr. Poland [a prosecutor] rose and begged that such unseemly demonstrations might be checked, observing that to him it was a matter of surprise that a body of Englishmen could regard an inquiry of such grave importance in such a spirit. The learned magistrate remarked that it was certainly "no laughing matter," but neither the admonition of the Bench nor the repeated remonstrances of the chief clerk and officers of the court had any appreciable effect upon a certain portion of the public. (May 30, 1870)

it not manifest that there must have been some very intimate relation between them for Mr. Fiske to write in this way?" (6:97)—and to take seriously its allusions:

> "The thought of you, Lais and Antinous in one, is ravishing." Lais and Antinous in one! Gentlemen, as I before observed, what is the meaning of this? What can it be but that this dainty boy, as I think Mr. Matthews called him, this dainty boy, this effeminate boy who was treated as a woman, combined in his own person the attractions of one of the most famous prostitutes in antiquity and, if Antinous is not wronged, of a male prostitute also. Lais and Antinous in one! Does not that give some key to the dressing up in women's clothes: sometimes a male prostitute, sometimes a female, sometimes a Lais, sometimes an Antinous. Lais and Antinous in one! (6:98)

Through his incantatory repetition of the letters' "vile phrases," the attorney general implies that homosexual prostitution is the "key to the dressing up in women's clothes." That Fiske would even dare to make such an allusion is seen by the editors of the *Pall Mall Gazette* to implicate him:

> Lais and Antinous have no business anywhere but in the classical dictionary. As long as they remain there, they will, like the rest of the heroes and monsters of antiquity, be mere phantoms, with very little power for evil or for good. Antinous in "drag" in the Burlington Arcade, in the police-court, and in the columns of the *Daily Telegraph* (supposing him to be a really existing creature) is infinitely more formidable than his half-forgotten prototypes. (May 30, 1870)

If, to the prosecution, a defendant's allusion to figures from antiquity in itself seems suspicious, the defense not only rationalizes this highbrow tone, but makes a virtue of the style. One defense attorney states:

> In modern times, for any man to suppose it possible that that kind of attachment—which must subsist between two persons who have this horrible and guilty relation—can be coupled with any other state of mind than one of gross sensuality and one of self-abasement, or [with] anything resembling the poetry and sentiment which attaches to tenderness of feeling between a man and a woman, is, I think—almost to anybody who will consider in what way the human mind and the human conscience are consti-

tuted — inconceivable. It is inconceivable that two Christians in the nineteenth century, having towards each other the relations that are imputed to the two young men, should express their mutual attachment in language savoring of sentiment, refinement, or of respect. . . . Is it in this way that persons committing unnatural crimes express themselves when writing to the object of them? Is it by far-fetched similes and metaphors drawn from classic learning that such things are spoken of? (4:1:242–43; 256)

The barrister for the defense here professes his client's innocence by invoking certain assumptions about the class and cultural ascription of sexual categories. Extravagance and folly are the alibi for the refined young men in the dock, whereas, by contrast, the kind of person seeking only "gross sensuality and self-abasement" is imagined to be slovenly and poorly bred. The very fact of the letter's elegant phrases — "the poetry and sentiment which attaches to tenderness of feeling" — tends to exonerate the defendants, he claims, because such language can be yoked only to sexual desire that subsists "between a man and a woman." Healthy heterosexuality, that is to say, is coterminous with good breeding, and such forays into genteel dalliance as the defendants' language (not to mention their consorting with noblemen) suggests are still arguably exculpatory.

That high literary culture should supply one column of the defense in this trial suggests that its centrality to Wilde's 1895 scandal may not be so anomalous as is sometimes thought. It is no coincidence that both cases should focus on literary subjects, for an emergent British literary culture came in this period to be marked with a perceptible taint of male homosexuality. This unfolding literary sensibility was rooted in Hellenistic studies, and the invocation of ancient Greek texts, the study of which was at the heart of a university education, had an equivocal valence by the date of this scandal. Linda Dowling has shown that classical studies at Oxford, in the wake of the Tractarian movement, provided the ideological basis for a renewal of British national culture in the works of John Stuart Mill and Matthew Arnold. At the same time, it made available to protogay literary writers (such as John Addington Symonds and Walter Pater) a Platonic discourse of incipient homoeroticism.[35] The im-

---

35. I am indebted to Linda Dowling, *Hellenism and Homosexuality in Victorian Oxford* (Ithaca: Cornell University Press, 1994), for my sense of the significance of Greek allusions in this period.

plication of elite literary culture in effete homosexuality and vice versa, which would become conventional by the fin de siècle, is not yet clearly established by 1870, however, and the use of classical allusions can still, to some auditors, pass for erudition, even for wholesomeness.

While the defense attorneys use evidence of literary proficiency to vindicate their clients, they depend as much upon a repudiation of homoeroticism as does the Crown. The judge presiding over *The Queen v. Boulton and Others* goes a step further in justifying ancient Greek references, feeling it incumbent upon him to exculpate Hellenistic pedagogy itself from charges of sexual depravity. Though utterly unprovoked, the justice brings up Socrates in his charge to the jury, raising the question of Greek pederasty in order thoroughly to desexualize it:

> It may be that all this was a species of erotic passion which had not for its object the gratification of any unnatural sensuality, but upon that you must judge. Such things have existed not only with one sex but with the other. . . . The learned, the wise, and the good in every age have come to the belief that the sentiment which undoubtedly Socrates entertained for the youths with whom he delighted to associate was one of a spiritual and ethereal character in which no sensual desire was mired. We have all believed, and do believe from the descriptions of those sentiments, which are to be found in the writings of his greatest scholars, that there was nothing beyond that which was purely spiritual and had nothing to do with gross and degrading sensuality; that the soul of that great philosopher who in all his aspirations loved beauty in its purity and virtue, its holiness, was never contaminated and soiled by the sensuality of gross and unnatural and loathsome lust. It may be the explanation here, but you will not say so unless you are satisfied of it from the absence of any evidence tending in an opposite direction, that this was the spirit in which this strange language, which in our age comes upon us only as calculated to excite odium and detestation, was used; that it was in that strain, I say, that these letters were written. (6:260–62)

Poignant in its defensiveness about the possibility for a healthy and virtuous love between men, this statement works to absolve the accused. It draws upon a conventional series of attributes—"purity," "holiness," spiritualism—to exonerate Socratic teaching from sexual corruption. In so doing, however, it also helps to make this high-cultural tradition available to sexual nonconformists who wish to draw upon it. The justice's remarks make Oscar Wilde's courtroom claim that his love letter to Lord Alfred Douglas was "a kind of prose poem" seem less disingenuous than it might otherwise, suggesting how plausible this justification had been only a generation earlier. By linking the transvestites to Socratic tradition, the judge makes clear the two directions in which classical allusions could lead: on one side, the touchstone for an English literary culture undergoing renovation, on the other, Hellenism is the basis on which the predominant discourse of gay male self-identification—the elite, literary language that culminated in Wilde—would rely for the next thirty years.

Reference to antiquity serves this double purpose by dint of its indeterminacy: at any given moment, it would never be entirely clear which strand of Greek significance was being suggested. Dickens's novel has shown us how indeterminacy itself comes to be one of the hallmarks of sexual expression, and the erotic suggestiveness of the defendants' epistles makes questions of interpretation imperative in this trial. Boulton, Park, and their correspondents draw upon an argot largely unintelligible to those outside their subculture, and it is therefore the prosecution that has to decipher their criminal language.[36] The attorney general

36. At points, the interpretive task is a perplexing one for the prosecutor, particularly when faced with translating gay subcultural slang into the Queen's English. The terms *drag* and *camp* occur frequently in the evidentiary letters, and while their genealogy is obscure, it is noteworthy that they appear so regularly at this early date. The words were clearly not in general circulation, for they have to be glossed in court and are always placed between quotation marks in the newspapers and trial transcripts. During a preliminary hearing, for example, the treasury solicitor "explained that the term 'drag' was a slang phrase employed in certain circles to mean 'wearing women's clothes.' He could give evidence of this fact if necessary" (*Times*, May 16, 1870). The OED supplement records the first written use of *drag* in this sense from a *Reynolds's News* report of this trial on May 29, 1870. The problems of this new terminology were compounded by one letter from Park to Lord Arthur, which contains the following passage:

> I cannot echo your wish that I should live to be a hundred, though I should like to live to a green old age. Green, did I say? Oh! *ciel*, the amount of paint that will be required to hide that very unbecoming tint. My campish undertakings are not at present meeting with the success they deserve. Whatever I do seems to get me into hot water somewhere; but *n'importe*, what's the odds as long as you're *rappy*? Believe me, your affectionate sister-in-law, Fanny Winnifred Park. (*Times*, May 30, 1870)

When this letter was entered into the court record, the word *campish* was misread as "crawfish," and a debate ensued over its meaning. While the court was clearly confused about what "sodomitical practices" might entail, that it could imagine them somehow

finds himself in the awkward position of having to put the worst possible construction upon ambiguous letters, and he ventures perilously deep into the world inhabited by the young men to comprehend, and to make comprehensible, their language. Here, for example, is a letter from Hurt to Boulton, dated April 4, 1870, which he had to parse:

> My darling Ernie,
>
> I had another cry in the train after leaving you, then lay back and managed to get to sleep. After all, as you say, after a few weeks we shall meet again and I must look forward to that. I hope I shall manage to sleep in my train tonight.
>
> The landlord of the inn from which I write tells me that all the men whom we saw here the other day were positive you are a woman. He assured them you were not to no purpose, although he seems to have been certain himself. He said you moved about and stood like one but that your thighs, which he examined when you were going upstairs, were not so plump as a woman's. (6:87–89)

Reading through the letter, the prosecutor interpolates the following comments:

> Gentlemen, what language is this? A man crying at parting for a few weeks with another man. "I had a cry in the train!" What language is that? Is it the language of friendship or is it the language of love? It seems to me very strange. . . . Gentlemen, you may put your own interpretation upon that, but it seems to me very strange and I do not understand it, I confess. A landlord examining Mr. Boulton's thighs! . . . These letters are so remarkable — they are so astounding that you must forgive me for calling your attention to [Hurt's] own account [that] he scarcely knew and had only seen a few times "my darling Ernie." What does it mean? (6:87–93)

The precariousness of the attorney general's posture drives him to claim at once that the letter's perversity is self-evident (he can therefore leave it to the jury to "put [their] own interpretation upon" it) and that he

---

to involve crustaceans is rather startling. (Roughead transcribes the phrase as "caw fish undertakings" [169]. *Crawfish out*, it should be noted, is an informal expression meaning "to withdraw from an undertaking" current from at least 1838 in the United States; both the form of the adjective here and the fact that it was not current in England, however, make it unlikely that the confusion in the trial arose from this meaning.)

"do[es] not understand it," thereby exonerating himself from any complicity in the perversion. His argument consists in iterating the letters' most outrageous phrases and posing rhetorical questions, both techniques that rely on insinuation, on an implied interpretation that does the work of incrimination. Illicit sexuality has clearly developed a language of its own, and the defenders of public morals are vexed by having to apprehend it while remaining uncorrupted by its depravity. The moment sex can be spoken, it can be overheard; if young men wearing dresses can learn the language, so too can barristers in powdered wigs.

In contrast to the prosecution's evocative, winking interpretation, the defense attorneys insist that the letters be taken simply as expressions of affection (however exaggerated by "theatrical propensities" [3:228]), that no correspondence can be established between such genteel language and criminally sexual acts: "all is purity and innocence" (3:240). By denouncing the Crown's readings as not only urbane and subtle but downright perverse, the young men's counselors can claim that the letters have been subject to gross misapprehension: "No word, no act of impropriety was either uttered or committed by them; there was no word suggesting commission of crime, nothing whatever to encourage or suggest anything of the kind, or even anything with a view of ascertaining whether [Boulton's] mind was capable of the infamous thoughts or deeds which my friend suggests was the main source of the conduct of these young men" (3:225).

In the debate over deciphering obscure sexual meanings, the hermeneutic disputes about how to construe evidence, usual in any criminal trial, are intensified, thanks to the crime's defining unknowability. Even with evidence that is not textual, the opposing camps of attorneys employ a consistent set of interpretive procedures for articulating a relation between public and private behavior. In addition to the letters, the prosecutors have to explicate the sexual significance of female costumes, face-powdering, and the rest of the public evidence, and they soon confront the difficulty of proving that an activity ordinarily so private as sexual intercourse has taken place. Making an asset of this problem, however, the attorney general takes the very lack of direct evidence for sodomy to demonstrate that the crime was committed: "This is a crime which from its very nature must necessarily be very difficult to prove. It is a description of crime which if committed is of course always or almost always committed with great precaution" (1:8–9).

Were it only a question of sodomy, the defense could take this absence of witnesses to exonerate the accused; but the conspiracy approach adopted by the government requires that the criminal sexuality merely implied by transvestism be disproved. Through a precise reversal of their antagonists' reasoning, the defense counselors claim that their clients' public antics are the very proof of their private innocence. "Do you think if these men were pursuing a course of criminal indulgence together at home that they would invite public criticism upon their private acts, and that they would create a public scandal by [such] conduct as would call attention to the very act which they were committing and which would be the best means of putting down their professional gains?" (3:256). That the young men sought so much publicity finally works in their favor, for obviously, the argument runs, if they were committing unnatural offenses, they would seek to hide, not to advertise themselves; their outrageous appearance comes to signal not perversity but guiltlessness. This dispute now casts the relation between transvestism and homosexuality as a question of interpretive persuasion. The moralism and gothicism of the following peroration by Digby Seymour, who represented Boulton, exemplify the high stakes in fixing the meaning of public appearance:

> My friend [the attorney general] I think used the expression that crimes of this kind are always committed with great precaution. True, gentlemen, from the very nature of the crime and its unnatural character, of course it would be one which those who indulge in it, and who unsex themselves for the commission of such an outrage upon decency, morality, and upon nature itself, would not be likely to bring public attention to in their acts, but would try by their conduct and by their dealings in the relations in which they stood to each other to avoid exciting the suspicion of others. . . . But here in this case the very course which my friend has taken by producing evidence of visits to theaters, visits to casinos, visits to arcades and other places of public resort and amusement and other acts — improper and unjustifiable acts, if you please, acts of extravagance and folly on the part of these persons to whom I refer — yet those very acts themselves, in place of showing that they were contemplating something over which the pall of darkness was to be withdrawn — something which was to be drawn away from the public light, which was to be the indulgence of some such horrible crime that men would shrink from suggesting even a trace or

a suspicion to those who might be suspicious of their intention—I say the mere fact of all this publicity is of itself a strong argument at the outset in favor of my clients. (3:218–20)

While the prosecution relies on insinuation and connotation to establish connections between cross-dressing and sexual crimes, the defense maintains a literal interpretation, insisting that the young men are merely dressed up as ladies for a bit of fun and nothing more. The link between the sexual life and the public one requires a certain body of knowledge to be recognized as such, and to the extent that the defense can claim ignorance of this information, it can thwart the contaminating allegations. The defense consistently feigns a wide-eyed guilelessness about the meanings the government puts on the evidence. In a remarkable literalization of this figurative myopia about the significance of going around in drag, Park's representative, Serjeant Parry, claims not to be able to see what all the fuss is: "I am so short sighted that without a glass I cannot discern the features of the jury whom I have the honor of addressing, but I am told by those who have a better and sharper sight than I have that a sort of thrill of horror ran through the jury box when all those dresses appeared upon the floor of the court" (4:1:147–48). Against the prosecution's connotation of the unspeakable, the faux naïveté of the defense resists recognizing the legibility of perversion.

Beyond the differences between the opposing counselors' interpretive procedures, each party to the trial depends upon a series of narrative conventions to make its case persuasive. Composed of a collection of texts that teaches its public lessons in private, scandal mimics the practices of the most familiar Victorian narratives of instruction about private life, the realist novel. Unlike novels, scandals have real-world referents, yet even so, scandals generate stories that need not be true, but merely plausible. In invoking conventional narrative codes, scandal, like the novel, attempts a reconciliation—however wishful or magical—between the private and public spheres of social and sexual life.

While newspaper accounts lend the case an overarching narrative structure, even within the courtroom certain familiar stories are put strategically into play. To legitimate the young men's transvestism, for example, the defense brings to the stand Boulton's mother, who chronicles her son's career as an actor. In recapitulating this evidence, Boulton's representative provides an account that reads as a drag queen's coming-of-age story:

So early as some ten or eleven years of age he showed extreme
fondness for appearing in female dress, sometimes putting on the
dress of his mother, sometimes that of a servant, and showing a
talent for the imitation of female characters, which he performed
for the amusement of his friends and which won the admiration
and applause of those who had the opportunity of seeing his performance. Year after year his taste improved. There was nothing in
his early taste for these theatricals which caused any other than a
feeling of admiration for the genius he had. . . . He grew gradually
fond of assuming these female characters; sometimes when friends
were at his father's house he would dress himself in the character of a parlor maid and come into the room and by his manner
and appearance show at once a cleverness and ability in getting up
female characters. (3:223–24)

And so the biography continues, until Boulton determines this "assuming female characters" to be his vocation. Within twenty-five years this
narrative could never have been used in *defense* of a man up on sodomy
charges, for rather than testifying to the innocence of his female imper-
sonation, it would demonstrate a nearly genetic predisposition for gay
style. Such proclivities would be the signifier of homosexuality, not its
alibi, by the time Havelock Ellis would codify life stories like this one in
Sexual Inversion. This difference is not only a matter of interpretation, for
it illustrates a conceptual shift: while Boulton's story could function in
1871 as a narrative of professional growth, it would be comprehensible
only as one of psychological development by 1897. The assumption that
self-presentation testifies less to the psychological constitution of sexuality than to its occupational status holds for the prosecution as well—
the difference lying in what that occupation is thought to be: acting or
prostitution.[37] The narratives mobilized to determine the criminality or
innocence of the defendants' private subject status are emphatically public in purview, relying not on a pathologizing depth-psychology but on
the evidence for vocational legitimacy.

The scandal draws upon the range of narrative forms we have consid-

---

37. On the increasing detachment of occupation from personal identity more generally
through the first half of the nineteenth century, see Leonore Davidoff and Catherine
Hall, *Family Fortunes: Men and Women of the English Middle Class, 1780–1850* (London: Hutchin-
son, 1987). On the narrative conventions of legal proceedings, see Christine L. Krueger,
"Naming Privates in Public: Indecent Assault Depositions, 1830–1860," *Mosaic* 27, no. 4
(December 1994): 121–40.

ered, from personal records of professional development to gothic tales of medical discovery, from the comical drag escapades recounted in the letters to the horror stories of men deceived by the defendants' female appearance. Yet as much as scandal spins out competing narratives for the pleasurable consumption of a horrified audience, it also aims at the ultimate revelation of a singular, true story. In this punitive truth-seeking mode, scandal abhors ambiguity: it attempts to fix meanings, exacting public morality through private exposure. Not in its production of narrative, then, but in its drive toward closure, scandal evinces hostility to the late-nineteenth-century literary project I have identified, of encrypting sexual sensations even while demonstrating their prohibition. The literary inscription of sexuality we witnessed in *Great Expectations* is complex and contradictory, neither verifiably intentional nor necessarily unconscious, but a writing *available* to interpretation. The indeterminacy of texts construed as literary allows (in the Boulton and Park trial) for exoneration as much as (in the Wilde case) for condemnation—but only because the scandal form itself requires that, after deferral, debate, and indecision, meanings be resolved unequivocally.

Between the literary and the scandalous attitude toward sexuality's discursive status, a middle road insinuates itself—one that partakes of literature's self-conscious and highly textured language without sharing its aptitude for sexual self-censorship; one that also joins in scandal's exuberant thralldom to salacious material without exercising its moralizing righteousness. I refer to literature's bastard sibling, pornography, the genre whose content is no longer governed by secrecy and discretion, but whose circulation is. Through the illusion it propagates of absolute speakability—a world in which nothing cannot be said—pornography negates the censoring impulses of both literature and scandal reporting, however different these two may be from each other. The restriction on pornography's circulation strictly limits audience access to such material: only through the severe circumscription of its marketplace and readership can pornography afford to express itself (or so it claims) unhindered. Certainly in the nineteenth century, and arguably by definition, pornography is consumed in private; it thus appears inversely to mirror scandal discourse, which trades publicity for necessary feints and indirection.[38] Even as pornography intercedes between litera-

---

38. By some definitions, pornography provides only the most extreme example of censorship; in *Hard Core: Power, Pleasure, and the "Frenzy of the Visible"* (Berkeley: University of

ture and scandal reporting, it shows these two discourses to be alike in still another way: as a medium whose constrained access allows for relatively unbounded substance, pornography exposes the centrality of censorship to the content of more freely available texts. It has been argued that censorship is constitutive of all discursive production:[39] subject to it, though in differing degrees, are both unequivocally public language (courtroom speeches and newspaper editorials, for example) and novels, with their peculiar mixture of availability in public and consumption in (as well as almost uniform concern with) private life. Only by virtue of its decidedly private status does pornography appear to escape—or, more accurately, does it resituate—the censoring mechanisms that help to compose sexuality.

Concluding by way of a pornographic coda, we can revisit some of the issues that have structured this investigation as they surface in one final account of Ernest Boulton and Frederick Park's sexual lives. Happily for us, the publicity surrounding the trial appears in at least one instance to have stimulated a sympathetic, protoliterary imagination to spin out a properly pornographic text. In addition to the constructions put on the transvestites' behavior by the legal, medical, and popular press accounts, a radically different version is available. This is the report of Jack Saul, a male prostitute notorious in Dublin and London, made infamous by the sensational testimony he gave in the Cleveland Street scandal, which threatened to expose the homosexual activities of several high-ranking men. Eight years before Cleveland Street—and ten years after Boulton and Park's acquittal—Saul produced a supposed memoir, *The Sins of the Cities of the Plain; or, the Recollections of a Mary-Ann, with Short Essays on Sodomy and Tribadism.* By its own account, the work was written at the behest of a nobleman whom Saul picked up in Leicester Square, in return for five

---

California Press, 1989), Linda Williams writes with reference to Kendrick's *Secret Museum:* "Pornography is simply whatever representations a particular dominant class or group does not want in the hands of another, less dominant class or group. Those in power construct the definition of pornography through their power to censor it. . . . Kendrick argues, for example, that in the nineteenth century the objectionable texts might be realistic novels, sensational melodramas, reports on prostitution, bawdy limericks" (12).

39. In a theorization that draws from Foucault, Francis Barker writes in *The Tremulous Private Body: Essays on Subjection* (London: Methuen, 1984) of "bourgeois discursivity . . . being conditional on censorship not in its elisions but in its substantial articulation. . . . The very structure of *all* bourgeois enunciation is governed by its relation to censorship as a determinant condition" (51).

pounds a week during the several weeks it took to compose; according to the title page, it was privately published in an edition limited to 250 copies.[40] *Sins* is a peculiar mixture of programmatic pornographic narrative with apparently factual, and potentially exposing, information; in this sense it reads much like the deposition that Saul gave in the Cleveland Street trial, which contained such inflammatory material that it actually protected him from being prosecuted.

Saul's rendition of Boulton and Park's conduct provides a piquant complement to the other narratives of their lives, valuable both for radically shifting the perspective and for highlighting the tendentiousness of any report about "sodomitical practices." It is clear from his account that Saul is familiar with the history of the two drag queens; his lengthy description, for instance, of a ball thrown at Haxell's Hotel — one of the principal incidents that was supposed to incriminate them — corresponds plausibly with the report of it in the trial. Saul's chronicle plainly savors its erotic content, yet it also mimics and transforms the trial's portrayal of Boulton and Park's antics: like the legal documents, it is exacting in such factual details as names, dates, and places; like the medical evidence, it is unflinchingly explicit in recounting their sexual practices. And like the scandalmongering press, the memoir depends for its force upon the exposure of private life, of revealing bedroom escapades to an interested readership.

As much as all the other accounts, *The Sins of the Cities of the Plain* makes use of Boulton and Park as objects of visual delectation. In so doing, the pornographic text throws the other versions into relief, exposing them

---

40. *The Sins of the Cities of the Plain; or, the Recollections of a Mary-Ann, with Short Essays on Sodomy and Tribadism,* 2 vols. (London: privately printed, 1881); quotations reproduced by permission of the British Library. A seriously distorted modern edition is also available (New York: Masquerade, 1992). Hyde, *History of Pornography,* writes: "Although some of the details of the incidents in *The Sins* . . . may be exaggerated for effect, the work is based upon fact and no doubt gives a faithful enough picture of a seamy side of contemporary London life" (141). Saul's testimony in court in the Cleveland Street scandal was restricted to the supposed proclivities of Lord Euston, plaintiff in the libel case against newspaper editor Ernest Parke, who had attempted to expose the government's cover-up of the homosexual prostitution ring. For more on Saul's role in the case, see Chester et al., *Cleveland Street Affair,* and Hyde, *Cleveland Street Scandal.* Another obscene rendering of the Boulton and Park case, likewise in pseudoliterary form, appears in a popular limerick that curiously registers an anachronistic conflation of sodomy and bestiality: "There was an old person of Sark / Who buggered a pig in the dark; / The swine in surprise / Murmured: 'God blast your eyes, / Do you take me for Boulton or Park?' " (Chester et al., *Cleveland Street Affair,* 59).

as fabrications that also serve particular interests. The following excerpt illustrates the ways in which information on the case was adapted to serve Saul's erotic purposes.

The extent to which pederasty is carried on in London between gentlemen and young fellows is little dreamed of by the outside public. You remember the Boulton and Park case? Well, I was present at the ball given at Haxell's Hotel in the Strand. No doubt the proprietor was quite innocent of any idea of what our fun really was; but there were two or three dressing-rooms into which company could retire at pleasure.

Boulton was superbly got up as a beautiful lady, and I observed Lord Arthur was very spooney upon her.

During the evening I noticed them slip away together, and made up my mind to try and get a peep at their little game, so followed them as quietly as possible, and saw them pass down a corridor to another apartment, not one of the dressing-rooms which I knew had been provided for the use of the party, but one which I suppose his lordship had secured for his own personal use.

I was close enough behind them to hear the key turned in the lock. Foiled thus for a moment, I turned the handle of the next door, which admitted me to an unoccupied room, and to my great delight a beam of bright light streamed from the keyhole of a door of communication between that and the one my birds had taken refuge in.

Quietly kneeling down I put my eye to the hole, and found I had a famous view of all that was going on in the next room. It put me in mind of the two youths which Fanny Hill relates to have seen through a peephole at a roadside inn. I could both see and hear everything that was passing.

Lord Arthur and Boulton, whom he addressed as Laura, were standing before a large mirror. He had his arm round her waist, and every now and then drew Laura's lips to his for a long, luscious kiss. His inamorata was not idle, for I could see her unbuttoning his trousers, and soon she let out a beautiful specimen of the *arbor vitae*, at least nine inches long and very thick. It was in glorious condition, with a great, glowing red head.

Laura at once knelt down and kissed this jewel of love, and would I believe have sucked him to a spend, but Lord Arthur was too impatient, as he raised his companion from her stooping position, and passing his hands under Laura's clothes, as she gave a very pretty scream and pretended to be shocked at this rudeness, he turned everything up and tossed her on the bed.

As yet there was nothing to see but a beautiful pair of legs, lovely knickerbocker drawers, prettily trimmed with the finest lace, also pink silk stockings and the most fascinating little shoes with silver buckles. His lordship quickly opened Laura's thighs, and, putting his hand into her drawers, soon brought to light as manly a weapon as any lady could desire to see, and very different from the crinkum-crankum one usually expects to find when one throws up a lady's petticoats and proceeds to take liberties with her; but his lordship's love was only a man in woman's clothes, as everyone knows it was Boulton's practice to make himself up as a lovely girl. There seems such a peculiar fascination to gentlemen in the idea of having a beautiful creature, such as an ordinary observer would take for a beautiful lady, to dance and flirt with, knowing all the while that his inamorata is a youth in disguise.

"What's this beautiful plaything, Laura darling? Are you an hermaphrodite, my love? Oh, I must kiss it; it's such a treasure! Will it spend like a man's love?"

I heard Lord Arthur say all this, as he fondled and caressed Boulton's prick, passing his hand up and down the ivory-white shaft and kissing the dark, ruby-coloured head every time it was uncovered.

How excited I became at the sight you may be sure. I also longed to caress and enjoy both the fine pegos I had seen; but although my own prick was stiff almost to bursting, I determined not to frig myself, as I was sure of finding a nice partner when I returned to the ball-room. Still, I would rather have had Boulton than anyone. His make-up was so sweetly pretty that I longed to have him, and him have me.

But to go on. I could see that the assumed Laura was greatly agitated. Her whole frame shook, whilst one of his lordship's hands seemed to be under Laura's bottom, and no doubt was postillioning her bottom-hole; and presently, seeing how agitated he had made her, he took that splendid prick fairly into his mouth and sucked away with all the ardour of a male gamahucher; his eyes almost emitted sparks as the crisis seemed to come, and he must have swallowed every drop of the creamy emission he had worked so hard to obtain.

His other hand frigged the shaft of Boulton's prick rapidly as he sucked its delicious head.

After a minute or two he wiped his mouth, and turned Laura round so as to present her bottom over the edge of the bed, then threw up all the skirts over her back, and opening the drawers behind he kissed each cheek of the lovely white bum, and tickled the little hole with his tongue, but he was too impatient to waste much time in kissing, so at once he presented his prick to Boulton's fundament, as he held the two cheeks of his pretty arse open with his hands.

Although such a fine cock, it did not seem to have a very difficult task to get in, and he was so excited that he appeared to come at once; but keeping his place, he soon commenced a proper bottom fuck, which both of them gave signs of enjoying intensely, for I could fairly hear his belly flop against Boulton's buttocks at every home push, whilst each of them called the other by the most endearing terms, such as:

"Oh, Laura, Laura, what a darling you are! Tell me, love that you love me! tell me it's a nice fuck!"

And then the other would exclaim:

"Push; push; fuck me; ram your darling prick in as fast as it will go! oh! oh! oh! quicker, quicker; do come now, dearest Arthur; my love, my pet! oh! oh!! oh!!!"

After seeing so much, I slipped away from the keyhole and went back to the company in the dancing room. (1:96–104)

Here is the proof the prosecution had sought of the defendants' private lives. As graphic, in its way, as the physicians' accounts of deviant sexual practices, this testimony bears witness to the sexual activity the Crown assumed, but could not prove, was associated with transvestism and public campishness. For all of its factual precision, however, this may well be the fantasy that the attorney general's insinuations provoked: if cross-dressing is linked unequivocally to buggery, then this is how an empathetic Victorian imagination gleefully elaborates that pathology. Yet while the scandal profits by exposing the defendants' private behavior, pornographic conventions require that this privacy be kept intact in order to maintain the erotic force of voyeurism. No doubt the treasury department would have jumped at the chance to peep through that keyhole, but only to follow by breaking down the door. The public work of private subject-making that I have recounted in the scandal is here subverted: the titillation of the pornographic text, unlike that of the scandal sheet, requires the preservation of privacy, both within its narrative and through its own status as contraband reading matter. Saul's account depends not only on seeing everything that happens but on maintaining the voyeuristic pose which engenders the narrative; just as the narrator crouches at the peephole, aroused by what he sees, so the imagined consumer, running his eyes over the comparably secret scene of the page before him, is positioned in a masturbatory relation to this material.

Furthermore, while the crisis for the scandal's valuation of the general public arises in its account of gender, the untruth of femininity in the pornographic work reveals what may be the truth outside the text: that the putative divide of gender masks the uniformity of phallic heterosexuality, which determines femininity only as negative, gullible, and defenseless. In *Sins*, that is to say, there is no pretense of a female presence, either in the readership or among the participants in the scene. The work frankly addresses itself to elite and strictly homosexual men (no fiction of that squeamish young person here), and in this portion of the memoir all of the women turn out to be men in drag: "I do not for a moment believe there was one real female in the room, for I groped ever so many of them, and always found a nice little cock under the petticoats, most of them quite slimy with spendings, they had been frigged so often" (1:106). Saul stages the revelation, so horrifically hinted in the scandal, that behind "lovely knickerbocker drawers, prettily trimmed with the finest lace" there might lurk "as manly a weapon as any lady could desire to see." Like her collective representation in the general public, the subject of this vision, the lady, is an entirely abstract entity. In this context, rather than precipitating a crisis over its public reception, the exhibition serves the private fantasy—dependent on a certain misogyny—of a gay male sexual paradise. The pornographer rejects the equation between femininity and credulous innocence as well as the panicky defensiveness of heteromasculinity that cowers behind its petticoats. Refusing the hypocrisy of a public discourse that both identifies itself as female and works to keep women ignorant, the gay pornographic narrative tells the truth of that discourse: like the real world, this imagined one has two *apparent* sexes according to which difference can be accounted; but making a utopia of the inadmissible reality, the fiction reveals a single significant organ, a single sexual plenitude, without necessitating a complementary figure of lack. No place for women here, but also no masquerade of a place.

Finally, *The Sins of the Cities of the Plain* takes seriously the importance of literature to the Boulton and Park scandal—not, like the court, by seeking to incriminate or exculpate the defendants on the basis of textual exegesis, but by self-consciously inscribing the transvestites within its own protoliterary form. Through the frankness of its voyeurism, *Sins* not only emphasizes its own formal status, but elucidates the literary structuration already inherent in scandal. Though it abjures the connotative aspect of literary language (no need for discretion here), Saul's memoir still relies on fiction: its narrative technique—plot, characterization, voice, and so on—both underscores its allegiance to conventional forms and accommodates the special erotic requirements of pornography. As if to enunciate the slippage between the facts and their fictional analogue, the narrator invokes the novelistic precedent of *Fanny Hill* just before—as though to justify—pornography's usual trope of omniscience: "I could both see and hear everything that was passing."[41] Unabashedly orthodox in its adherence to the conventions of the genre, *Sins* also demonstrates the ways in which any narrative representation of Boulton and Park's career—any narrative, for that matter, of the sexual life—is so prescripted as to recall to its readers lessons that their bodies, constituted through a phantasmatic privacy, have no doubt already learned.

41. In "Seeing Things: Representation, the Scene of Surveillance, and the Spectacle of Gay Male Sex," in *Homographesis: Essays in Gay Literary and Cultural Theory* (New York: Routledge, 1994), 173–91, Lee Edelman discusses the peep-show scene of male homosexuality in *Fanny Hill* as an "instance of sodomy's capacity to implicate those who would envision or observe it" (186).

FOUR

SCHADENFREUDE IN

THE MILL ON THE FLOSS

Among the many indiscretions that Maggie Tulliver commits, giving herself an impromptu haircut is scarcely the most egregious. Immediately after the impetuous young protagonist of George Eliot's novel *The Mill on the Floss* (1860) shears off her "dark heavy locks,"[1] however, she realizes from her family's horrified reaction that she has flown in the face of respectable femininity. With a certain percipience, Maggie soon recognizes that the community's response is distilled in the attitude of one person in particular: the coiffeur. "The hairdresser from St. Ogg's . . . had spoken in the severest terms of the condition in which he had found her hair, holding up one jagged lock after another and saying, 'See here! tut—tut—tut!' in a tone of mingled disgust and pity, which to Maggie's imagination was equivalent to the strongest expression of public opinion" (85). Maggie feels the sting of Mr. Rappit's disapproval and understands his finger-wagging to convey all the shame and humiliation that "public opinion" aims to instill in rebellious girls.

Everyone knows the mortification a hairdresser can induce, standing, as he does, not only as the expert but also as the representative of all who judge one's appearance. In reproving Maggie for her defiance of taste in hairstyles, Mr. Rappit works in the service of the feminine com-

---

1. George Eliot, *The Mill on the Floss* (Oxford: Oxford University Press, 1980), 13; further references will be made parenthetically to this edition.

munity whose concerns are codified in the fashion system. Yet however feminized the police who typically implement fashion's ordinances, this public itself answers to the higher authority of what it imagines men to desire in women. When the coiffeur speaks on behalf of female opinion, then, he actually ventriloquizes the women saying what they think men want to hear. If Mr. Rappit voices the opinion of Maggie's hairstyle that derives from a conventional masculine aesthetic, however, it is only his distance from normative masculinity that enables him to enforce its rules so well. That the source of Maggie's chastening lesson in gender-appropriate behavior should be the figure destined to epitomize compromised masculinity—the hairdresser—suggests how fragile the system is that requires such vigilant maintenance. For the security of Mr. Rappit's location on the gender map is thrown into doubt as much by his fastidious attention to female fashion-correctness as by his own remarkable hairdo: "his well-anointed coronal locks tend[ed] wavily upward, like the simulated pyramid of flame on a monumental urn" (85). All but literally flamboyant, the hairstylist makes an ironic—if for that, all the more powerful—source for the administration of codes of gender conduct, and the beauty-parlor world we glimpse around him models in miniature the complex gendering of the public, which passes judgment on sexual transgressions, throughout *The Mill on the Floss*.

In Mr. Rappit's "tut—tut—tut!" moreover, even in his "tone of mingled disgust and pity," there is a hint of fussy satisfaction at meting out the punishment deserved by the rascally iconoclast, Maggie. This is a bitter sort of enjoyment, exacted by one who stands at the margins of heterosexual hegemony, and taken at the expense of another who ought—but has failed—to abide by that order. *The Mill on the Floss* is replete with characters who derive pleasure from Maggie Tulliver's afflictions, and the novel bids us not to sympathize with them. The Germans give the name *schadenfreude* to the type of pleasure taken in the tribulations of others, a reaction central to the propagation of scandal. It is a form of scandal reception that particularly compels George Eliot, because it focuses her usual interest in the ethics of responding to others' troubles. Pleasure is perhaps the most callous response to adversity, though one which attaches tenaciously to the misfortune that is scandal. The full range of unsympathetic reactions—including not only "disgust and pity," but delight, condescension, righteousness, and vindictiveness—belong to the scope of Eliot's project.

We have seen in the previous chapter how a sex scandal in the press excites in its readers some of these affective responses, through its circulation of fantasies about both deviant private bodies and an endangered public sphere. Having considered the professedly nonfiction case, I want in this chapter and the following one to return to fiction, investigating the ways in which novels about scandals also construct a responsive reading public for their own purposes. The two works I take up here provide critical accounts of scandal's capacity to produce an audience for sexual unspeakability, and they suggest two different modes of reacting to news about sex. Each of these modes elaborates upon an element of scandal reception we witnessed in the newspaper case. Eliot admonishes the public within The Mill on the Floss for its fascination with and castigation of the story's scandal victim; she uses the response to scandal as a means of distinguishing the public inside the novel from the cultivated audience she imagines, and seeks to propagate, for her own work. Anthony Trollope, by contrast, creates a narrator in The Eustace Diamonds who occupies the position of the supercilious scandalmonger, and his pose of urbane disavowal with respect to his material allows him both to tell a racy story and to distance himself from its raciness. Imagination of the public—both the audience for scandal and the one for the novel—becomes central to literature's own emerging self-definitions, and this imagination shapes the novel's representation of sexuality.

Why should the scandals in these novels concern female heterosexuality, while the nonfiction cases I examine—the Boulton and Park trial, and the Wilde affair—treat male homosexuality? In part, the answer to this question has to do with the differing narrative capacities of novelistic, as opposed to newspaper, scandals. In considering material that lies at the limits of what the popular press can report, I have taken up the type of case that most vividly confronts the rhetorical problem of sexual unspeakability, male homosexuality. While novels regulate their language at least as highly as do scandal sheets, this is not simply a question of available material: sexually heterodox characters of all sorts undeniably appear in Victorian fiction. But the conventions and the history of the genre—as an imaginatively feminized form—produce the problem of female sexuality as its primum mobile. The story of a female heterosexual scandal is consequently more evocative and pervasive than any other in the Victorian novel, although this does not necessarily correspond—nor should it—with the cases most sensationally reported in the press. With both the fiction and the nonfiction, I consider the type of story that most characteristically, because most dramatically, illustrates the features of the genre.

The Mill on the Floss provides an exemplary account of the conditions and effects of female sexual scandal. The story anatomizes the relation between fiction and public opinion—manifested as respectability, reputation, and gossip—and this representation prepares the way for the novel's censure of the scandal audience at its end. Through her account of the scandal audience within the story, Eliot highlights the novel's own subjection to public opinion, but by sharply differentiating the novel's public from scandal's prurient audience, she clearly elevates the former. The difference between the two publics is enunciated in gender terms, for scandal's self-righteous female spectators especially come in for criticism, while the novel's exalted audience is imagined as male. The fundamental distinction between these publics has to do with their differing capacities to make ethical distinctions. The vulgar audience for scandal jumps to conclusions and passes judgment without knowledge of particulars, while the elite audience for the novel learns to discriminate carefully. Despite Eliot's insistence on this difference, however, it is strangely undercut by her own narrative technique, which is shot through with a rhetoric of generalization that both asserts the value of the story beyond its depiction of particular, provincial lives and ironizes the impulse to generalize itself. The gap that opens up between plot and narrative voice with the question of generalization affords a space in Eliot as it does in Dickens (and again, we will see in the next chapter, in Trollope) for aberrant sexual material to be at once evoked and eluded. This material is suggestive not only of adultery and incest, but also of both female and male homoeroticism. To our ongoing compendium of techniques for rendering sex unspeakable in the Victorian period, Eliot contributes her project, of raising the novel to a form of high art for cultivated readers.

Although the general public represented in *The Mill on the Floss* has its most powerful effects on the scandal plot that makes up the final third of the novel, public opinion emerges as an influential force long before Stephen Guest, admiring Maggie Tulliver's arms, persuades her to fall into his. The Dodson clan is obsessed with the respectable reputation their family enjoys, and well in advance of the introduction of her more finely discriminating sisters, Mrs. Tulliver worries that " 'Folks 'ull think it's a judgment on me as I've got such a child [as Maggie]— they'll think I've done summat wicked' " (28). Little worry that Bessy Tulliver née Dodson might actually have "done something wicked to deserve her maternal troubles"—her concern is with what "people would think" (102). If the Dodsons' consuming interest in family prestige seems at first glance attributable to their petit-bourgeois nervousness, we need only look to another site on the class spectrum—scampish young Bob Jakin's realm of rat-catching and bird-frightening—to discover that anxiety about reputation makes the well-polished and the mud-splattered worlds seem as socially similar as they are geographically continuous. Not unlike the St. Ogg's elite, Bob concerns himself with the respectability of his actions in others' eyes: he swallows what little pride he has in order to retrieve the pocketknife that he scornfully sought to return to Tom, and he is sure not to regurgitate that pride when he encounters "the public opinion of Kennel Yard, which was the very focus or heart of Bob's world" (52).

From fashionable Mr. Rappit's milieu to Dorlcote Mill to the Kennel Yard, public opinion pervades the characters' self-conception from the start. As the haircutting incident suggests, public opinion is most thoroughly exacting in the demands it makes of gender performance—even when (as with Mr. Rappit) the source of that opinion is itself a site of precarious gender identification. Consider, first of all, the novel's principal male characters. Tom Tulliver receives a gentleman's education that handicaps his masculinity almost as fully as his hunchbacked schoolmate, Philip Wakem: as a result of his tutoring, "Tom became more like a girl than he had ever been in his life before" (141). Tom recovers his virility in the face not only of adversity but of public evaluation: he "astonishes" his family and his father's creditors when he discovers a "sudden manliness of tone" (213), and he determines to "provide for his mother and sister, and make every one say that he was a man of high character" (225). Like any of his maternal aunts, Tom focuses on reputation: so far as "everyone" is concerned, Tom Tulliver will be no milksop.[2] The novel's other central male characters have their masculinity equally impugned by public assessment. Stephen Guest is suspect for being the exemplar of that paradoxical persona, the ladies' man: he displays his heterosexuality so flagrantly that his success with women

---

2. In another instance, Tom "was even getting rather proud of [Maggie]: several persons had remarked in his hearing that his sister was a very fine girl" (338). The punctuation of this sentence implies a causal relation between others' assessments of Maggie and Tom's pride in her. For an enlightening account of the ways in which gossip and its attendant narrative forms serve regulatory functions within a circumscribed novelistic community, see Casey Finch and Peter Bowen, " 'The Tittle-Tattle of Highbury': Gossip and the Free Indirect Style in *Emma*," *Representations* 31 (Summer 1991): 1–18.

seems to derive not so much from his distinguishing masculinity as from the femininity he is imagined to understand *too well*.[3] Philip, by contrast, "by nature half feminine in sensitiveness" (331), must learn through its public exposure how compromising such sensitivity is. Tom's physical threat—" 'I'll thrash you' "—is immediately reinforced by a more socially costly one: " 'I'll hold you up to public scorn. Who wouldn't laugh at the idea of *your* turning lover to a fine girl?' " (345). The threat of disgrace circulates around impoverished, excessive, or debilitated masculinity, each of which fails to meet the demanding, if not unattainable, public standards of decent manliness.

The sexual instability on which the novel focuses most centrally, however, is not male but female, and if public opinion is rigorous in the demands it makes of masculinity, its imperatives for femininity are, at least in Maggie's case, ruinous. Although education and an interest in artistic or domestic affairs threaten to weaken the men through feminization, a girl's scorn for femininity does not correspondingly empower her through masculinization. The fact that Maggie is, as her father says, " 'twice as 'cute as Tom [and] too 'cute for a woman' " (12) hardly works to her advantage; her rebellion against conventional female behavior, in the initial form of cutting off her hair, is met with "a chorus of reproach and derision" (68) from her first public, the extended family. The young heroine's impudent refusal of proper femininity has led many readers to apply the moniker *tomboy* to her (though the term is never used in the text), a label apt not only in its usual sense but in its onomastic and etymological suggestions as well. In addition to indicating her excessive concern with the estimation of her brother Tom, the term has an older meaning—harlot—that allows it accurately to condense Maggie's youthful repudiation of femininity with her adult sexual mis-

---

3. The introductory portrait of Stephen, which designates him a fop, could in this period still signal his virility, but Eliot's portrayal predicts the perversity that his decadence would soon come to connote: "Mr. Stephen Guest, whose diamond ring, attar of roses, and air of nonchalant leisure, at twelve o'clock in the day, are the graceful and odoriferous result of the largest oil-mill and the most extensive wharf in St. Ogg's" (363). F. R. Leavis, in *The Great Tradition* (London: Chatto & Windus, 1973), states, "That the presentment of Stephen Guest is unmistakably feminine no one will be disposed to deny," and cites Leslie Stephen's comment, which cannily yokes Stephen's femininity both to Mr. Rappit's compromising profession and to the problems of Eliot's authorial transvestism: "George Eliot did not herself understand what a mere hairdresser's block she was describing in Mr. Stephen Guest. . . . No man could have introduced such a character without perceiving what an impression must be made upon his readers" (40).

conduct. For Maggie's ungirlishness serves decisively as the precursor of her fallen womanhood: years after her seditious haircut, when she returns to St. Ogg's from her elopement with Stephen, a young man-about-town "bow[s] to her with that air of nonchalance which he might have bestowed on a friendly bar-maid" (493–94).

The admixture of rigorous public opinion with unstable gender identifications makes a scandal come to seem inevitable, and the novel's scandal engine is well greased even before Stephen Guest arrives in book 6. From such trivial occurrences as Maggie's haircut or her dumping cousin Lucy into the mud, to weightier ones, like the exposure of her trysts with Philip in the Red Deeps, scandal is long in the offing. The events that largely organize the plot up until Stephen's appearance—Mr. Tulliver's loss of the mill—compose a scandal in the financial register. The rapid decline, in the public mind, of the family name is as damaging as the substantive deprivations that follow Mr. Tulliver's failure in court. While the legal debacle is brought about almost entirely by the intransigence of Tulliver père, his Dodson wife serves as the receptacle for the family's trauma over its devastated reputation. Mrs. Tulliver demonstrates from the first that the value of a name derives from its public currency—"she could not help thinking that her case was a hard one, since it appeared that other people thought it hard" (96)—and even her husband, at least to her understanding, appears "very often . . . [to have] done something because other people had said he was not able to do it, or had pitied him for his supposed inability" (129). As much as her conformity, his resistance is a reaction to the compulsions of reputation.

As with most scandals, material loss becomes subordinate to the humiliation of having one's private troubles put into public circulation. The dispersal of the Tulliver housewares through "the hateful publicity of the Golden Lion" (236) literalizes this devaluation, as the Dodson sisters thoroughly comprehend:

> "Ah, dear, dear!" said Aunt Pullet, shaking her head with deep sadness, "it's very bad—to think o' the family initials going about everywhere. . . ."
>
> "As to disgrace o' the family," said Mrs. Glegg, "that can't be helped wi' buying teapots. . . . The disgrace is, as they're to be sold up. We can't hinder the country from knowing that." (213)

While the women's worry over the family name is framed in terms of "disgrace," the men's is phrased more usually as "discredit"—not only because repaying creditors falls within a male purview, but because it is the explicitly financial value of the name that tends to concern them. Mr. Tulliver "hurried away from market, he refused all invitations to stay and chat" because "in all behaviour towards him, whether kind or cold, he detected an allusion to the change in his circumstances" (278); and, as earnest Tom says to Mr. Deane, " 'I hope I should never do you any discredit, uncle. . . . I care about my own credit too much for that' " (232). The scourge of public opinion damages personal as much as fiduciary reputation, so much so that the two stand in for each other.

The destruction of the Tulliver family's reputation functions as punishment for the business miscalculation of its paterfamilias. While the scandal in the masculine world of commerce offers at least a hope of recovery—through Tom's assiduity, the relatives' compassion, and Bob Jakin's entrepreneurial assistance—Maggie's later, more decisive scandal, for which her father's trial with the mill serves effectively as a narrative dry run, offers fewer possibilities of recuperation.[4] Maggie's spectacular scandal takes place in the feminine sphere, where it is far more difficult to lend credit to chastity than it is to recover the currency of a good name in the economic realm. Even Maggie's principal defender, Dr. Kenn— who, by name, ought to *know* better—comes to understand that scandal and its ensuing damage to reputation have nothing to do with facts and everything to do with popular opinion: "Even on the supposition that required the utmost stretch of belief—namely, that none of the things said about Miss Tulliver were true—still, since they *had* been said about her, they had cast an odour round her which must cause her to be

---

4. Dickens's work suggests a different strategy for navigating the difficulties of the sex scandal: displace it onto a more tolerable, though less pungent, financial one. *Bleak House* (1852–53) and *Little Dorrit* (1855–57), for instance, are both impelled by the fear of sexual scandal, though neither novel finally sees a scandal—or, to be more precise, sees the one it fears—carried out: Lady Dedlock's secret, debased liaison is revealed only in her death (and functions, despite all previous anxiety, to liberate rather than to castigate her daughter, Esther); and Mrs. Clennam's concealment of Arthur's parentage remains a secret from him, the character whom it concerns most closely. In both works, however, financial scandals—the mockery that ends Jarndyce and Jarndyce, and the fraud and resulting suicide of Merdle—*are* worked through, and these exposés serve to deflect the personal revelations threatened by the sexual scandals. Even if one were reluctant to assert that financial or political scandals take their form from the sex scandal, such plots at least suggest the frequent proximity of the two. While Eliot shows, through the narrative of Mr. Tulliver's ruin, that a financial scandal occasions lessons about reputation, private life, and public opinion, she (unlike Dickens) is not content to leave the full-blown sex scandal untold.

shrunk from by every woman who had to take care of her own reputation—and of Society" (505). The Society that condemns Maggie for
her apparent sexual indiscretion has a remarkably broad span, stretch-
ing from those nearest to her—her brother, who insists that "the worst
that could happen [was] not death, but disgrace" (483)—to figures so
anonymous and déclassé as to personify the very generality of the public: "the circumstances which in any case gave a disastrous character to
her elopement, had passed beyond the more polite circles of St. Ogg's,
and had become matter of common talk, accessible to the grooms and
errand-boys" (486).

If public opinion shapes expectations and judgments about sexuality
and gender throughout the novel, the reverse is true as well, for gender
inflects the public itself. However expansive, variegated, or amorphous
this public seems, when St. Ogg's Passes Judgment, Eliot is explicit about
its most apposite embodiment: "not the world, but the world's wife"
(490). No wonder Maggie has a harder time recovering her good name
than her father and brother do: since "public opinion, in these cases, is
always of the feminine gender" (490), sexual offenses—those that trans-
gress middle-class domestic and conjugal standards, and therefore take
place on a ground designated female—will appear more egregious than
masculine outrages, whose credit finds a tangible correlative in the bank.
Maggie's crime affirms the righteously respectable femininity—in particular, married femininity—ascribed to the audience for her scandal.[5]
The narrator can afford a punishing severity with respect to "the ladies of
St. Ogg's . . . [who] had their favourite abstraction, called Society, which
served to make their consciences perfectly easy in doing what satisfied
their own egoism—thinking and speaking the worst of Maggie Tulliver, and turning their backs upon her" (505).[6] Like the public conceived

5. Patricia Meyer Spacks suggests in *Gossip* (New York: Alfred A. Knopf, 1985) that slander
and gossip have long been considered primarily feminine weapons (38–42). The narrator confirms this sense, calling the period in which the story is set "a time when cheap
periodicals were not, and when country surgeons never thought of asking their female
patients if they were fond of reading, but simply took it for granted that they preferred
gossip" (119).

6. Like Eliot's narrator, John Stuart Mill in *The Subjection of Women* (1869) embodies the vulgar public in unintelligent married women and cites their tendency, through influence
over their husbands, to level public opinion: "The wife's influence tends, as far as it goes,
to prevent the husband from falling below the common standard of approbation of the
country. It tends quite as strongly to hinder him from rising above it. The wife is the

in the Boulton and Park case, the one for Maggie's scandal is imagined as female, but while reports of the buggery trial feminize the public in order to justify shielding it from dangerous information, Eliot has the general public speak in the voice of the world's wife so as to denigrate it.

Eliot carefully delineates the scandal audience within her story, and in addition to her extra-narrative disquisitions on the gender of the public, certain characters are made to emblematize its membership. Long before the narrator explicitly generalizes about the femininity of public opinion, the Dodson sisters epitomize that community. With two more members than the plot strictly requires, an obsession with reputation, and a penchant for gossip, the matrilineal Dodson clan personifies the world's wife (even to the extent that the sisters are known almost exclusively by their married names). This remains their role throughout Maggie's childhood, but just at the moment when Maggie loses her own concern for public opinion, the Dodsons, formerly its almost undifferentiated representatives, become distinctly individual. Mrs. Glegg, the sister previously associated most closely with a ruthless standard for reputation, surprisingly rallies to Maggie's defense. The narrative enables this transformation in Mrs. Glegg—from one among many gossiping voices to a clearly distinguished character—by theorizing a new feminine public *apart* from Maggie's extended family. Once the world's wife has been designated elsewhere, Aunt Glegg, by virtue of her "hereditary rectitude and personal strength of character" (499), comes within the realm of Maggie's private life—not least because she understands that her own family reputation has a stake in Maggie's fate. The embodiment of anonymous opinion subsequently shifts to female characters extraneous to the plot: "Mrs. Glegg only hoped that Mrs. Wooll, or any one else, would come to her with their false tales about her own niece, and she would know what to say to that ill-advised person!" (499).

In the novel's ongoing specification of the public, the Dodson sisters are replaced by another sorority, the thoroughly undifferentiated coterie of their social betters, "the Miss Guests, who associated chiefly on terms of condescension with the families of St. Ogg's, and were the glass of fashion there" (400). Stephen's sisters have little admiration for Maggie's unself-conscious manners, and it does not take long for this censorious female public to find reasons to criticize her—as much for

---

auxiliary of the common public opinion"; *On Liberty with The Subjection of Women and Chapters on Socialism*, ed. Stefan Collini (Cambridge: Cambridge University Press), 205.

her unwillingness to play by their rules as for any action she intentionally undertakes. At the bazaar, for example,

> the ladies who had commodities of their own to sell . . . saw at
> once the frivolity and bad taste of this masculine preference for
> [Maggie's] goods . . . and it is possible that the emphatic notice of
> various kinds which was drawn towards Miss Tulliver on this pub-
> lic occasion, threw a very strong and unmistakable light on her
> subsequent conduct in many minds then present. . . . There was
> something rather bold in Miss Tulliver's direct gaze, and something
> undefinably coarse in the style of her beauty . . . in the opinion of
> all feminine judges. (430–31)

Paralleling the transformation in the Dodsons' role from representative of public opinion to bulwark against it, Maggie also changes: from
her childish thralldom to others' estimation of her (evidenced, for instance, in her embarrassment before Mr. Rappit, even in her "desire to
conciliate gypsy opinion" [109]), she becomes woefully unmindful of
the diurnal maintenance required of a well-tended reputation. Her very
lack of attention to the public stock in her name is just what enables it
to fall so dramatically. As an adult, Maggie is almost alone among the
novel's characters in her disregard for the community's collective opinion, concerning herself instead with her moral duty to individuals. Even
when public opinion approves of her, she remains unconscious of it.
Fashion—so often the index of feminine opinion—could serve her, but
Maggie fails to make use of it. In imitation of her,

> several young ladies went home intending to have short sleeves
> with black lace, and to plait their hair in a broad coronet at the back
> of their head—"That cousin of Miss Deane's looked so very well."
> In fact, poor Maggie, with all her inward consciousness of a pain-
> ful past and her presentiment of a troublous future, was on the way
> to become an object of some envy—a topic of discussion in the
> newly-established billiard-room, and between fair friends who had
> no secrets from each other on the subject of trimmings. (399–400)

To be, like Maggie, oblivious of public opinion is to scorn it; and to scorn
public opinion is the surest way of becoming its victim. That Maggie is
the erotic object of masculine billiard-room talk should, were she more
attentive, alert her to the dangers of her public appearance. That she is
the "object of some envy" among women like the Misses Guest should

perhaps alarm her even more, for envy is the complement to (and thus never very far from) the schadenfreude that lends scandal its pleasure.

While from the narrator's point of view, the Dodson and Guest sororities seem overly concerned with public opinion, from their perspective, Maggie could stand to be somewhat more so. The text delineates the problematic of scandal, showing it to be bounded on one side by an excessive worrying over reputation and on the other by insufficient attention to it. This conflict reaches a pitch in Maggie's elopement with Stephen, when she disregards her reputation and expresses only her moral responsibility to family and friends: "Among her thoughts, what others would say and think of her conduct was hardly present. Love and deep pity and remorseful anguish left no room for that" (479). In his attempt to persuade Maggie to marry him, Stephen likewise makes claims for honor and duty; but when these fail, he speaks on behalf of "the world" and reveals the inevitability of scandal: " 'You *are* mine now—the world believes it—duty must spring out of that now' " (478). Stephen's argument surprises Maggie, to whom such an idea seems never to have occurred, and when she insists that her obligations to individuals take precedence over what "the world believes," he is shocked at her genuine naïveté: " 'Good God, Maggie!' said Stephen, rising too and grasping her arm, 'you rave. How can you go back without marrying me? You don't know what will be said, dearest. You see nothing as it really is' " (478). Maggie's intransigence about her personal integrity is entirely at odds with the movement of scandal, which claims for itself the ground of honor.[7]

In order to demonstrate the powerful effects of public opinion, and its distance from genuine morality, Eliot deliberately narrates a scandal based in a falsehood. Yet even if Maggie had committed the sexual crime of which she is accused, Eliot demonstrates that public reaction would still depend fundamentally on an imaginary account of the story. The popular presumption of Maggie's unchastity renders meaningless her actual virtue; she would have done better with "the ladies of St. Ogg's" had she followed through her elopement rather than repenting it. In the crazily acid voice that the narrator assumes in order to mimic these women, we hear an extended fantasy about what would have hap-

---

7. Alexander Welsh, in *George Eliot and Blackmail* (Cambridge, Mass.: Harvard University Press, 1985), 141–54, supplies an astute analysis of how Maggie can "[lose] her reputation without losing her virtue" (145).

pened "if Miss Tulliver, after a few months of well-chosen travel, had returned as Mrs. Stephen Guest" (490): namely, that justifications would have been produced and the newlyweds shortly welcomed back to St. Ogg's ("Society couldn't be carried on if we inquired into private conduct in that way—and Christianity tells us to think no evil" [491]). This fantasized future for the imaginary Guests[8] reflects as poorly on the hypocrisy of female public opinion as the events that transpire, for in both cases the scandalmongers appear more committed to gossip itself than to the moral code from which such judgments purport to derive.

The narrator rebukes the censorious public in gendered terms not because of some inherent quality of femininity, but because female gossips serve as scapegoats for a pious moralism to which the men themselves are too craven to own up:

> Until every good man is brave, we must expect to find many good women timid: too timid even to believe in the correctness of their own best promptings, when these would place them in a minority. And the men at St. Ogg's were not all brave by any means: some of them were even fond of scandal—and to an extent that might have given their conversation an effeminate character, if it had not been distinguished by masculine jokes, and by an occasional shrug of the shoulders at the mutual hatred of women. It was the general feeling of the masculine mind at St. Ogg's that women were not to be interfered with in their treatment of each other. (506)

In a classic illustration of scandal's regulatory capacity, Eliot's analysis shows that the men find it more effective to have the women chasten one of their own than to exercise that discipline themselves. That scandalmongering is felt to confer "an effeminate character" on its practitioners suggests how useful it is for rigidly dichotomized gender relations to keep the world's wife gossiping—and to restrain the world's wife's husband from doing so. The feminization of sex scandal derives from a fundamental misogyny, that "mutual hatred of women" shared by the men of St. Ogg's (a lesson in which Mr. Wakem supplies Philip

---

8. At least one contemporary reader was taken in, perhaps unconsciously, by this fantasy; if only in the common form of the proper name, "Maggie Guest" lurks in the imagination of the anonymous reviewer for the Spectator (April 7, 1860): "Few persons in the novel-dramas which make so much of our literature now-a-days are so distinctly embodied and vividly coloured as the Maggie Tulliver who has just been introduced as a new guest in so many thousand English homes"; reprinted in George Eliot: The Critical Heritage, ed. David Carroll (London: Routledge & Kegan Paul, 1971), 109.

by telling him, " 'We don't ask what a woman does—we ask whom she belongs to' " [426]). The wives' participation in scandal has the status in Eliot's account of false consciousness about gender. The feminine public pronounces patriarchal *idées reçues* much more effectively than the men could, and Eliot excoriates the women for the pleasure they take in this self-deception.

Eliot accounts this public, which frankly enjoys seeing Maggie ruined, as vulgar, both because it judges its victim on appearances and because it speaks on behalf of what it thinks others wish to hear. Precisely to the extent that she condemns this practice, moreover, Eliot depicts the savory pleasures to be had in humiliating one's neighbor. As much as the narrator evokes scandal's disciplinary function, that is to say, the novelist relishes showing us its titillations. The most earnest of Victorian novelists is thus the one to afford us the fullest account of scandal's flesh-tingling delights.

To take pleasure in another's ruination—to find a resource for community allegiance in the affirmation of values against a transgressor—these are the satisfactions of scandal. Rebuking the world's wife by portraying the enjoyment of scandal as vindictiveness or prurience, the narrator inculcates novel-readers in the rather more refined pleasures of *resisting* scandal. Placed in a position of superior knowledge (knowing the whole story) and of superior ethics (making fine discriminations), readers are shown how not to be scandalized, even in the face of apparent sexual misconduct.

As if to prevent the reader of the fictional scandal story from recapitulating the pleasure taken by the prurient audience depicted within the novel, Eliot carefully differentiates the reading public she imagines for her work from the invidious gossips within *The Mill on the Floss*. The distinction between these publics consists in their differing sensibility, intellect, and capacity for careful ethical discrimination. What makes an audience vulgar, in Eliot's analysis, is its failure to distinguish a particular case, such as Maggie's, from the scandal script that public obdurately presumes to follow. In the following much-discussed passage, Eliot theorizes the ability of an audience to generalize correctly on the basis of novelistic or scandalous particulars:

> The great problem of the shifting relation between passion and duty is clear to no man who is capable of apprehending it: the question . . . is one for which we have no master-key that will

fit all cases. The casuists have become a byword of reproach; but their perverted spirit of minute discrimination was the shadow of a truth to which eyes and hearts are too often fatally sealed—the truth, that moral judgments must remain false and hollow, unless they are checked and enlightened by a perpetual reference to the special circumstances that mark the individual lot.

All people of broad, strong sense have an instinctive repugnance to the man of maxims; because such people early discern that the mysterious complexity of our life is not to be embraced by maxims, and that to lace ourselves up in formulas of that sort is to repress all the divine promptings and inspirations that spring from growing insight and sympathy. And the man of maxims is the popular representative of the minds that are guided in their moral judgment solely by general rules, thinking that these will lead them to justice by a ready-made patent method, without the trouble of exerting patience, discrimination, impartiality—without any care to assure themselves whether they have the insight that comes from a hardly-earned estimate of temptation, or from a life vivid and intense enough to have created a wide fellow-feeling with all that is human. (497–98)

This passage distinguishes between two types of response to morally difficult material. On one side is the "man of maxims," who, with his blindingly indiscriminate "general rules," differs from feminine public opinion only to the extent that his precipitate judgment lacks in vulgar hypocrisy. As the "popular representative" of the reception that greets Maggie when she returns to St. Ogg's, the man of maxims colludes with the world's wife in failing to sympathize and to make "minute discriminations." This complicity is tightened, moreover, by his being "laced up" in formulas that sound distinctly like corsets.[9] On the other side, by

9. Passages like the following one might tempt us to associate generalization with masculinity, as opposed to the particularity of the feminine: "[Tom's] physiognomy in which it seems impossible to discern anything but the generic character of boyhood [was] as different as possible from poor Maggie's phiz, which Nature seemed to have moulded and coloured with the most decided intention" (33). But this sentence, which relies on conventional alignments (male/female: general/particular: public/private), is contradicted by a statement such as, "[Tom] was not a boy in the abstract, existing solely to illustrate the evils of a mistaken education, but a boy made of flesh and blood, with dispositions not entirely at the mercy of circumstances" (170). While the second quotation effectively disarms any easy parallelism between gender and generalization, the conflict between the two passages points up the problematic nature of exemplarity itself in Eliot's work.

contrast, are those people capable of attending to "the special circumstances that mark the individual lot," whom the narrator valorizes.

The conflict between what Eliot says about audience judgment in this passage and the means she uses to say it has often gone unnoticed. She contends that to generalize is an ethically dubious prospect, but, abstracting from the case at hand, she makes this assertion in thoroughly general terms. Even within the extra-narrative form this discussion takes, unthinking collective opinion at least finds a "representative" in a single individual, relatively rich in embodied particulars, while the capacity for fine discrimination is attributed to an undifferentiated class of humanity—"all people of broad, strong sense." [10] The appropriate audience *cannot* be described too specifically, for the terms in which it is evoked must be general enough to allow a reader to identify with it.

Even as Eliot disparages the moral effects of the impulse to generalize, in other words, in her fictional method she wields a broad brush of universalization. There is a pivotal conflict between, on the one hand, the ethical principles Eliot enunciates in metanarrative passages such as those I have been discussing, and, on the other, the rhetorical devices she employs in the narrative proper, such as generalization and aphorism, which I want now to consider. Generalizing discourse saturates *The Mill*

---

10. The two most influential recent accounts of this scene verge on the same contradiction that besets Eliot's own prose. In writing about this passage, Nancy Miller, in "Emphasis Added: Plots and Plausibilities in Women's Fiction," in *The New Feminist Criticism*, ed. Elaine Showalter (New York: Pantheon, 1985), 339–60, recasts Eliot's formulation about generality and particularity as a male/female binary; she then generalizes Maggie's particular story to apply to all female experience, which she proposes is the singularly valued term: "The attack on female plots and plausibilities . . . does not see, nor does it want to, that the fictions of desire behind the desiderata of fiction are masculine and not universal constructs. It does not see that the maxims that pass for the truth of human experience, and the encoding of that experience in literature, are organizations, when they are not fantasies, of the dominant culture" (357). While such maxims derive from patriarchy, Eliot is clear about the "public opinion" that condemns Maggie being "always of the feminine gender" (490). Eliot's view is neither so straightforwardly feminist nor so dichotomizing as to align the public/private opposition neatly with a male/female one. Mary Jacobus, in "The Question of Language: Men of Maxims and *The Mill on the Floss*," *Critical Inquiry* 8, no. 2 (Winter 1981): 207–22, seeks instances of *écriture féminine* in the novel, and equally falls into what, by her own reasoning, would have to be called a patriarchal strategy of generalization: she slides from proposing (with Eliot) that "An argument for the individual makes itself felt by an argument against generalities" to suggesting that Maggie's story "could be said to be all women's story" (212). This seemingly unconscious tendency among critics to generalize particularities amplifies the logical and pedagogic contradiction that *The Mill on the Floss* itself exemplifies.

on the Floss, as it does most of Eliot's novels, and supplies the means by which particular events of the plot are shown to have relevance for the world outside the story.[11] The narrative procedure for this generalization follows a consistent pattern: it begins with a description of behavior ("She rushed to him and clung round his neck, sobbing, 'O Tom, please forgive me—I can't bear it—I will always be good' "); from the incident, an ironic universal lesson is drawn ("We learn to restrain ourselves as we get older. We keep apart when we have quarrelled, express ourselves in well-bred phrases, and in this way preserve a dignified alienation. . . . We no longer approximate in our behaviour to the mere impulsiveness of the lower animals, but conduct ourselves in every respect like members of a highly civilized society"); finally, the case at hand is shown to illustrate the law we have just learned—which, however, derived in the first place from the example ("Maggie and Tom were still very much like young animals, and so she could rub her cheek against his, and kiss his ear in a random, sobbing way" [39]). Strictly speaking, such argument is neither deductive nor inductive—or rather, it is by turns deductive and inductive, and so tends to function tautologically: the example proves the rule that was gleaned from the example. By late in the story, the mock-syllogism is reduced to a basic three-sentence form: "Maggie was hardly conscious of having said or done anything decisive. All yielding is attended with a less vivid consciousness than resistance; it is the partial sleep of thought; it is the submergence of our own personality by another. Every influence tended to lull her into acquiescence" (467). The sequence that moves from "Maggie" to "all yielding" to "her acquiescence" makes a Möbius strip of narrative logic.

Despite Eliot's professed aversion to generalization, then, her work relies on narrative techniques that look suspiciously like those of a man of maxims. This method finds its most condensed and characteristic form

11. Susan Sniader Lanser, in *Fictions of Authority: Women Writers and Narrative Voice* (Ithaca: Cornell University Press, 1992), provides the fullest discussion of Eliot's generalizing strategies, showing how "Eliot's professed dislike of quotations, abstractions, and 'maxims' stands . . . in unresolved tension with the pervasive system of generalization in her work and especially with her practices of epigraphy" (100). Lanser demonstrates that Eliot's questioning of authority in the abstract serves ultimately to shore up her own narrative power, through narrative techniques such as epigraphy, which "mediates the tension in [Eliot's] work between a semantics of indeterminacy and a syntax of authority" (99). See also Gillian Beer, *George Eliot*, in Key Women Writers (Bloomington: Indiana University Press, 1986), 19–29.

in the aphorisms that punctuate virtually every page of Eliot's prose. "People who live at a distance are naturally less faulty than those immediately under our own eyes" (206), we are told at one point; "Poor relations are undeniably irritating—their existence is so entirely uncalled for on our part, and they are almost always very faulty people" (83), we learn at another. Such aphorisms do not simply contradict the indictment of the man of maxims, however, for they work in a double way that reveals the complexity of generalizing rhetoric. In one sense, they take an absolute form, thanks to their diction ("naturally," "undeniably," "always") and the voice of disembodied authority in which they are enunciated. These aphorisms court the reader's assent almost before they are recognized, lending broad, general meaning to the action at hand. At the same time, however, this assent is undermined by a narratorial irony that derides both the characters with whose consciousness the aphorisms are associated (Mrs. Glegg in the first instance just quoted, Mr. Tulliver in the second) and the reader who would take them at face value. At the expense of characters and undiscerning readers, the trope elevates the superior consciousness both of the narrator and of that special, intended reading audience, which understands that truths asserted by generalization and aphorism must always be tempered with a dose of irony.[12]

In condensing common sense, aphorism serves as a novelistic surrogate for public opinion; but the arch narrative tone behind it distances readers from the force of generalization and thereby transvalues public opinion by insisting it attend to particular circumstances. The mutually reinforcing oscillation between generality and particularity allows Eliot to establish a basis for readerly empathy and to enunciate the features of the reading audience she aims to construct for her work. This audience is meant to draw generalizable lessons from Maggie's story, but to do so

---

12. Rosemarie Bodenheimer, *The Real Life of Mary Ann Evans: George Eliot, Her Letters and Fiction* (Ithaca: Cornell University Press, 1994), supplies a useful discussion of Eliot's double construction of her readership.

> The appeals to readers and the sudden shifts of perspective that are so central to the effect of George Eliot's prose originate in this always double activity, in which the writer both immerses herself in writing and assumes the position of a suddenly critical reading audience. . . . The reading audience is not so much addressed as called to witness a confrontation between the writer and an audience located in some fearful and scornful part of her consciousness. To be an actual reader, then, is to be audience to George Eliot's imaginary audiences; that is what her writing asks, and what it performs. (46, 51–52)

by way of forswearing, not participating in, prurience.[13] Eliot instructs her readers in how not to be scandalized by a tale of ostensible sexual indiscretion by making it impossible for us to respond to Maggie's story with the same measure of schadenfreude as the discredited world's wife. Yet just as scandal renders sex unspeakable through its insistence on the fascination of what it refuses to tell, so Eliot's novelistic antidote to it— an anti-philistine, nearly imperious appeal to ethics and the intellect— equally suggests that sexual content might as well go without saying. As loudly as the prurience it condemns, this superior, compassionate re-nunciation of scandal announces the imperative for evading sexuality.

One of the powerful attributes of generalizing rhetoric is that, like public opinion, it brooks no refusal—as much in the mouths of the gossips and puritans as in Eliot's aphoristic writing. Both as an avenue for the moralizing compulsions by which scandal profits and as a fea-ture of the ethical inculcation that the high-culture novel takes as its mission, generalization represents a component in the technology of sexual unspeakability. Scenes of erotic arousal in Eliot's prose, I want to show, shift as rapidly into the realm of universal experience as, in the hands of scandalmongers, they are assumed to violate a rigid code of propriety. The swiftness with which these narrative gestures are per-formed preempts any demurral, so that they, as much as Dickens's thick silences, leave no room for discussion. Writ large now instead of mar-ginally, sexuality comes to seem nearly as displaced in *The Mill on the Floss* as it is in *Great Expectations*. The disjunction between the articulated plot of Dickens's novel and its narrative voice, which I argued provides an opening into which sexual meanings can be insinuated as unspeakable subjects, reappears in different form in Eliot's work, now as a productive contradiction between the narrow-mindedness of the world's wife, con-demned in the plot, and the valorized, if ironized, generalizing method of the narrator. Like that other contradiction, this one is both generative

13. In an essay on authorship, "Leaves from a Note-book," *Essays of George Eliot*, ed. Thomas Pinney (London: Routledge & Kegan Paul, 1963), Eliot writes of the novel as a pedagogic vehicle:

> Man or woman who publishes writings inevitably assumes that office of teacher or influencer of the public mind. Let him protest as he will that he only seeks to amuse, and has no pretension to do more than while away an hour of leisure or weariness—"the idle singer of an empty day"—he can no more escape influencing the moral taste, and with it the action of the intelligence, than a setter of fashions in furniture and dress can fill the shops with his designs and leave the garniture of persons and houses unaffected by his industry. (440)

of, and evasive about, sexual meanings, on one side condemning them as vulgar, on the other abstracting them to such an extent that they are not open to disputation.

To discern this process, let us again follow the erotic trajectory of an arm:

> "Do take my arm," [Stephen] said, in a low tone, as if it were a secret.
>
> There is something strangely winning to most women in that offer of the firm arm: the help is not wanted physically at that moment, but the sense of help—the presence of strength that is outside them and yet theirs—meets a continual want of the imagination. Either on that ground or some other, Maggie took the arm. (408)

The narrator discovers a "continual want of the imagination" in "most women"—a lack that can be satiated only by an intersubjective "presence of strength," which plausibly constitutes sexual desire. Yet just when it has generalized about such desire and prepares to move back to the case at hand, the narrative falters, temporarily backing away from its usual omniscience: it tergiversates over whether it was "on that ground or some other" that "Maggie took the arm." Lest one imagine that this faltering disrupts the narrator's absolute knowledge, however, it need only be indicated that in making the description of the action itself unsteady—the very "ground" is unsure—the narrative figure redoubles Maggie's own hesitancy. In equivocating about its comprehension, the narrative mimetically reproduces the protagonist's momentary lack of self-possession, thereby paradoxically shoring up its full command of the scene. While such uncertainty about Maggie's motives makes a pointed contrast with the malicious assumptions of public opinion, the narrator's authority is secured all the more firmly for having relaxed its omniscience.

While this passage generalizes, on the basis of Stephen's appendage, about the satisfactions of a generic "firm arm" for "most women," it does not depend for its effect upon an embodied fantasy of its reader. In what is no doubt the sexiest passage in the book, however, when an arm is once again eroticized, desire is as fully predicated of the character as of an imagined audience:

> Stephen was mute; he was incapable of putting a sentence together, and Maggie bent her arm a little upward towards the large half-opened rose that had attracted her. Who has not felt the beauty

of a woman's arm?—the unspeakable suggestions of tenderness
that lie in the dimpled elbow, and all the varied gently-lessening
curves down to the delicate wrist, with its tiniest, almost imper-
ceptible nicks in the firm softness. A woman's arm touched the soul
of a great sculptor two thousand years ago, so that he wrought an
image of it for the Parthenon which moves us still as it clasps lov-
ingly the time-worn marble of a headless trunk. Maggie's was such
an arm as that—and it had the warm tints of life.

A mad impulse seized on Stephen; he darted towards the arm,
and showered kisses on it, clasping the wrist. (441–42)

The narrative is licensed to indulge such a lavish and titillating appraisal
of the female limb thanks to a question—"Who has not felt the beauty
of a woman's arm?"—that can, within the bounds of normative heterosexuality, remain purely rhetorical only so long as the reader's desire is
imagined to be that of a man. Modulating through the usual sequence,
these lines show Stephen's desire to be the desire of all men—of all pro-
jected readers—which in turn proves that his particular "mad impulse"
is not perhaps as mad as Maggie might think.[14]

The indications in this passage, about how the novel conceives of its
audience when it generalizes about sexuality, raise the question of who
Eliot posits as her readership elsewhere in the work. One sure way for
the author to effect a distinction between her highbrow readers and the
audience for scandal within the story is to construe her public, unlike
Maggie's, as male. Critics have often taken passages such as the following one for proof of the narrator's masculinity, but we might do better
to consider it instead as a fantasy of the reader's gender:[15]

Every one of those keen moments has left its trace, and lives in us
still, but such traces have blent themselves irrecoverably with the
firmer texture of our youth and manhood. . . . Is there any one
who can recover the experience of his childhood, not merely with

14. For a very different discussion of Eliot's variable capacity to narrate sexuality, see
Barbara Hardy, "Implication and Incompleteness in *Middlemarch*," in *Particularities: Readings
in George Eliot* (Athens, Ohio: Ohio University Press, 1982), 15–36.
15. Penny Boumelha, for instance, makes a case for the maleness of Eliot's narrators in
"George Eliot and the End of Realism," in *Women Reading Women's Writing*, ed. Sue Roe
(Brighton: Harvester, 1987), 13–35. For an account of the alignments among female char-
acter, narrator, and author in the novel, see Michael Ragussis, *Acts of Naming: The Family
Plot in Fiction* (New York: Oxford University Press, 1986), 130–34.

a memory of what he did and what happened to him, of what he liked and disliked when he was in frock and trousers, but with an intimate penetration, a revived consciousness of what he felt . . . when his schoolfellows shut him out of their game because he would pitch the ball wrong out of mere wilfulness . . . or when his mother absolutely refused to let him have a tailed coat that "half," although every other boy of his age had gone into tails already? (66)

Through its use of the first-person plural and the generic "any one" (antecedent of "he"), this passage aims at an identification more with readers than with an embodied narrator. As the novel's opening pages demonstrate, Eliot is perfectly capable of assuming a narratorial "I," and in that case the narrator's gender is indefinite. But the "experience" cited in generalizing passages such as this one is decisively male, despite the narrative's close identification elsewhere with Maggie's powerful consciousness. With all the criticism that the ostensibly female scandal audience comes in for during the novel's last third, Eliot clearly benefits from distinguishing her audience by designating it male. Even so, invocations of the novel's readers cease in book 6, for this is the point at which the scandal blows open and in which the narrator undertakes the dissection of feminized public opinion; to conjure up the novel's own audience at this stage would perhaps draw it uncomfortably near the vulgar public under attack.

To propose even a notionally male fiction-reading audience may seem insupportable, since from its inception the English novel has been thought of as a female genre, both in its producers and consumers and in its cultural milieux.[16] The audience that Eliot posits must be understood not as genuinely male, but rather as male in the same rhetorical and ideological ways that the scandal audience is female. Regardless of the actual gender of its membership, the public that consumes scandal is, when imagined as endangered, embodied in an innocent schoolgirl, and, when condemned for its prurience, in the world's wife. When the novel seeks to exalt its audience as consumers of high art and adjudi-

16. Kate Flint, *The Woman Reader, 1837–1914* (Oxford: Clarendon Press, 1993), provides a rich account of how Victorian women were imagined and instructed to consume fiction. "There was," Flint notes, "a popular perception that women, particularly young women, formed the most likely readership for novels" (49). While novels in general were not aimed exclusively at a female readership, the idea of the novel-reader as a young woman—especially when the work in question was at all morally questionable—is the cultural stereotype against which Eliot positions her work.

cators of high moral sense, it correspondingly construes a masculine reading public. The novel's audience is male to the same extent, then, and in the same way as its author: performatively and pseudonymously. Decked out in transparent coattails, George Eliot dresses up "his" readers in equally diaphanous—but nonetheless necessary—male drag. The first of Eliot's novels to be widely recognized as the work of a woman, *The Mill on the Floss* preserves the open secret of narrative cross-dressing by displacing it onto the putative readership.[17] As in her acerbic essay "Silly Novels by Lady Novelists," Eliot assumes the voice of a man speaking to men in order to make persuasive a critique of a suspiciously feminine institution.[18]

The imaginary nature of this gendering must be emphasized, for while the difference between the audience for scandal and the one for the novel is exemplified by gender, it cannot precisely be attributed to it. Actual men who enjoy scandal take refuge behind a female public; actual women who engage the moral issues raised by Eliot's fiction comport themselves as male readers. Keeping in mind the active construction of the readership performed by the narrative, let us now return to, and take seriously, the question posed at the moment of high erotic drama, "Who has not felt the beauty of a woman's arm?" Putting aside the pro-

17. An unsigned notice in the *Saturday Review* of April 14, 1860 (rpt. *Critical Heritage*, ed. Carroll), begins:

> A year ago, most readers who had just finished *Adam Bede* would have been greatly surprised to hear two things which we now know to be true. It would have been very strange news that *Adam Bede* was written by a woman, and it would have been equally surprising to learn that within a twelvemonth the authoress would produce another tale quite worthy to rank beside its predecessor. Now that we are wise after the event, we can detect many subtle signs of female authorship in *Adam Bede*; but at the time it was generally accepted as the work of a man. To speak the simple truth, without affectation of politeness, it was thought to be too good for a woman's story. It turns out that a woman was not only able to write it, but that she did not write it by any lucky accident. The *Mill on the Floss* may not, perhaps, be so popular as *Adam Bede*, but it shows no falling off nor any exhaustion of power. . . . No one can now doubt that the lady who, with the usual pretty affectation of her sex, likes to look on paper as much like a man as possible, and so calls herself George Eliot, has established her place in the first rank of our female novelists. (114–15)

18. The masculinity of the essay's critical voice virtually goes without saying; that its imagined (if not necessarily intended) audience is also male is suggested by the passage in which Eliot speaks for—and against—the men who would generalize from silly lady novelists to deny all women an education. See "Silly Novels by Lady Novelists," *Selected Essays, Poems and Other Writings*, ed. A. S. Byatt and Nicholas Warren (London: Penguin, 1990), 155.

priety requisite to keeping the question rhetorical, we can identify the sexual reverberations that Eliot's domineering narrative voice works so sedulously to diminish. Left out by the apparent capaciousness of such a formulation are all readers who do not number women's limbs among their erotic objects. Included in the question's address, however, is not only the heterosexual male reader but the lesbian as well—even if she must route her cathexis through the heteromasculine desire of Stephen, the narrator, and the Parthenon sculptor. By holding erotic significa-tion in check, such generalization suggests all the more powerfully the counternormative potential entailed by a woman, disguised as a man, portraying and provoking the sexual desire of a reading audience com-posed, at least in part, of women disguised as men. The access to and authority over heterosexuality, which this shared transvestism grants the author and a lesbian readership, is achieved under the guise of male homosociality: the female writer, impersonating a masculine author, solicits the concurrence of her imaginary male readership over generic masculine desire for the female character. In its vertiginous suggestions for both female and male "homosexual" relations between narrator and reader, this process indicates how effective a closet—and yet how sexu-ally charged what it closets—the pseudonymity of George Eliot is.

In combination with her ambition to foster a serious, discerning audi-ence for the novel, the scandalous circumstances of George Eliot's adult life necessitated this complex layering of disguises. Like many forms of constraint, however, the requisite secrecy of Eliot's authorship proved an enabling condition for her writing. The scandal of Eliot's adulter-ous relationship with George Henry Lewes, and the inextricability of it from the secret of her authorship, resonate with the themes of illicit sexuality, alienation from community, and the invidiousness of public opinion in *The Mill on the Floss*. Writing successful novels under a nom de plume provided Eliot a means of both justifying and protecting herself, and her attacks on female gossips, along with her cultivation of sensi-tive novel readers, work to preempt the scandal of having her own illicit marital status exposed.[19]

By masculinizing both herself and her reading audience, Eliot lends

19. See Welsh, *George Eliot*, chap. 6: "But now Marian's success changed the aspect of their other secret, which they had refused to treat as such. A scandal that could be withstood in strictly private life was directly injurious to the publicity which George Eliot's suc-cess required. . . . The affairs of unorthodox marriage and pseudonymous writing had become permanently linked" (126).

legitimacy to the novelistic enterprise (no silly novel by a lady novelist this). But once the author's identity had been discovered to the public, the generalizing cast that she gave to sexual transgression could no longer exonerate the passages of vivid eroticism. One of the protections masculine pseudonymity had afforded Eliot up to the publication of *The Mill on the Floss* was impunity from the standards of propriety applied to female writers. Narrating from a perspective sympathetic to Stephen's sexual motives proved dangerous for Eliot, as the following notice in the *Saturday Review*, keenly attuned to the vibrant seductiveness of Maggie's arm, suggests:

> There is a kind of love-making which seems to possess a strange fascination for the modern female novelist. . . . They all like to describe these sensations as they conceive them to exist in men. We are bound to say that their conceptions are true and adequate. But we are not sure that it is quite consistent with feminine delicacy to lay so much stress on the bodily feelings of the other sex. . . . We cannot think that the conflict of sensation and principle raised in a man's mind by gazing at a woman's arm is a theme that a female novelist can touch on without leaving behind a feeling of hesitation, if not repulsion, in the reader. In points like these, it may be observed that men are more delicate than women. There are very few men who would not shrink from putting into words what they might imagine to be the physical effects of love in a woman. Perhaps we may go further, and say that the whole delineation of passionate love, as painted by modern female novelists, is open to very serious criticism. There are emotions over which we ought to throw a veil; and no one can say that, in order to portray an ardent and tender love, it is necessary to describe the conquest of a beautiful arm over honour and principle. As it seems to us, the defect of the *Mill on the Floss* is that there is too much that is painful in it.[20]

Once exposed, the "female novelist" cannot justify her "strange fascination" with "love-making," for it conflicts with her "feminine delicacy." The argument consequently suggests that a male novelist should be able to narrate such "sensations," at least so far as they pertain to

---

20. *Critical Heritage*, ed. Carroll, 118–19. Merle Mowbray Bevington lists no attribution for the review in the appendix of known authors to *The Saturday Review, 1855–1868: Representative Educated Opinion in Victorian England* (New York: Columbia University Press, 1941).

men. But male novelists, the reviewer goes on to assert, "are more delicate than women," and they therefore "shrink from putting into words"
such sexual feelings. This critic—whose own gender is shielded by the
conventions of anonymous reviewing—sees the primary problem as
cross-gender narration itself: women who describe male sexuality are
too bold, while men who portray female passion are indelicate. This
impasse of narrative transvestism goes to prove what George Eliot had
already recognized as the only viable solution: to raise transvestism to a
higher level and institute it authorially.

Cross-gender pseudonymity, which served as Eliot's defense against
a scandalmongering public and a puritanical press, produced in some
of her audience precisely the sort of lesbian identification that narrative
generalization about the beauty of the female arm might have predicted.
Reading Eliot's fiction with a consciousness about the conditions of her
pseudonymity, women who felt alienated from institutions of heterosexuality—for reasons however different than Eliot's—sought out her
counsel and came to regard her as an erotic object. Edith Simcox, Eliot's
friend and admirer, wrote frankly of this desire in her autobiography:

> I kissed her again and again and murmured broken words of love.
> She bade me not exaggerate. I said I didn't—nor could, and then
> scolded her for not being satisfied with letting me love her as I
> did—as in present reality—and proposing instead that I should
> save my love for some imaginary he. She said—expressly what she
> has often before implied to my distress—that the love of men and
> women for each other must always be more and better than any
> other and bade me not wish to be wiser than "God who made
> me"—in pious phrase. I hung over her caressingly and she bade
> me not think too much of her—she knew all her own frailty and
> if I went on, she would have to confess some of it to me. Then she
> said—perhaps it would shock me—she had never all her life cared
> very much for women—it must seem monstrous to me.—I said I
> had always known it. She went on to say, what I also knew, that
> she cared for the womanly ideal, sympathised with women and
> liked for them to come to her in their troubles, but while feeling
> near to them in one way, she felt far off in another—the friendship
> and intimacy of men was more to her. Then she tried to add what
> I had already imagined in explanation that when she was young,
> girls and women seemed to look on her as somehow "uncanny"

while men were always kind. I kissed her again, and said I did not mind—if she did not mind having holes kissed in her cheek.—She said I gave her a very beautiful affection—and then again she called me a silly child, and I asked if she would never say anything kind to me. I asked her to kiss me—let a trembling lover tell of the intense consciousness of the first deliberate touch of the dear one's lips. I returned the kiss to the lips that gave it and started to go.[21]

Despite her condescending response to Simcox's affection, her advice to Simcox to pursue heterosexuality, and her careless profession of an aversion to female company, Eliot, though unwittingly, attained the status for her devotees of an idol. These idolaters had come to know Eliot from her fiction, and when they sought her out in person generally had to visit her secluded in ignominy. Eliot's unlawful relationship enforced the ongoing transvestism of her writing persona, and in combination with the imagined cross-dressing of her audience, the scandal enabled protolesbian readers to identify their own exclusion from marital orthodoxy with her more public violation of that order. Eliot's "pious" advice to Simcox to "save [her] love for some imaginary he" suggests a lapse in just the sort of sympathetic understanding that she advocates in The Mill on the Floss: she seems, when she has become the object of female affection, unable to make sense of the other ways, besides her own particular circumstances, in which a woman could feel excluded from normative heterosexuality.

If Eliot was restrained in her personal relations with women, her writing, at least in The Mill on the Floss, nevertheless proliferates alternatives to the usual romance plot. In part, the shamelessly tragic, unconventionally unromantic ending—so rare among the work's contemporaries—simply refuses the coupling logic of heterosexuality. The cost of this refusal, of course, is annihilation, and if Maggie declines sexual object choices in the form of fornication (Stephen) and incest (Tom)—as well as deformity (Philip)—she also repudiates the standard novelistic

---

21. Quoted in K. A. McKenzie, Edith Simcox and George Eliot (London: Oxford University Press, 1961), 97. Gordon S. Haight's account in George Eliot: A Biography (New York: Oxford University Press, 1968), though homophobic, provides evidence for the intense attractiveness of Eliot to numerous women who were her readers (451–54, 492–97). Elma Stuart, for instance, sent various gifts to attest her devotion to Eliot, and, Haight notes unaccountably, "was constantly advising [Eliot] about undergarments, which Edith Simcox got made for her" (459). For a reading of desire between female characters in Middlemarch, see Kathryn Bond Stockton, God Between Their Lips: Desire Between Women in Irigaray, Brontë, and Eliot (Stanford: Stanford University Press, 1994), chap. 7.

resolution of marriage. Yet as the gender convolutions in its narrative stance suggest, the novel's anticonventionalism is not simply negative. In one other, rather dramatic way, the novel poses an alternative to heterosexual romance, through the inscription that opens and closes it: "In their death they were not divided." By virtue of its status as both epigraph and epitaph, this line purports to express the truth of the story at so general a level that it can serve as the work's grand, overarching aphorism. While readers may recall that the line originates in the biblical story of David and Jonathan in the book of Samuel, few have paused to consider its radical inapplicability to the case at hand. One might, on the analogy of the same-sex relations I have intimated, imagine it is in the death of the two heroic figures that love is apotheosized—especially since, with that love between them "passing the love of women," David and Jonathan constitute a central locus in the nineteenth century for what Wilde was to call the "great affection of an elder for a younger man." In fact, however, the quotation is David's lament over the death in battle together of his beloved Jonathan and Jonathan's father, Saul, the latter whose efforts at exterminating David proved unsuccessful only by dint of divine intervention. Rather than construing the relation between Maggie and Tom as one of male lovers on the Israelite model, then, Eliot alludes implicitly to their shared conflict with their father.

Eliot emphasizes (placing it even on the title page) a line that invokes, perhaps misleadingly, a homoerotic union, and, more accurately if more distantly, a military masculine rivalry. The intermale or intergenerational conjunction amplifies the fraternal-sororal bond, the link between Maggie and Tom that readers have often felt to be inexorable and incestuous. Whether taken as homosexual or paternal, the epigraph allows the siblings' relationship to continue acting as a break upon the engine of heterosexual romance. But by translating the terms of this relationship onto an all-male terrain, the biblical line also elides the distinctively female character of Maggie's misfortunes. Like the ground opened by George Eliot for "his" "male" readers, the gesture condensed in the epigraph should not surprise us with its suggestion that a principal strategy by which Victorian women writers can make themselves be taken seriously is to assume male disguise. What is surprising, however, is that invocation of a male homosexual alliance should enable rather than diminish this discourse; and that the gynephobic hostility—in the form of attacks on the world's wife, or an erasure of any specifically female plight in the allusion of the epigraph—which so often accompanies male homosociality (and, phantasmatically, male homosexuality) should so powerfully undergird this relation even when it is impersonated by a woman.

Like *Great Expectations*, then, Eliot's novel accommodates a range of alternatives to the marriage plot. From the cross-gender incestuous energy the story harnesses, to the male homosexual relations it insinuates, to the lesbian reader-response it provokes, to the adulterous relationship that can be said to have motivated its account of scandal, *The Mill on the Floss* comes to seem as fully perverse a work as one could desire. The novel's presentation of itself as an acculturating remedy for the hideous exactions of vulgar, generalizing public opinion enables this perversity, even while it insists that such possibilities be banished to locations beyond the articulated representation: for the heterosexual order, against which such perversity asserts itself, finds its promise fulfilled in the tragedy that terminates the story and in the epilogue, anticipating reproductive renewal, that closes it. The scandalous situation of the adulterous, pseudonymous female author enables the novel's imperious narrative voice. This voice is so commanding that it can aver the ethics of relegating sexuality to the status of unspeakability at the same moment that it cultivates places of refuge for the sexual alienation in which it shares.

FIVE

TROLLOPE'S TROLLOP

"When a woman thinks that her house is on fire, her instinct is at once to rush to the thing which she values most. It is a perfectly overpowering impulse, and I have more than once taken advantage of it. . . . A married woman grabs at her baby—an unmarried one reaches for her jewel box."—Sherlock Holmes, in "A Scandal in Bohemia"[1]

On that day she wore at her waist . . . a small reticule of a shape which had just come into fashion; and, as she lay on the sofa and talked, she kept playing with it—opening it, putting a finger into it, shutting it again, and so on.—Sigmund Freud, Dora[2]

Though it hardly seems to warrant the scrupulous attention of detectives as eminent as Holmes and Freud, the symbolic substitution of female genitals with receptacles for valuables nonetheless requires constant proof. Of course Dora's fingering her reticule signifies her desire to masturbate; and yet, of course, this interpretation can in no way be substantiated.[3] The concatenation of the glaringly obvious with the strictly

1. Arthur Conan Doyle, "A Scandal in Bohemia" (1891), in *The Complete Adventures and Memoirs of Sherlock Holmes* (New York: Bramhall House, 1975), 12.
2. Sigmund Freud, *Dora: An Analysis of a Case of Hysteria* (1905), ed. Philip Rieff (New York: Collier, 1963), 94; further references will be made parenthetically to this edition.
3. Freud clearly recognizes that the heavy-handedness of an interpretation has little bearing on its persuasiveness:

unverifiable, as earlier chapters have argued, points at once in two directions: toward the sexual and toward the literary. First, not simply as the
record of sexual censorship but as an active agent of it, this combination
signals the particular linguistic status of sexuality in the late nineteenth
century. Perhaps because of his critical attitude toward its repression,
Freud could describe the situation of sexual signification so astutely:
"He that has eyes to see and ears to hear may convince himself that no
mortal can keep a secret. If his lips are silent, he chatters with his finger-
tips; betrayal oozes out of him at every pore" (96). As if reflexively to
corroborate the point, at the very moment he seeks to prove the unprovable meaning of the reticule, Freud's unctuous and purulent diction di-
vulges—embarrassingly, but for that, no more verifiably—its own erotic
investment in extricating others' secrets. Second, long before the theorization of an unconscious whose continual censorship serves continually
to betray it, nineteenth-century literary texts had been the repository
for the obvious-and-yet-unprovable symbol. The Victorian imagination
of the literary, that is to say, is thoroughly vested in this particular brand
of ambiguity, a version of what I have been calling the unspeakable.

Sexual unspeakability generates linguistic cruxes that lavishly draw
attention to themselves, though they never repay that attention with self-
disclosure. A vivid instance of the specifically linguistic compensations
sponsored by sexual subjects arises in the principal entry under which a
nineteenth-century slang dictionary lists the terms for female genitals:
monosyllable (or, alternately, "the divine monosyllable").[4] In elevating this

---

Dora found no difficulty in producing a motive: "Why should I not wear a reticule
like this, as it is now the fashion to do?" But a justification of this kind does not dis-
miss the possibility of the action in question having an unconscious origin. Though
on the other hand the existence of such an origin and the meaning attributed to the
act cannot be conclusively established. We must content ourselves with recording
the fact that such a meaning fits in quite extraordinarily well with the situation as
a whole and with the order of the day as laid down by the unconscious. (95)

4. John S. Farmer, *A Dictionary of Slang*, 7 vols. in 2 (1890; rpt. Ware, Hertfordshire: Wordsworth, 1987), 4:336–45. One of Farmer's citations under the lemma *monosyllable*, an 1823
dictionary, itself suggests an abyssal regression into linguistic self-reference as the sign
of sexual unspeakability: after making it clear that the reference is to *pudenda muliebris*, the
earlier lexicon indicates, "Of all the thousand monosyllables in our language, this *one*
only is designated by the definite article—THE MONOSYLLABLE; therefore do some men
call it 'the article,' 'my article,' and 'her article,' as the case may be." Now no longer even
a linguistic description of the slang term, the article itself—"the monosyllable," or perhaps simply "the"—functions as the periphrastic substantive. Another dictionary citation
(from 1811) states more economically: "MONOSYLLABLE. A woman's commodity" (4:345).

particular term to the lexicon's main heading for twelve hundred slang synonyms, the compiler pays a strange kind of tribute to the censorship that necessitated production of such a dictionary in the first place. Frankly euphemistic in its identification of the subject, the dictionary anticipates Freud's self-canceling insistence that he does not hesitate to "call bodily organs and processes by their technical names. . . . *J'appelle un chat un chat*" (65). In both cases, the expletive is occluded in the process of being explicated. The very effort to give a name to the subject constitutes it as unspeakable, for it draws attention to the materiality of the term under erasure, in the one case by referring to the apparently irrelevant quantity of its syllables, in the other by translating its "technical name" into a foreign tongue. Such a paradoxical linguistic occasion, when writ large in the novel, contributes to the production of the literary itself.

Anthony Trollope's novel *The Eustace Diamonds* (1871–72) supplies an especially remunerative instance of such signification, not only because it encodes sexuality in relatively overt ways, but because its central figure —the eponymous jewels—reveals a great deal about the representation of sexuality in *addition* to the imperative to keep it silent. The jewels, that is to say, are so suggestive that, even as they stand in for sexual meanings, they make use of the opportunities availed by unspeakability and lend their own status as objects of monetary value back to sexuality. The gems, which form the centerpiece in a series of overlapping scandals, at once metaphorize sexuality and literalize the economics of sexual difference.

In using the diamonds to render explicit the putative differences between male and female property, the novel relies on a distinction between two conflicting accounts of their legal status: one, which takes them to have a price determined in the marketplace, and the other, which values them according to absolute, immutable standards. The clash between these two paradigms pertains not only to the struggle, depicted in the novel's plot, of a widow to retain her property, however; it pervades the story as a whole through a conjoined conflict of values in regard to the very source of the narrative's authority. For the novel is everywhere concerned to account for the basis of its own entitlement to tell a scandal story, and this account is itself split between, on the one hand, an authority derived from an imaginary market in public opinion and, on the other, an appeal on the part of the narrator to precisely the sort of external authority that would seem to oppose the capricious sentiments of a public audience. The scandalous public contest over possession of the jewels thus analogizes—and has serious consequences for—Trollope's imagination of his own license to produce works of literary art. The symbolic artifact that announces even as it effaces its sexualization—the diamonds—provides the novel extraordinary opportunities to reflect on the nineteenth-century project of generating texts whose demurrals and evasions appear most literary precisely when they are most sexual.

Even if one did not entirely concur with the character in *The Eustace Diamonds* who calls the novel's protagonist, Lizzie Eustace, "false, dishonest, heartless, cruel, irreligious, ungrateful, mean, ignorant, greedy, and vile,"[5] one would probably still be suspicious of her. A general odor of iniquity envelops Lizzie, and for most of the novel this malevolence expresses itself in her refusal to cede the family jewels to her late husband's estate. Lizzie insists that the £10,000 worth of diamonds are her own, and just when the scandal of her possessing them seems in danger of flagging, the stakes in the property contest are raised: first, by the theft from Lizzie's hotel room in Carlisle of the iron box in which her jewels are supposed to be encased (and her actual, secret retention of them), and, second, by the subsequent theft of the diamonds themselves from her lodgings in London. The novel focuses so pointedly both on this object of vast monetary and symbolic value and on its container that our first order of business, as Trollope might say, is to dispense with the diamonds and their box.

Like the women whom Freud and Holmes describe, Lizzie Eustace pays her jewel box an extravagant amount of attention. To safeguard the gems her husband presented to her, she orders an iron box on her own initiative; in its synecdochal relation to its precious contents, the box itself becomes a thing of value and accrues a potent sexual charge. Following Freud, we can indicate the (utterly conventional) genital attributes of the high-profile jewel box, here displaced downward:

> They were like a load upon her chest, a load as heavy as though she were compelled to sit with the iron box on her lap day and night. In her sobbing she felt the thing under her feet, and knew that she could not get rid of it. She hated the box, and yet she must cling to it now. She was thoroughly ashamed of the box, and yet she must seem to take a pride in it. She was horribly afraid of the box, and yet she must keep it in her own very bed-room. (1:187–88)[6]

5. The appraisal is Lady Linlithgow's. Anthony Trollope, *The Eustace Diamonds*, 2 vols. in 1 (Oxford: Oxford University Press, 1973), 1:311; further references will be made parenthetically to this edition.

6. The overdetermination of the shameful, fearful, bedchamber box for Lizzie's puden-

According to an elementary substitutive logic, the box is suggestive of female genitals. Its function as a repository for patrilineal property, moreover, augments its appropriateness as a figure for female sexuality, whose traditional purpose is to transfer property between men of different generations. The contents of the box, the family jewels, in turn designate the supposedly scarce resource of reproductive male sexuality, materialized in the seat of spermatic production: the testes. Insinuating the testicular referent between two of its principal symbolic containers, one of Lizzie's suitors, Lord George de Bruce Carruthers, establishes the metaphoric utility of speaking of jewels as nuts: "'You had got the kernel yourself, and thought that I had taken all the trouble to crack the nut and had found myself with nothing but the shell. Then, when you found you couldn't eat the kernel; that you couldn't get rid of the swag without assistance, you came to me to help you'" (2:326). If the jewels signify the male contribution to procreation, they also represent the uneasy dependence of patriarchy upon a female vessel to pass along wealth.

To a first glance, which aligns inanimate objects with human reproductive organs, jewels metaphorize the male genitals just as the box does the female. But such symbolic suggestions can sustain a literary interest only so long as they resist becoming ossified. Staying for the moment in the symbolic register, we note that Trollope's representation of female sexuality extends beyond the box itself: through its proximity to Lizzie's body, the protective contrivance suggests the metonymic relation of the

---

dum is the primary dirty joke in the novel, but by no means the only one. Drawing on the conventional misogyny that associates female sexuality with rancid fish, the narrative introduces an invidious non sequitur:

> When rumours reached [Mr. Emilius] prejudicial to Lizzie in respect of the diamonds, he perceived that such prejudice might work weal for him. A gentleman once, on ordering a mackerel for dinner, was told that a fresh mackerel would come to a shilling. He could have a stale mackerel for sixpence. "Then bring me a stale mackerel," said the gentleman. Mr. Emilius coveted fish, but was aware that his position did not justify him in expecting the best fish on the market. (2:239–40)

Trollope employs an identical narrative strategy, though without the same putrescent overtones, in describing the doubts of another suitor:

> There was very much in the whole affair of which he would not be proud as he led his bride to the altar; — but a man does not expect to get four thousand pounds a year for nothing. Lord George, at any rate, did not conceive himself to be in a position to do so. Had there not been something crooked about Lizzie, — a screw loose, as people say, — she would never have been within his reach. There are men who always ride lame horses, and yet see as much of the hunting as others. (2:217–18)

diamonds and all their trappings to her sexual prowess—and to the false modesty in which she envelops her rather voracious charms.

> "Heaven and earth! To suppose that I should ever keep them under less than seven keys, and that there should be any of the locks that anybody should be able to open except myself!"
> "And where are the seven keys?" asked Frank.
> "Next to my heart," said Lizzie, putting her hand on her left side. "And when I sleep they are always tied round my neck in a bag, and the bag never escapes from my grasp. And I have such a knife under my pillow, ready for Mr. Camperdown, should he come to seize them!" Then she ran out of the room, and in a couple of minutes returned with the necklace, hanging loose in her hand. It was part of her little play to show by her speed that the close locking of the jewels was a joke, and that the ornament, precious as it was, received at her hands no other treatment than might any indifferent feminine bauble. (1:285)

If in this case the keys touch Lizzie's skin, it does not take much reflection to recognize that, when the diamonds themselves arrive, their metonymic rubbing up against her body also signifies sexually: "'I ain't noways sure as she ain't got them very diamonds themselves locked up, or, perhaps, tied round her person'" (2:91), suggests a policeman; and her confidant, Lord George, reassures her, "'They would never ask to search your person. . . . Keep them in your pocket while you are in the house during the day. They will hardly bring a woman with them to search you'" (2:106). The safest bet, as any latter-day drug smuggler could affirm, is to encase contraband goods within a bodily "pocket," and thereby evade any but the most invasive personal search.

The jewels' metaphoric relation to male sexuality thus slides—by virtue of their always adorning women—into a metonymic representation of female sexuality as well. Female governance of the male-inflected jewels extends from the protective custody of the box to the very display upon the body, as though to render explicit the question of whether the woman possesses the necklace or the necklace (like a choker) possesses the woman. In appropriating the gems as her own property, Lizzie does not simply exhibit female self-assertiveness but enacts a wholesale symbolic revaluation of jewels themselves. The story forms an erotic drama of protecting, transporting, concealing, and revealing the necklace, and in every case its extraordinary value (never its beauty) is what fascinates the characters. In order to assert her rights to the property, Lizzie boldly wears it out in public:

> Lady Glencora's rooms were already very full when Lizzie entered them, but she was without a gentleman, and room was made for her to pass quickly up the stairs. The diamonds had been recognised by many before she had reached the drawing-room;—not that these very diamonds were known, or that there was a special memory for that necklace;—but the subject had been so generally discussed, that the blaze of the stones immediately brought it to the minds of men and women. (1:158)

The public interest evinced in Lizzie's neck is matched by her private obsession with the security of her valuables—a concern that, once compounded by her retaining the jewels after claiming they have been stolen, blurs into a sexualized secret: "She could not keep herself from unlocking her desk and looking at it twenty times a day, although she knew the peril of such nervous solicitude. . . . And then she was aware of a morbid desire on her own part to tell the secret,—of a desire that amounted almost to a disease" (2:80–81).

Lizzie's propensity for bibelots long antedates her acquisition of the Eustace diamonds, as does the association of her sexuality with jewelry. In the novel's first paragraph we learn that, "when she was little more than a child, [she] went about everywhere with jewels on her fingers, and red gems hanging round her neck, and yellow gems pendent from her ears, and white gems shining in her black hair" (1:2). This prepossessing child's acquisitive instinct is coterminous with her sexual precocity: she knows how to use her bejeweled charms to ensnare a wealthy husband—Sir Florian Eustace, who repays the pawnbrokers for the gems she took out on credit even before he unwittingly bestows his family diamonds upon her. Assimilating Lizzie's jewelry to the more general blush of her sex appeal, the narrator notes, "It was true that Sir Florian was at her feet; and that by a proper use of her various charms,—the pawned jewels included,—she might bring him to an offer" (1:4). Through the circulation of credit that follows the path of her own circulation between men, Lizzie pawns the jewels that her father gave her in order to amass the funds necessary for acquiring a husband; she then craftily retrieves the jewels, so as to charm the young man, on the promise that her (as yet unaffianced) suitor will redeem them.

In addition to the connections I have adduced between the jewels and

Lizzie's sexuality, a final link ensures the impossibility of disentangling the two. The narrative tracks Lizzie's criminal possession of the diamonds, and while this scandal for a long time bears a faint aroma of impropriety, the sexual aspect of her case eventually becomes overwhelming. The switchpoint between the property question and the sexual one arises in the plot of Lizzie's second engagement, to Lord Fawn, who cannot decide which scenario will be more shameful: marrying a woman whose reputation has been damaged by the accusation that she illegally possesses another man's family jewels, or withdrawing from an engagement that has been publicly announced. Fawn's sister, Mrs. Hittaway, raises the moral stakes by exposing Lizzie's indiscreet flirtation with Frank Greystock, her cousin and possible paramour; she is now openly accused of the whorishness that was previously only implied:

> Then had come Mrs. Hittaway's evidence as to Lizzie's wicked doings down in Scotland. . . . And that which had been at first, as it were, added to the diamonds, as a supplementary weight thrown into the scale, so that Lizzie's iniquities might bring her absolutely to the ground, had gradually assumed the position of being the first charge against her. Lady Fawn had felt no aversion to discussing the diamonds. . . . It was well that the fact should be known, so that everybody might be aware that her son was doing right in refusing to marry so wicked a lady. But when the other thing was added to it; when the story was told of what Mr. Gowran had seen among the rocks, and when gradually that became the special crime which was to justify her son in dropping the lady's acquaintance, then Lady Fawn became very unhappy, and found the subject to be, as Mrs. Hittaway had described it, very distasteful. (2:179–80)

The sexual connotations hovering around the theft solidify into denotation, and the two crimes are yoked together under the rubric of scandal with as little concern for accuracy as is usual in such matters. The collapse of the two scandals into one is realized in the simple substitution, through Lady Fawn's imagination, of the sexual indiscretion that "Mr. Gowran had seen among the rocks" for Lizzie's misconduct with those other rocks, the diamonds. Sexual unspeakability germinates in the interstices between her crimes as a generalized and unspecifiable sense that " 'Lizzie,' as she was not uncommonly called by people who had hardly ever seen her,—had something amiss with it all. 'I don't know where it is she's lame,' said that very clever man . . . 'but she don't go flat all round' " (1:153).

We have seen how, by means of symbolic substitution, the diamond necklace represents forms of sexuality that would otherwise be inarticulable. Yet the necklace's status as an authentic repository of monetary value ensures that it functions not only as a symbol. For this lapidary emblem allows the heterosexual contract to be conceived in literal financial terms, manifesting, as it does, the economic realities of the marriage market. I now want to suggest that in the text's economy, this sexualized and gendered property vacillates between two opposing paradigms—one, which conforms to a model of commodity exchange, the other, which appears to resist it. The story distinguishes between these two property formations through the competing legal definitions ascribed to the jewels. The judicial question that preoccupies the characters throughout the novel is whether the diamonds constitute an "heirloom"—and therefore belong to the scion of the Eustace estate, Lizzie's son—or whether they are partible and exchangeable property, which can be given as a gift and which Lizzie could therefore retain as "paraphernalia." The learned barrister, Mr. Dove, supplies the opinion that a diamond necklace cannot be an heirloom because there is no guarantee that it will be "maintained in its original form":

> "[It] is not only alterable, but constantly altered, and cannot easily be traced. . . . Heirlooms have become so, not that the future owners of them may be assured of so much wealth, whatever the value of the thing so settled may be,—but that the son or grandson or descendant may enjoy the satisfaction which is derived from saying, my father or my grandfather or my ancestor sat in that chair, or looked as he now looks in that picture, or was graced by wearing on his breast that very ornament which you now see lying beneath the glass." (1:258–59)

Heirlooms, by this reasoning, preserve value through their originality and constancy, and lie outside an exchange economy; they are quintessentially male property, since they belong to the estate and are conveyed by primogeniture. Paraphernalia, on the other hand, is property belonging to a married woman exclusive of what her husband appropriates from her (her dowry); up until 1870, paraphernalia was virtually the only property a married woman possessed, and could dispose of, as her own.[7] Though Dove is uncertain whether the court would actually deem

---

7. *Paraphernalia* (etymologically, "beyond the dowry") is defined in the *Oxford English Dictionary* as "Those articles of personal property which the law allows a married woman to

the jewels paraphernalia (that is, Lizzie's exclusive property), he is persuaded that the necklace *cannot* be an heirloom because it is mutable and divisible, and because its value therefore subsists in its potential for exchange. He does, however, argue that even if the jewels were considered "paraphernalia belonging to her station," Lizzie would still be "debarred from selling" them because of their extraordinary value (1:228–29). Although the assurance that Lizzie will be prevented from cashing in the jewels should comfort the Eustace family attorney, Mr. Camperdown, he justifiably persists in fearing she will sell them: "Were she once to get hold of that word, paraphernalia, it would be as a tower of strength to her. . . . He was as certain as ever that the woman was robbing the estate which it was his duty to guard, and that should he cease to be active in the matter, the necklace would be broken up and the property sold and scattered before a year was out, and then the woman would have got the better of him!" (1:231).

For the purposes of the Eustace estate, it would be far preferable to have the jewels adjudged an heirloom, and everyone in the novel (except Dove) is incredulous that they cannot be: "A pot or a pan might be an heirloom, but not a necklace! Mr. Camperdown could hardly bring himself to believe that this was law. And then as to paraphernalia! Up to this moment, though he had been called upon to arrange great dealings in reference to widows, he had never as yet heard of a claim made

---

keep and, to a certain extent, deal with as her own." The dictionary then elaborates, in an explanatory note:

> The word *parapherna* was used by the Roman jurists to indicate all property which a married woman *sui juris* held apart from her *dos* (dower). Over such property the husband could exercise no rights without his wife's consent. . . . In English and Scottish Common law, under which all personal or movable property of a wife vested *ipso jure* in the husband, the *paraphernalia* became restricted to such purely personal belongings of a wife as dress, jewels, and the like. These latter were regarded as, in a sense, appropriated to the wife, and on the husband's death they were not treated as part of his succession, and the right of a trustee over them, in the event of the husband's bankruptcy, was restricted. . . . The effect of the "Married Woman's Property Acts" of 1870, etc., will ultimately be to deprive the term of all significance in English and Scottish legal practice.

Though the 1870 law allowed married women certain property rights, significant legislative changes did not come about until 1882. For a history of the law, including the contemporary context for Trollope's novel, see Lee Holcombe, *Wives and Property: Reform of the Married Women's Property Law in Nineteenth-Century England* (Toronto: University of Toronto Press, 1983).

by a widow for paraphernalia" (1:254). Camperdown's logic betrays the following contradiction: the only reason he wants the jewels treated as an heirloom—and so excluded from an exchange economy—is because their worth, as determined by the market in diamonds, is so great. The official distinction, then, between the two types of property—that the worth of paraphernalia, like any commodity, is governed by the market-place, and the value of an heirloom derives from its traditional associations and its immutability—is, in practice, undermined. On the one hand, the only heirloom worth designating as such is one with a high commodity valuation. On the other, Lizzie's original claim (however disingenuous) to possession of the diamonds as paraphernalia—that her late husband gave them to her as a sign of his affection—itself prevents her from selling them, since it effectively revalues them *as* heirlooms (that is, property whose value lies in its familial and chivalric associations). Despite her legal right to redeem the diamonds, their enormous symbolic value as expropriated patrilineal property precludes the possibility of her doing so: "She could not bring herself to let them out of her own hands. Ten thousand pounds! If she could only sell them and get the money, from what a world of trouble would she be relieved. And the sale, for another reason, would have been convenient; for Lady Eustace was already a little in debt. But she could not sell them, and therefore when she got into the carriage there was the box under her feet" (1:185).

Although the terms of this opposition seem to break down, the plot nonetheless depends upon the appearance of a stable distinction for the property battle to be meaningful. Since, as I have suggested, the novel inextricably binds up the story of the diamonds with female sexuality, we can now ask what the status of the jewels has to teach us about the economy of gender relations. In other words, if the legal issue is whether jewels accord with or resist a model of commodity valuation, can the same be said of female sexual property? According to the paraphernalia model, women retain possession of their sexual goods and simply retail them to the highest bidder. Lizzie clearly conforms to this paradigm, even though she has several incommensurable markets in which to consider her prospects: wealth (Sir Florian), respectability (Lord Fawn), and sentiment (Frank Greystock). That she ends up with the odious Mr. Emilius simply suggests how little her worth has come to by the end of the story. If it were not clear enough from Trollope, the terms of Sherlock Holmes's formulation would indicate just how unnatural Lizzie's sexuality is (thanks to the diamonds) felt to be: she confounds Holmes's conventional morality since she reaches for her jewels, not her baby, when she is in danger. Acting like a single woman who knows the value of her sexual goods, the widow Lizzie finally makes those goods valueless precisely by putting them in circulation.

Lizzie serves as a negative exemplar, as the narrator's frankly hostile presentation of her suggests: "There shall be no whitewashing of Lizzie Eustace. She was abominable" (1:321). She disturbs patriarchal institutions both through her recognition of her function within that order—as a vehicle for the transfer of property between her husband and her son—and through her attempt to subvert that process. The novel, however, also subscribes to a fantasy of female sexuality according to the heirloom pattern, embodied in its domestic heroine, Lucy Morris. Despite extraordinary tortures of doubt and discouragement, Lucy sustains her love for Frank Greystock; by setting her in heavily underscored counterpoint to Lizzie, Trollope affirms the latter's status as a whore with respect to both jewels and men. To use Dove's words, Lucy's heart is steadfastly "maintained in its original form," while Lizzie's desire (as the long succession of her lovers indicates) "is not only alterable, but constantly altered." Jewels once again both metaphorize and literalize female worth, now serving the broad strokes of the contrast between the two women. In figurative terms, the formulation is quite simple: "Lucy held her ground because she was real. You may knock about a diamond, and not even scratch it; whereas paste in rough usage betrays itself. Lizzie, with all her self-assuring protestations, knew that she was paste, and knew that Lucy was real stone" (2:230).[8] Literally speaking, Lucy supplies an ornament of genuine sentimental worth, as Frank informs Lizzie:

> "If you were to attempt to sell the diamonds they would stop you, and would not give you credit for the generous purpose afterwards."
>
> "They wouldn't stop you if you sold the ring you wear." The ring had been given to him by Lucy, after their engagement, and was the only present she had ever made him. It had been purchased out of her own earnings, and had been put on his finger by her

---

8. Another instance, from Frank's consciousness: "How unlike [Lizzie] was to Lucy! . . . When Lucy was much in earnest, in her eye, too, a tear would sparkle, the smallest drop, a bright liquid diamond that never fell; and all her face would be bright and eloquent with feeling;—but how unlike were the two! He knew that the difference was that between truth and falsehood;—and yet he partly believed the falsehood!" (1:177).

own hand. . . . "Let me look at the ring," she said. . . . "What is the price?" she asked.

"It is not in the market, Lizzie. Nor should your diamonds be there." (1:283)

By contrast with Lizzie's diamonds, Lucy's ring has a worth—its affectional symbolism—far in excess of its strict market price. Since it has little monetary value, Lucy's jewelry ironically serves as a much better demonstration of heirloom economics than Lizzie's, whose contradictory status (an heirloom prized for its pecuniary worth) it thus exposes. Finally, the metaphoric and literal distinctions between the two women converge on a single jewel—the hundred-guinea brooch with which Lizzie attempts to bribe Lucy (1:141). In offering her the bauble, Lizzie tries to infect Lucy with an imagination of both jewels and feminine wiles as commodities, an idea so anathema to the pristine governess that she rebuffs her former friend altogether.

The evidence for this bipolar construction of femininity is so overwhelming that it cannot but seem suspicious. It should come as no surprise that, although the narrative superficially posits this opposition as the organizing principle in its representation of women, Lizzie and Lucy compose two sides of the same coin. The presentation of the two women taken together elucidates the ideology that directs women to imagine their desires on the heirloom model and yet treats them as commodities, condemning them when they seek to govern their own value in the exchange economy in which they really do circulate. Frank Greystock's classic romantic bind epitomizes this conundrum: his career demands a wealthy wife while his desire aims at the pure girl with no property. In the collapse of the literal and metaphorical aspects of Lucy-as-jewel, the economics of the marriage plot become clear to Frank: "There was no doubt about Lucy being as good as gold;—only that real gold, vile as it is, was the one thing that Frank so much needed" (1:276).[9]

9. The parallel between Lizzie and Lucy in terms of their jewels also extends at one point to the box: comparable to Lizzie's jewels stored in the iron box, the object of greatest value to Lucy—Frank's letter proposing to marry her—resides in a much-emphasized "iron post": "If Lucy could only have known of the letter, which was already her own property though lying in the pillar letter-box in Fleet Street. . . . It was so hard upon her that she should be so interrogated while that letter was lying in the iron box!" (1:132–33). The letter-box yokes together Lizzie's pervasive strong box with Trollope's professional career in the post office—and, in particular, his role as "originator" of the pillar letter-box. See Anthony Trollope, An Autobiography (Oxford: Oxford University Press, 1980), 282.

The gross binarism of the Lucy/Lizzie relation announces itself not only in the symbolism of their reciprocal relation to jewels, but also in the proto-Barthesian phonetic distinction between their given names. As with the jewels, the text again transcends the simple opposition, now through the complex phonemic interrelation of their full names: Lucy Morris and Lizzie Eustace. The sibilant placidity of Lucy's *uc* converges on the first syllable of Lizzie's married surname, while the brazen buzzing of Lizzie's *iz* almost—but does not quite—terminate Lucy's maiden name. Indeed, the failure of "Lucy Morris" to voice the final consonant and thus incorporate "Lizzie"—by analogy with the capacity of "Lizzie Eustace" to assimilate "Lucy"—suggests the breakdown of the symmetry just where one might expect it to be secured. The noncomplementarity of the characters' nomenclature both confirms and belies the opposition between them. If this seems an excessive amount of attention to pay to proper names, it need merely be pointed out that their significance has the same status as that of the sexual connotations attaching to jewel boxes: their obviousness makes them appear unnoteworthy even as their meaning is strictly unprovable.

A genuine difference in the representation of female sexuality arises more pointedly midway through the novel, with that female figure apparently midway between Lizzie and Lucy: she is called Lucinda. The introduction of Lucinda both augments and muddles the embodiment of characterological distinctions in nominal ones. Just as her name begins like Lucy's, she too arrives a penurious but highly marriageable young woman with a certain charm; but Lucinda rapidly veers away from the sentimentalized domesticity to which Lucy accedes—though not by the same route as Lizzie. While Lizzie's protofeminist independence patently shores up the patriarchy it resists, Lucinda's hysterical refusal of heterosexual conformity is so pathological as to exceed the norms that structure both Lucy's submission and Lizzie's rebellion. At first, her mediating role appears as if it may simply reinforce, rather than challenge, the Lizzie/Lucy binary:

> It had seemed to her that all the men who came near her were men whom she could not fail to dislike. She was hurried here and

---

The novel's narrator makes a joke on the subject, referring to "the post-office, with that accuracy in the performance of its duties for which it is conspicuous among all offices" (1:134).

hurried there, and knew nothing of real social intimacies. As she told her aunt in her wickedness, she would almost have preferred a shoemaker, — if she could have become acquainted with a shoemaker in a manner that should be unforced and genuine. There was a savageness of antipathy in her to the mode of life which her circumstances had produced for her. (2:4)

The fantasy common to Lucy, Lizzie, and the ideology of the narrative as a whole — that a poor marriage is always and only a loving one, a rich marriage always and only mercenary — clearly organizes Lucinda's romantic imagination too. But Lucinda's history represents a fundamental break with the novel's other versions of female sexuality — a break with the romantic imagination itself. At first, she conforms to conventions of the femme fatale (she is compared to Cleopatra and the French murderess Brinvilliers); her potential suitors, "so used to softness and flattery from women," are said to "have learned to think that a woman silent, arrogant, and hard of approach, must be always meditating murder" (1:330). Her contemptuous hostility is soon turned inward until (like a forebear of Hardy's Sue Bridehead), in her frigid mortification, she refuses to put herself in circulation at all. After the first kiss from her fiancé: "Never before had she been thus polluted. The embrace had disgusted her. It made her odious to herself. . . . For the sake of this man who was to be her husband, she hated all men" (2:24); and on her wedding day: " 'I will never trust myself alone in his presence. I could not do it. When he touches me my whole body is in agony. To be kissed by him is madness' " (2:273). Though she imagines at first that Sir Griffin Tewett is simply the wrong man, she ends by rejecting the whole of his sex: " 'I don't think I could feel to any man as though I loved him' " (2:273). Lucinda's frank repugnance for male sexuality, and for all the obligations of marriage, poses an alternative — however psychotic in its depiction — to the heterosexual order that organizes the other women's desire. Her refusal of heterosexuality can only be portrayed as a frigid lack of desire, as against Lizzie's candid libidinousness and Lucy's more respectable (but no less fierce) devotion to her man.[10]

10. While Lucinda is revolted by a man's touch, Lizzie knows how to make use of a posture of supplication, laying her head on the breast of each of her lovers in succession (Sir Florian [1:8], Lord Fawn [1:74], Frank [1:291], Lord George [2:104]). Even when she settles for (and on) Emilius, she eroticizes the very qualities that make him repellent: "The man was a nasty, greasy, lying, squinting Jew preacher . . . but there was a certain

Lucinda's aborted engagement makes for a scandal in miniature, as the plaint of her guardian, Mrs. Carbuncle, indicates: " 'Oh, Lucinda, this is the unkindest and the wickedest, and the most horrible thing that anybody ever did! I shall never, never be able to hold up my head again' " (2:277). This scandal both corresponds to and revises the drama that Lizzie enacts on the novel's main stage. As in Lizzie's case, sexual misconduct aligns with property difficulties: the relation of Lucinda's frigidity to her poverty parallels that of Lizzie's nymphomania to her ill-gotten wealth. As in Lizzie's case, also, the scandal makes it unclear whether sexuality propels the other issues or masks them—whether, that is to say, Lucinda's sexual crisis is the cause or the effect of her sensational refusal to go through with the marriage. By virtue of this ambiguity, the story can insinuate sexual meanings by promoting their unspeakability.

If the novel's principal technique for encoding women's sexuality consists in the representation of female property, what property formation does the text attribute to Lucinda? The term associated most closely with her plight is *tribute*, the title of the chapter in which Mrs. Carbuncle exacts expensive wedding gifts for Lucinda from everyone she knows. "The presents to be made to Lucinda were very much thought of in Hertford Street at this time, and Lizzie . . . did all she could to assist the collection of tribute. It was quite understood that as a girl can only be married once . . . everything should be done to gather toll from the tax-payers of society. It was quite fair on such an occasion that men should be given to understand that something worth having was expected" (2:232). Unlike the heirloom, this "toll" is mutable and exchangeable, but unlike paraphernalia, its female possessor has little to say about its disposition; it is both uninheritable and unregenerate property, which simply goes to pay off the accumulated debt of the impoverished women. The ultimate fate of all this tribute indicates the dead end to which such property relations lead—not nuptial bliss, but merely remunerated creditors:

> It was rumoured that Mrs. Carbuncle, with her niece, had gone to join her husband at New York. At any rate, she disappeared altogether from London, leaving behind her an amount of debts which showed how extremely liberal in their dealings the great

---

manliness in him. . . . While he was making his speech she almost liked his squint. She certainly liked the grease and nastiness. Presuming, as she naturally did, that something of what he said was false, she liked the lies" (2:314).

tradesmen of London will occasionally be. . . . One account, however, she had honestly settled. The hotel-keeper in Albemarle Street
had been paid, and all the tribute had been packed and carried off
from the scene of the proposed wedding banquet. (2:359)

As the stolen diamond necklace parallels Lizzie's story, and the sentimental ring Lucy's, so the fifty-pound silver service (and £150 cash),
which Mrs. Carbuncle extorts from Lizzie on behalf of her niece, both
bespeaks and silences Lucinda's sexuality.[11]

The correlation between women's sexuality and objects of material
value extends across the representation of female characters in the novel.
The mobile symbolism of the jewels in particular makes manifest the
economic relations that organize sexual difference in Victorian Britain—
both the difference between men and women and differences within
the imagination of female sexuality. The exigency, I have suggested, of
portraying sexuality in mitigated and deflected form itself affords certain literary opportunities. The compulsion for encoding indicates the
unspeakability of what is covered, while the transparency of the code
suggests how manageable literature has nonetheless made it. The ideological incitement to such displacement, in the case of The Eustace Diamonds,
lies in the simultaneous imperative and refusal to acknowledge the relationship between female sexuality and property. But when, as we will
shortly see, a male author identifies himself in certain conspicuous ways
with a woman at the center of a sex scandal, we have to ask whether his
own property—his literary work—is equally divided between the two

11. Still more evidence for a correspondence between female sexuality and the economics
of jewelry arises in the contest over the inadequacy of Mrs. Hanbury Smith's tribute.
Mrs. Carbuncle replies to her former friend's gift:
    "Lucinda has received your little brooch, and is much obliged to you for thinking
    of her; but you must remember that, when you were married, I sent you a bracelet
    which cost £10. If I had a daughter of my own, I should, of course, expect that she
    would reap the benefit of this on her marriage;—and my niece is the same to me
    as a daughter. I think that this is quite understood now among people in society.
    Lucinda will be disappointed much if you do not send her what she thinks she has
    a right to expect. Of course you can deduct the brooch if you please." (2:235)
In this exclusively female system of exchange, the operative unit of currency continues
to be the bauble. Extending the thematics of the novel's main action, the incident derives
its comic effect from the fact that Mrs. Carbuncle makes too obvious the concatenation
of jewelry, property, and sexuality which is supposed ("among people in society") to
remain inexplicit.

models, heirloom and paraphernalia, on which the woman-as-jewel is constructed.

The distinction between a text's fabricated author-function and its narrator enables us to locate a peculiar identification between the former—call it "Trollope"—and the story's protagonist. As if to complement or compensate for the narrator's contemptuous antipathy toward Lizzie, the author behind the narrator exhibits an uncanny likeness to her. From at least the evidence of the Lizzie/Lucy opposition, we know that names are scarcely coincidental in this work, and there is no reason to think that the common meaning of the author's proper name is lost upon the text: "trollop," a strumpet or harlot, clearly identifies the novel's anti-heroine, though the word is never used explicitly in reference to her.

It is by means of a term that encapsulates Lizzie's chief characteristics—her avarice and her lubricity—that the author nominally identifies himself with her. But is the connection merely onomastic, or do these attributes apply as aptly to the author as to the character? Is there also an analogy, that is to say, between the forms of property—authorial commodities and female sexual goods—according to which each "trollop" is defined?[12] One place to begin looking for an answer to this question is the text in which "Trollope," as a purveyor of literary properties, is most fully realized: the *Autobiography* (1883). In this work, the author in fact imagines his literary manuscripts to be his own jewels, which, as he attests, he had a habit of keeping locked up in an iron box at just the period during which he wrote *The Eustace Diamonds*. Before embarking on an eighteenth-months' sojourn in Australia, for instance, Trollope arranges the publication of works while he is away:

> I . . . left in the hands of the editor of *The Fortnightly*, ready for production on the 1st of July following, a story called *The Eustace Diamonds*. . . . I also left behind, in a strong box, the manuscript of *Phineas Redux* . . . [and,] in the same strong box, another novel, called *An Eye for an Eye*, which then had been some time written, and of which, as it has not even yet [in 1876] been published, I will not further

12. On the relations among women, jewels, and authorship in an exchange economy, I am indebted to Catherine Gallagher, "George Eliot and *Daniel Deronda*: The Prostitute and the Jewish Question," in *Sex, Politics, and Science in the Nineteenth-Century Novel: Selected Papers from the English Institute, 1983–84*, ed. Ruth Bernard Yeazell (Baltimore: Johns Hopkins University Press, 1986), 39–62.

speak. It will probably be published some day, though, looking forward, I can see no room for it, at any rate, for the next two years.

If therefore The Great Britain, in which we sailed for Melbourne, had gone to the bottom, I had so provided that there would be new novels ready to come out under my name for some years to come.[13]

While explicitly subordinating his work to his name, Trollope implicitly draws an analogy between his authorial labors and Lizzie's work at maintaining possession of the diamonds: like her, he circulates his valuables in a competitive marketplace, holding out for the highest bidder and reserving his merchandise in a strong box until the market can bear it.[14]

Also like his character's, the author's allegiances are divided between a self-professed desire for profit and self-aggrandizing claims for the moral authenticity of his production. The figurative congruence between literary property and female jewels suggests that both the novelist and the protagonist advertise themselves according to the heirloom model—his motivation is moral improvement through art, hers is affection—while their monetary incentives indicate that they function like paraphernalia. What the representation of women and jewels in The Eustace Diamonds has taught us to recognize, however, is that the ostensive antagonism between these two economic modes masks an underlying collusion. Verbal art and sexual desire are no less authentic for being marketed, that is to say, but neither are they worth more for being real.

Though the two models of female sexuality appeared chasmally divided under our initial analytic rubric, they finally showed themselves to be fundamentally confederate. And just as with the woman-as-jewel, so too with the novel-as-commodity. Even at the moment of its inception, in fact, the distinction between the two basic types of property

13. Autobiography, 343–45.

14. As does Lizzie, Trollope abjures a paradigm of genital procreativity for his work. According to N. John Hall, Trollope: A Biography (Oxford: Clarendon, 1991), his literary ingenuity flowed instead on an anal-expulsive model: Trollope is said to have remarked to George Eliot, " 'With my mechanical stuff it's a sheer matter of industry. It's not the head that does it [i.e., produces "imaginative work"]—it's the cobbler's wax on the seat and the sticking to my chair!' And, according to another account, he drove home his point about the seat of inspiration with 'an inelegant vigour of gesture that sent a thrill of horror through the polite circle there assembled' " (363). For a fuller consideration of the mode of literary production theorized and exemplified in Trollope's autobiography, see Walter M. Kendrick, The Novel-Machine: The Theory and Fiction of Anthony Trollope (Baltimore: Johns Hopkins University Press, 1980).

(heirloom and paraphernalia) seems already to have collapsed. On the one hand, despite being foremost among major Victorian novelists to conceive of himself as a workman producing literary commodities for the market,[15] Trollope subscribes at least minimally to a Romantic ideology of original authorship: "I think that an author, when he uses either the words or the plot of another, should own as much, demanding to be credited with no more of the work than he has himself produced. I may say also that I have never printed as my own a word that has been written by others." This valuation of work, which, in its indivisible integrity, belongs exclusively to its author, comports with a model of literature as heirloom. On the other hand, however, at precisely the moment that Trollope explicitly articulates the paraphernalia/heirloom distinction in the novel—that is, in the recounting of Dove's legal opinion—this claim on behalf of immutable authorial property falls apart around him. The account of Dove's opinion is unique in Trollope's literary output, he states in the *Autobiography*, as the sole case of his publishing someone else's material under his own name. In a footnote to the passage just quoted, he writes: "I must make one exception to this declaration. The legal opinion as to heirlooms in *The Eustace Diamonds* was written for me by Charles Merewether, the present Member for Northampton. I am told that it has become the ruling authority on the subject."[16] Trollope appropriates Merewether's words without acknowledging their authorship, taking writing as one more exchangeable, changeable commodity whose worth is determined not by its originality but by the value that can be derived from it in the literary marketplace. In treating as paraphernalia the very passage that differentiates between forms of property, and then, in his posthumously published *Autobiography*, renouncing such use

15. "There are those who would be ashamed to subject themselves to such a taskmaster, and who think that the man who works with his imagination should allow himself to wait till—inspiration moves him. When I have heard such doctrine preached, I have hardly been able to repress my scorn. To me it would not be more absurd if the shoemaker were to wait for inspiration, or the tallow-chandler for the divine moment of melting. . . . The author wants [inspiration] as does every other workman,—that and a habit of industry" (*Autobiography*, 120–21).

16. *Autobiography*, 116. Later in the same text, Trollope explains "what we all mean when we talk of literary plagiarism and literary honesty. The sin of which the author is accused is not that of taking another man's property, but of passing off as his own creation that which he did not himself create. When an author puts his name to a book he claims to have written all that there is therein, unless he makes direct signification to the contrary" (254).

of the passage in favor of an ideology of literature as heirloom, Trollope has it both ways with the distinction even in the course of proposing it.

The analogy between the novelist's property and the character's holds: divided by the terms of a putative difference and then reconsolidated, both sorts of assets are secured all the more firmly in both the heirloom and the paraphernalia models for value. We can now understand this bifurcated account, of how worth is assigned to property, to extend to one other arena as well: to the scandal narrative that composes the text. This less material but no less consequential realm of value—truth value—supplies the very medium through which the novel makes its assertions about other kinds of property. And just as lapidary and literary commodities are defined simultaneously in market-valued and extra-market terms, so is the narrative ground on which the novel establishes the validity of its own avowals. While the definition of female capital in the novel's plot takes shape through a dispute over *legal* authority, however, the material that constitutes the novel is organized around a parallel conflict over *narrative* authority. This epistemology of the novel determines the means by which information about sexuality, as both vehicle and tenor of the economic metaphors, is simultaneously conveyed and held back—in short, the means by which it is rendered unspeakable.

Within the novel's plot, assertions about the truth of things seem to derive entirely from what people—"the public"—believe them to be. Like *The Mill on the Floss*, *The Eustace Diamonds* makes it clear that scandal stories derive from public opinion propped upon fictions. While Maggie's scandal is fictional because it is based on incorrect facts, however, Lizzie's is so in the sense that it accrues all the public attention of a scandal which it actually is not—a sex scandal—but which everyone in the novel imagines it to be (and which, *a fortiori*, it eventually becomes). The public in Trollope's novel self-consciously does not care about the truth, desiring only a scoop ("'Upon the whole, the little mystery is quite delightful. . . . Nobody now cares for anything except the Eustace diamonds'" [2:72], writes Barrington Erle) or a fashion tip ("'Nobody will dare to wear a diamond at all next season,' said Lady Glencora" [2:73]). The wrongness of the St. Ogg's community, and the indifference to facts of the one at Matching Priory, consequently point to markedly different conclusions about the relation of scandal stories to their audiences. Like Eliot, Trollope suggests that capricious public opinion determines what is taken for the truth; but while *The Mill on the Floss* attacks the narrow moralism of the world's wife, *The Eustace Diamonds*, we will see, comes close to endorsing the judgments made by "the world."

Within the world of Trollope's novel, fickle public opinion—whose media range from a cross-class gossip network to high-society newspapers—both supplies the means by which scandal circulates and registers its effects.[17] Lizzie regularly employs the rumor machine to achieve her purposes, as when she keeps Lord Fawn in check by putting his name in traffic with hers: "Lord Fawn was, therefore, well aware that Lady Eustace had published the engagement. It was known to everybody, and could not be broken off without public scandal" (1:106). Though Lizzie is consistently surrounded by scandal, Fawn is the character most threatened by gossip and newspaper stories:

> To have his hands quite clean, to be above all evil report, to be respectable, as it were, all round, was Lord Fawn's special ambition. He was a poor man, and a greedy man, but he would have abandoned his official salary at a moment's notice, rather than there should have fallen on him a breath of public opinion hinting that it ought to be abandoned. He was especially timid, and lived in a perpetual fear lest the newspapers should say something hard of him. (1:93)

Owning nothing but a respectable reputation, Lord Fawn is exceedingly sensitive to its damage, and his fiancée's defamation threatens to rob him of this sole possession. Lizzie, by contrast, makes use of scandal, purposely putting herself before "The Eye of the Public" (2:246), where she knows Lady Glencora's court of fashion will judge her less harshly than Mr. Camperdown's chancery court. Lizzie is always known to have a damaged reputation, and while such a name may be bad, Lizzie uses it—by keeping it in public view—to protect her from something worse: the loss of her sole possession, the diamonds. The public's capriciousness aggravates Lord Fawn, who at a certain point discovers "a change in general opinion about the diamonds. When he had taken upon himself with a high hand to dissolve his own engagement, everybody had, as he thought, acknowledged that Lizzie Eustace was keeping property which did not belong to her. Now people talked of her losses as though the diamonds had been undoubtedly her own" (2:146). When Lizzie even-

---

17. On the role of public opinion ("the world") as a "policing force" more efficacious in *The Eustace Diamonds* than the literal police force, see D. A. Miller, *The Novel and the Police* (Berkeley: University of California Press, 1988), 14–15.

tually loses her ability to manipulate public perceptions, she concurs with Fawn in begrudging the press and the public access to her private life. Noticing that "the fashionable evening paper" has demanded a full disclosure of her role in the theft, "Lizzie threw the paper from her with indignation, asking what right newspaper-scribblers could have to interfere with the private affairs of such persons as herself!" (2:305).

Scandal, as Lizzie Eustace recognizes, has far less to do with illegal or immoral private behavior than it does with public perceptions of the case. When Camperdown attempts to take the jewels from her in Mount Street, for example, Lizzie's problem is not so much the material one of losing her property as the *réclame* of exposure before everyone: "Hitherto there had been some secrecy, or at any rate some privacy attached to the matter; but now that odious lawyer had discussed the matter aloud, in the very streets, in the presence of the servants, and Lady Eustace had felt that it was discussed also by every porter on the railway from London down to Troon" (1:189). While the audience from which Lizzie wishes to shield herself in this instance is altogether plebeian, she soon takes to parading her drama before the public that composes high society, for the latter will defend her better than any lawyer can. Though fully realized as characters elsewhere in the Palliser series, Lady Glencora, Madame Max Goesler, the Duke of Omnium, and the other denizens of Matching Priory function in this novel merely as embodiments of "the world," engrossed by the scandal sheets and eager to correspond with one another about Lizzie's tribulations.[18]

> Before the end of January everybody in London had heard of the great robbery at Carlisle,—and most people had heard also that there was something very peculiar in the matter,—something more than a robbery. Various rumours were afloat. . . . There were strong parties formed in the matter,—whom we may call Lizzie-ites and anti-Lizzieites. The Lizzieites were of opinion that poor Lady Eustace was being very ill-treated. . . . It was worthy of re-

18. Patricia Meyer Spacks, *Gossip* (New York: Alfred A. Knopf, 1985), writes: "To say that Trollope's novels contain a lot of gossip says nothing very interesting about them. Nor does detailed examination of how the gossip works shed much light on the novels as wholes. . . . Trollope's characters talk obsessively about one another's dubious behavior: Lizzie Eustace keeps everyone busy and happy for years by her reprehensible conduct. In precisely the same way, she provides the reader of *The Eustace Diamonds* with occupation and pleasure" (190).

mark that these Lizzieites were all of them Conservatives. . . . When the matter at last became of such importance as to demand leading articles in the newspapers, those journals which had devoted themselves to upholding the conservative politicians of the day were very heavy indeed upon Lord Fawn. The whole force of the Government, however, was anti-Lizzieite; and as the controversy advanced, every good Liberal became aware that there was nothing so wicked, so rapacious, so bold, or so cunning but that Lady Eustace might have done it. (2:66–67)

Scandal metaphorizes activities both greater and lesser than itself. On the one hand, as Lord Fawn clearly recognizes, the scandal involves "something more than a robbery"—that is, Lizzie's sexual dubiousness. On the other hand, it stands in for something less as well, shielding partisan squabbles (devoid of any properly political content), which are here imagined as merely epiphenomenal to opinions about Lizzie's virtue.[19] Indeed, the political debate that forms the backdrop for the novel is entirely formal: when Frank and Fawn spar in Parliament over the Sawab of Mygawb, the interest not only of readers but of characters is solely in the personal fortunes of the opponents: "On neither side did the hearers care much for the Sawab's claims, but they felt that Greystock was making good his own claims to some future reward from his party" (1:61). The partisan ramifications of Lizzie's plot conform to the usual configuration of political scandal, which routinely works by yoking affairs of state to unrelated activities from private life. Mr. Palliser's equally vacuous political preoccupation—institution of a decimal monetary system—likewise holds our attention only so long as it provides the occasion for Lady Glencora to press Lizzie's cause with Fawn. The narrator thus indicates how little public concern nominally political topics arouse: "The great question of the day was settled in two minutes, before the guests went out of the drawing-room" (2:141).[20] Politics, in

19. The possibility of serious political fallout from a scandal of female sexual virtue is hardly implausible: as the 1838 case surrounding Queen Victoria's lady-in-waiting, Lady Flora Hastings, and the so-called Bedchamber crisis make clear, such scandals have the potential for far more than symbolic consequences. See R. B. Martin, *Enter Rumour: Four Early Victorian Scandals* (London: Faber and Faber, 1962), 19–80.

20. The subject of divisible monetary units does, however, assume more than simply formal significance insofar as it relates thematically to the question of the diamond necklace's separable status.

this novel at any rate, simply serves as a vehicle for putting scandalous talk about sexuality into circulation.

The novel depicts a world in which social values seem wholly determined by a scandal economy: devoid of political, moral, or even legal standards, the ethics of any action are entirely articulated upon its social reception, upon how public opinion comes down (or, what amounts to the same thing, how it is imagined to do) on questions of conduct. In this arena of competing individual interests, opinions function in a marketplace much like the system in which, as we have seen, Lizzie merchandises her sexual goods. Hence the phantasmatic entity of the general public behaves not only, according to a theatrical metaphor, as an audience for the scandal's drama,[21] but also, according to an economic one, as the consumer of news. The public is a consumer not merely in the sense that it purchases newspapers and retails gossip, but also in the sense that it composes the customers of the market in opinion: public confidence in a particular position (say, Lizzie's rights to the jewels) enhances its value as against another (say, Fawn's justification in withdrawing from the engagement). Like today's public opinion polls, which inherit this impulse to calibrate social attitudes, the novel quantifies audience response as if on an affective barometer: "Since the two robberies, public opinion had veered round three or four points in Lizzie's favour, and people were beginning to say that she had been ill-used" (2:179).[22]

Like other markets, the one in opinions is fickle, and merchants who fail to deliver promised goods are punished. In the police-court Lizzie's disingenuous performance wins her much sympathy:

> "I was in such a state, sir, from fear, that I did not know what I was saying," exclaimed Lizzie, bursting into tears and stretching forth towards the bench her two clasped hands with the air of a suppliant. From that moment the magistrate was altogether on her side, — and so were the public. Poor ignorant, ill-used young creature; — and then so lovely! That was the general feeling. (2:320)

---

21. For instance, in response to Madame Goesler's suggestion that the police might "unravel the mystery" of the Eustace diamonds, Lady Glencora responds: " 'I hope they won't do that. . . . The play is too good to come to an end so soon' " (2:73).

22. See Mary Poovey, "Figures of Arithmetic, Figures of Speech: The Discourse of Statistics in the 1830s," Critical Inquiry 19, no. 2 (Winter 1993): 256–76, on the invention of statistical thinking earlier in the century (which was requisite to the production of an objective public opinion) and the relation of this discourse, claimed by its proponents to be based in fact, to the figures that it finds unrepresentable.

But when Lizzie later refuses to testify at the trial, she declines precipitously in the opinion market:

> People who had heard of the inquiry before the magistrate, had postponed their excitement and interest on the occasion, because they knew that the day of the trial would be the great day; and when they heard that they were to be robbed of the pleasure of Lady Eustace's cross-examination, there arose almost a public feeling of wrath that justice should be thus outraged. (2:354)

Even so lofty an English value as justice, it turns out, is beholden to the vicissitudes of "public feeling." And as Lizzie comes to understand, the market in opinions, which determines her public worth, overlaps with that of sexuality, in which she retails herself, and thus has material consequences: as her public stock depreciates, so too do her marital prospects.

Not only does the public, in passing judgment, evaluate the events and construe them as scandal; as I have argued in earlier chapters, the scandal also reciprocally generates a representation of the public. Trollope's depiction of the audience is less constrained than Eliot's, with its characterization of scandal's consumers in concrete gender and class terms. The public for Lizzie's crime—now embodied in the Palliser society set, now in the servants on the street—is the capacious and virtually undifferentiated contemporary audience of gossips and newspaper readers; it is a public unlike the self-contained St. Ogg's community, passing judgment on one of its members, which Eliot nostalgically evokes. The power of "the world" in *The Eustace Diamonds* derives from its very generality, which also enables it to bleed over almost imperceptibly into the novel's readership—by contrast with Maggie's public, which Eliot sharply distinguishes from her own.

The Eustace Diamonds affirms that the significance of an event hinges upon the consensus of the public that judges it; such judgments cannot be referred to a higher authority, and the social institutions intended to regulate conduct (the courts, the Church, Parliament) must wait upon the tide of an imagined public opinion. Even Lady Eustace regards herself as a spectacle, for she has trouble distinguishing herself as object of the public's scrutiny from its subject position. She "was upon the whole disposed to think as everybody thought" (2:209), and when she attempts to confess her crime to her cousin, "she told him the whole story;—not the true story, but the story as it was believed by all the world. She found it to be impossible to tell him the true story" (2:53). Lizzie is as prone to believing the fictions upon which public opinion is founded as everyone else—even when she is the subject presumed to know the truth distorted by those opinions.

Although the plot has convinced us that the truth of a story is entirely contingent upon the public's feelings about it, we will, from our investigation of the jewels, be suspicious of any assignment of value that appears driven solely by the market. This last quotation itself begins to suggest an alternate current of belief that runs throughout the novel: namely, that such a thing as "the true story" exists objectively, and that the narrator has access to it. Even if, as I have been arguing, for the purposes of the plot, truth is imagined as a mutable social construction dependent on opinion, for the purposes of the enclosing narrative, such truth is understood to be absolute and determinable. The novel, that is to say, accommodates two conflicting models of truth-construction, one roughly identified with the plot, the other with the narrative voice. These paired models recapitulate the accounts of sexual and literary property whose structure we have already delineated: while the plot locates truth in the marketplace of opinion, like paraphernalia, the guiding narrative consciousness registers it outside of exchange, in a realm of immutable value, like the heirloom.[23]

Critics have associated the so-called realism of Trollope's fiction with the author's professed valuation of the actual (truth) over the possible (fiction).[24] The determination of truth within the story follows a different

23. In a related analysis, James R. Kincaid, in *The Novels of Anthony Trollope* (Oxford: Clarendon, 1977), writes about the tension in Trollope's work between "moral purism" (absolute standards) and "empiricism" or "relativism" (what I have been calling social contingency—in short, public opinion). Kincaid revises the theory of "situation ethics" that Ruth apRoberts proposes in *The Moral Trollope* (Athens, Ohio: Ohio University Press, 1971), suggesting instead a notion of flexible consistency:

> This is not to deny that empirical standards are present in Trollope, but they seldom if ever stand in a normative position. Ordinarily, empiricism is one extreme pole of the novel's value system, a position seductive but dangerous. It is usually played off against an opposite moral purism. . . . Trollope's method and his morality, then, appear to me very much tied to situations, but only because situations test and make solid an ethical code that would otherwise remain abstract and superficial. The situations can diversify, even break, codes, but the codes derive always from a civilized base independent of the situations. (14–16)

While I agree that such a conflict arises in *The Eustace Diamonds*, my effort is less to resolve it dialectically than to show how the putative difference was ideologically determined from the outset.

24. Kendrick fully elaborates such an analysis in *The Novel-Machine*, proposing that, for Trollope, literature would ideally convey "life" without mediation, and that only the inadequacies of the representational medium produce a reader's awareness of "textuality."

logic, whereby opinion—expectation based on probability—functions like a market: such is the paraphernalia model, as we have seen, of narrative truth. But the narrator of *The Eustace Diamonds* draws on the heirloom model, in which the representation corresponds directly to unchanging truths. Against the marketplace, in which the value of aesthetic representations (like other commodities) is artificially inflated, the narrator insists upon an author's responsibility to portray life in real, unidealized form: "Go into the market, either to buy or sell, and name the thing you desire to part with or to get, as it is, and the market is closed against you. . . . No assurance short of A 1. betokens even a pretence to merit. . . . In those delineations of life and character which we call novels a similarly superlative vein is desired. Our own friends around us are not always merry and wise . . . but neither are our friends villains" (1:319). By contrast with such corrupted notions of literature, the narrator presents his model:

> The persons whom you cannot care for in a novel, because they are so bad, are the very same that you so dearly love in your life, because they are so good. To make them and ourselves somewhat better . . . is, we may presume, the object of all teachers, leaders, legislators, spiritual pastors, and masters. He who writes tales such as this, probably also has, very humbly, some such object distantly before him. . . . When such a picture is painted, as intending to show what a man should be, it is true. If painted to show what men are, it is false. The true picture of life as it is, if it could be adequately painted, would show men what they are, and how they might rise, not, indeed, to perfection, but one step first, and then another on the ladder. (1:320)

As Walter Kendrick observes, in order to realize this claim for "truth" or "realism," the narrator assumes the prior existence of an objectively knowable world; he also depends upon an uncomplicated theory of representation, by which reality is translated almost automatically into

---

Kendrick argues that "both the characters and the novelist's knowledge of them are complete before any writing is done" (27), and that "in Trollope's theory it is precisely the recognition of this difference"—between "the novel world" and "the real world"—"that the novelist's labor is intended to suppress" (50). With reference to Trollope's authorial intrusions, Kendrick writes, "It is a typical tactic of Trollope's fiction that when it obeys literary conventions, it does so blatantly, grudgingly. Literature is different from and only partially adequate to life, and literature itself announces its inferiority" (75).

language. Such assumptions paradoxically motivate the counter-realistic intrusions by the narrator into the telling of the story.

Trollope inscribes this heirloom model—of narrative truth that can be objectively cited—in certain rhetorical positions. One exemplary trope, a minute but pervasive instance, he appears superficially to share with Eliot: the aphorism. The novel's innumerable aphorisms arise as if to justify the characters' and plot's motivations. "The world, in judging of people who are false and bad and selfish and prosperous to outward appearances, is apt to be hard upon them, and to forget the punishments which generally accompany such faults. Lizzie Eustace was very false and bad and selfish" (1:191). Such aphoristic rhetoric makes the specific incidents of the plot seem merely illustrative of universal truths. The narrator consistently points to the world outside the novel to validate the assertions made within it, positing general claims that the plot at hand is then seen to corroborate ("A man captivated by wiles was only captivated for a time, whereas a man won by simplicity would be won for ever" [1:194]). Eliot ironizes her aphoristic, generalizing language to expose the force of opinion-making *as* a fiction, and privileges the particular case over the general rule. Trollope inverts the priority of individual instance over universal dictum, and while his assertion of absolutes ("in truth" [2:76], and so on) might suggest a fundamental break with the socially determined, market-driven nature of truth portrayed in the story (like Eliot's), Trollope's immutable truths nevertheless align rather neatly with the opinion of the general public.

Trollope relies on aphorism to establish the rectitude of the truths that flow from an extra-novelistic order. Unlike a Dickens or Collins, who holds plot secrets in reserve until the precise moment for dénouement, Trollope famously gives away nearly all suspense and intrigue with a toss of the narrative head: "He who recounts these details has scorned to have a secret between himself and his readers. The diamonds were at this moment locked up within Lizzie's desk" (2:78–79). Only by virtue of his confidence in the story's prior existence, apart from this verbal rendering, can the narrator afford such flippancy. When, for instance, Lucinda Roanoke appears, a question arises for both characters and readers about her identity: "There was some difficulty about her,— as to who she was." Immediately "the world" inside the novel adduces its conviction: "That she was an American was the received opinion." Two sentences later, the reader learns the objective truth, which simply goes to show how accurate the public's assessment is: "The received opinion was correct" (1:331). As this example indicates, the difference between a truth ascertained by consensus ("the received opinion . . .") and one introduced by the ultimate authority of the narrator (". . . was correct") may in fact amount to very little.

Just as the distinction between paraphernalia and heirlooms elsewhere proved, however useful, to be spurious, so it seems to be in this case too. Witness the exemplary breakdown between the two modes of truth-determination in this epigrammatic form: "Everybody said so, and it was so" (2:189). On the paraphernalia model, we can read "and" in this sentence as "therefore"; on the heirloom model, as "because." Ultimately, the difference matters very little, since the two come down to the same in any case. This collapse only demonstrates the efficacy of the ideology that subtends both paradigms: either truth-values lie beyond the social, and public opinion simply happens to affirm them in every case; or public opinion determines social truths, which are then enshrined in absolute principles. Either way, the status quo regenerates itself, shored up on one side with an evacuated set of values that cannot quite be referred to a higher power (religion, ethics, or the law), on the other with the fantasy of a coherent public that always reaffirms the values that were assumed from the outset.[25]

If in the register of narrative truth the distinction between the paraphernalia model and the heirloom model collapses, we are left with a question of why the novel does not simply lapse into self-contradiction. The answer lies with the irony that regulates the relationship between the two paradigms, tempering both the narrator's appeal to absolutes and the story's cynicism about the contingency of opinion.[26] The narrator assumes an amoral, urbane distance from the plot he relates, and this determinedly antisensational style can treat its racy material as little more than the humdrum machinations of an ambitious and self-

25. In an effort to challenge the view of Trollope as an uncomplicated conservative, John Kucich makes a persuasive case for the ability of "transgressive" dishonesty to shore up middle-class hegemony in the process of challenging it in Trollope's fiction; "Transgression in Trollope: Dishonesty and the Antibourgeois Elite," ELH 56, no. 3 (Fall 1989): 593–618. It remains a question, however, whether any transgression that serves bourgeois ideology so effectively is worthy of the name in the first place.

26. For a discussion of Trollope's narrative voice, and the relation between its irony and its believability, see Paul Lyons, "The Morality of Irony and Unreliable Narrative in Trollope's The Warden and Barchester Towers," South Atlantic Review 54, no. 1 (January 1989): 41–54; Lyons reviews the considerable critical literature on Trollopian irony.

interested social elite. Yet the insouciant attitude that the narrator adopts screens a certain moralism, as if the ironic voice of indifference itself were being ironized. This double irony manages to evade the impasse of moral agnosticism and yet, at the same time, to avoid committing the novel to either of the two positions—absolutism or consensus—raised as possible bases for judgment. Take, for example, one of the many invocations of the reader: "That Lizzie Eustace had stolen the diamonds, as a pickpocket steals a watch, was a fact as to which Mr. Camperdown had in his mind no shadow of a doubt. And, as the reader knows, he was right. She had stolen them" (1:252). The narrator's unshakable conviction about "the true story" ("Lizzie Eustace had stolen the diamonds") provides ironic leverage on the characters' partial knowledge. Yet the suave indifference that such aplomb enables nonetheless allows an appeal to the reader, with an assurance that we recognize and concur about the true moral corruption of Lizzie.[27]

Although its narrative posture—an ironic lack of interest in fundamental truths—helps the novel to reconcile the conflicting models of value it has presented, this irony, like Eliot's doubly valenced use of generalization, represents a tactic already within the domain of Victorian sexual unspeakability. Trollope corners the market on that mode of scandal discourse whereby, in an attempt to sidestep the charge of producing scandal, scandal narratives arrogate to themselves the indifference to truth that inheres in the very form of scandal. As we witnessed in reports of the Boulton and Park trial, a principal means of exonerating the publication of salacious stories is to adopt a voice of cultivated indifference to their salaciousness. In depicting not only the production of scandal but also its second-order representation—as gossip, newspaper story, object of police and judicial inquiry—Trollope's narrator can invoke scandalous plot elements all the while keeping above the level of prurience by assuming a stance of haughty disdain for the public's interest in such affairs.[28]

In raising indifference to an art form, Trollope produces the illusion

27. On the invocation of the reader, see Patricia A. Vernon, "Reading and Misreading in *The Eustace Diamonds*," *VIJ* 12 (1984): 1–8, and "The Poor Fictionist's Conscience: Point of View in the Palliser Novels," *Victorian Newsletter* 71 (Spring 1987): 16–20.

28. This is to amplify Spacks's comments on how novelists, "often reliant on morally dubious raw material, may wish to justify it in fictional or in ethical terms": "The reader (to say nothing of the writer) thus has it both ways, free to contemplate the kind of behavior one whispers about, while remaining superior to mere scandal" (*Gossip*, 204).

of an escape from sensationalism, even as this resistance itself demonstrates the persistent fascination for his readers of lurid material.[29] While Eliot condemns scandal's audience for its prurience and moralistic intolerance in The Mill on the Floss, suggesting the fine discrimination required of novel-readers as an antidote to the scandalized response, Trollope aligns the audience for scandal with the one for the novel, though he provides the latter a justification for its spectatorial pleasures with his narrator's voice of ironic distance. And while Eliot discredits an interest in sexual meanings by casting it as philistinism, Trollope's super-sophistication relegates sexual significations to the realm of the unspeakable by implying that they are so flagrantly conspicuous as not to require any further elaboration. The embarrassment one endures in rendering explicit the genital designation of the unmarried woman's jewel box, in Holmes's figure, or of Dora's reticule, arises in the face of just such a genteel disavowal: one need not register libidinous meanings, and therefore one should not do so. Drawing upon the interdependence of public opinion and absolute standards, this process presents as already-agreed-upon what no one has discussed, and thereby lends to sexuality its peculiar linguistic status.

The pose that narrators such as Trollope's strike ("of course . . . everybody knows . . . so why bother saying so?") allows them to have it both ways with sexual meanings, and it marks a paradigmatic moment in the discourse of sexuality. For we can finally understand that the mutually reinforcing oppositions, which apply not only to property but to narrative language as well, constitute a central means of defining sexuality as the unspeakable subject in nineteenth-century Britain. This strategy makes it possible to mean things without saying them, to play upon a readership's fascination while disavowing any appeal to base interests. Analogizing the Eustace diamonds to both female sexuality and literary property, Trollope's work demonstrates the reciprocal and inextricable relationship between the two principal arenas of linguistic ambiguity in Victorian culture—the sexual and the literary. That the author's ambitions should align with a trollop's simply reinforces the relationship. Trollope only minimally disguises this similitude—conceals it, that is to say, only about as well as a jewel box conceals female sexuality.

29. For a consideration of one of the possible consequences of this strategy—boredom—see D. A. Miller, "The Novel as Usual: Trollope's Barchester Towers," in The Novel and the Police, 107–45.

SIX

INDETERMINATE WILDE

In the light of contemporary literary and historical scholarship, it can hardly seem surprising that Oscar Wilde's work encodes homoerotic themes in multiple and deliberate ways. Recent criticism of Wilde has proven the density and pervasiveness of this coding, demonstrating how certain linguistic formations function to express, while nonetheless concealing, sexual meanings.[1] Such scholarship has been crucial in enabling readers to locate and recover the obscured sexual signification in Wilde's work. Yet the consequent celebration of Wilde as the foundational figure in a century-long struggle for freedom of sexual expression has come at a certain cost: it has become difficult to acknowledge Wilde's documented *resistance* to admitting the legibility of homosexual

---

1. This work includes: Neil Bartlett, *Who Was That Man? A Present for Mr. Oscar Wilde* (London: Serpent's Tail, 1988); Ed Cohen, "Writing Gone Wilde: Homoerotic Desire in the Closet of Representation," PMLA 102, no. 5 (October 1987): 801–13; Christopher Craft, *Another Kind of Love: Male Homosexual Desire in English Discourse, 1850–1920* (Berkeley: University of California Press, 1994), chap. 4; Jonathan Dollimore, *Sexual Dissidence: Augustine to Wilde, Freud to Foucault* (Oxford: Clarendon Press, 1991); Kevin R. Kopelson, *Love's Litany: The Writing of Modern Homoerotics* (Stanford: Stanford University Press, 1994), chap. 1; Eve Kosofsky Sedgwick, *Epistemology of the Closet* (Berkeley: University of California Press, 1990), chap. 3, and "Tales of the Avunculate: *The Importance of Being Earnest*," in *Tendencies* (Durham: Duke University Press, 1993), 52–72; Gary Schmidgall, *The Stranger Wilde: Interpreting Oscar* (New York: Dutton, 1994); Alan Sinfield, *The Wilde Century: Oscar Wilde, Effeminacy and the Queer Moment* (New York: Columbia University Press, 1994).

meanings in his work, or at any rate to do so without dismissing this resistance as mere defensiveness. Wilde's energetic denial of precisely the kinds of readings that latter-day gay-affirmative critics propose, however, needs to be taken seriously, not written off as self-delusion.

In Wilde's day, of course, outside of a small group of supporters (themselves often gay-identified), only prosecutors for the Crown were producing such interpretations. Yet Wilde's defense against such readings is not sufficiently explained even by his need to protect himself against vicious attacks. Since, by biographical accounts, Wilde was recklessly unconcerned to defend himself against charges of homosexuality—and ineffectual at doing so even when he finally attempted it—why would he disavow the sexual component of his writing?[2] Is there an explanation other than expediency or incompetence?

What has tended to get lost in the pursuit of sexual representations through Wilde's oeuvre is its contribution to that other category of the late nineteenth century, besides sexuality, whose meanings were regularly open to interpretation: literature. For while Wilde encoded sexual meanings in his work more assiduously and self-consciously than any of the other literary writers I have considered in this study, he simultaneously reimagined the status of literature itself in ways analogous to that of sexuality. The mutual and reciprocal relation between the two formations of unspeakability—the sexual and the literary—that we have seen developing in earlier works coalesces in Wilde's writing. Wilde's scandal represents the failure of this reciprocity, signaling the decline of the historical moment in which literature could strategically encipher sexuality, and in which expressions of sexuality could take refuge under the banner of literature. In short, Wilde's career forms the horizon for a specifically literary practice of rendering sex unspeakable. Understood in this light, Wilde's case serves not as the point of origin for contemporary battles over sexual liberation, but as the culmination of both Victorian scandal and the literary project that I have been tracing through this book.

This chapter's argument begins by locating Wilde's formulation of the literary in his metacritical essays on aesthetics. In Wilde's theory, literature is inextricable from, and valued no more highly than, criticism, on

---

2. See, for instance, Richard Ellmann, *Oscar Wilde* (New York: Alfred A. Knopf, 1988), chaps. 17–18; Bartlett, *Who Was That Man?* chap. 5; and Schmidgall, *Stranger Wilde*, chap. 12 ("Why He Stayed").

which it converges in a conception of indeterminate, interpretable writing. Wilde's novella *The Portrait of Mr. W. H.* dramatizes these aesthetic principles, serving simultaneously as literature and as literary criticism. The indeterminacy that allows the story to function doubly enables its canny representation of sexuality as well; the novella undertakes literary and erotic signification at the same time, allowing each to hide itself behind a veil of the other's ambiguity. The balance struck in Wilde's work between the literary and the sexual was eventually upset by the eruption of scandal: in the trials, the Crown insisted on deciphering the connotativeness that Wilde argued was formative of literature. At the end of this chapter, I take up the question of what other outcome, besides the Wildean one, was possible for the sexual unspeakability of Victorian literary production. Turning to Henry James, I consider the splitting apart of the literary and the sexual as an alternative to their disastrous convergence in Wilde.

Wilde lays out his conception of literary art in a series of essays on aesthetics that culminate in a paradoxical reversal of Matthew Arnold's dictum from "The Function of Criticism at the Present Time": in Wilde's scheme, "the primary aim of the critic is to see the object as in itself it really is not."[3] Chief among Wilde's claims about literature, and the one that has become paramount in twentieth-century ideas of the literary, is its susceptibility to interpretation. In these essays, Wilde seeks to prove the superiority of art to nature and of criticism to art, demonstrating that art is constituted by interpretation. In "The Decay of Lying" (1889), for instance, Wilde argues for the value to artists of celebrating artificiality and lying, as against the vulgar imitation of nature ordained by realism. In "The Critic as Artist" (1890), moreover, the supremely creative individual turns out to be not the artist but the critic, since the latter bears no responsibility for achieving a resemblance between representation and the material world:

> The critic occupies the same relation to the work of art that he criticises as the artist does to the visible world of form and colour, or the unseen world of passion and of thought. He does not even require for the perfection of his art the finest materials. . . . I would say that the highest Criticism, being the purest form of personal impression, is in its way more creative than creation, as it

3. Oscar Wilde, "The Critic as Artist," in *The Complete Works* (New York: Harper & Row, 1989), 1030; further references to Wilde's essays on aesthetics will be made parenthetically to this edition.

has least reference to any standard external to itself, and is, in fact, its own reason for existing. . . . Certainly, it is never trammelled by any shackles of verisimilitude. No ignoble considerations of probability, that cowardly concession to the tedious repetitions of domestic or public life, affect it ever. (1027)

The modern artist's imperative is to turn from art to the more fertile, more "independent" (1026) field of criticism, which allows an even fuller realization of individual subjectivity than does artistic creation. Wilde elevates the responsive element in criticism, as against art's mere productivity, insisting that art is valuable only in its interaction with the one who perceives it, understands it, and uses it as the basis for a new creation—that is, the critic.

> To the critic the work of art is simply a suggestion for a new work of his own, that need not necessarily bear any obvious resemblance to the thing it criticises. The one characteristic of a beautiful form is that one can put into it whatever one wishes, and see in it whatever one chooses to see; and the Beauty, that gives to creation its universal and aesthetic element, makes the critic creator in his turn, and whispers of a thousand different things which were not present in the mind of him who carved the statue or painted the panel or graved the gem. (1030)

Once criticism is "more creative than creation," the traditional hierarchy between art and criticism is inverted, and interpretation takes precedence over productivity. The critic's task is to render meaning from the inert work of art, and although that meaning derives partly from the object, it has far more to do with the subjective impression of the one who responds. Paraphrasing Walter Pater, Wilde writes: "The aesthetic critic rejects . . . obvious modes of art that have but one message to deliver, and having delivered it become dumb and sterile, and seeks rather for such modes as suggest reverie and mood, and by their imaginative beauty make all interpretations true, and no interpretation final" (1031). Critics subjectively derive meaning from works of art, so the best works are those that are most indeterminate.

This aesthetic program results both in criticism "more creative than creation" and in literary works that incorporate guides to their own interpretation, and thereby function as art that is itself critical. "The Critic as Artist" initiates the former of these efforts, for Wilde enacts in it his claims for creative criticism.[4] In his story-cum-essay on the interpretation of Shakespeare's sonnets, *The Portrait of Mr. W. H.* (1889/1893), Wilde produces a text as truly critical as it is creative. The accomplishment of this work is partly a result of its reflexive treatment of a literary object, rather than (like the aestheticism essays) of art in general. Shakespeare's sonnets make a particularly apt focus for Wilde's aesthetic experiment, both because of the aura of interpretive mystery that surrounds them and because they (along with the narrative poems) represent the work of Shakespeare's that can be considered unequivocally as writing rather than as the citation for words spoken on stage, subject to the vagaries of performance.[5]

The Portrait of Mr. W. H. appears to fulfill the mandate of "The Critic as Artist": it functions as criticism, in that its interpretation of an artistic object serves as the basis for realizing the critic's own personality, and, at the same time, as creation, in that it foregrounds its own production of ambiguous meanings, and is therefore itself subject to interpretation. In its critical mode, *The Portrait of Mr. W. H.* contains a theory that suggests a positive identity for the young man to whom at least the first 126 of Shakespeare's sonnets (in the canonical arrangement) are addressed.

4. The essay is structured as a dialogue between two speakers who are, though barely realized as characters, distinguishable; in a comically self-conscious passage, Wilde has his spokesman, Gilbert, expostulate on the virtues of dialogue as a genre: "Dialogue, certainly, that wonderful literary form which . . . the creative critics of the world have always employed, can never lose for the thinker its attraction as a mode of expression. By its means he can both reveal and conceal himself, and give form to every fancy, and reality to every mood. By its means he can exhibit the object from each point of view, and show it to us in the round." Gilbert's somewhat dull (but eventually converted) interlocutor, Ernest, replies: "By its means, too, he can invent an imaginary antagonist, and convert him when he chooses by some absurdly sophistical argument" (1046). Through passages such as this one, and others of luxuriantly ornate, recognizably aesthetic prose, Wilde strives to fashion a metacritical piece nearly as creative—that is, as prone to interpretation—as his works of literary art.

5. The epigraph from Gertrude Stein to Joel Fineman's study *Shakespeare's Perjured Eye: The Invention of Poetic Subjectivity in the Sonnets* (Berkeley: University of California Press, 1986) suggests the uniquely written character of Shakespeare's poetry: "That is the difference between Shakespeare's plays and Shakespeare's sonnets. Shakespeare's plays were written as they were written. Shakespeare's sonnets were written as they were going to be written." This principle suggests one reason for limiting my argument to Wilde's non-dramatic work. My discussion of *The Portrait of Mr. W. H.* is indebted to Fineman's book, both for its general argument about the literary substance of the sonnets and for its comments on Wilde (28).

Based on an imputed narrative of the poems, the theory proposes that Mr. W. H., mysteriously indicated in the printer's famous epigraph to the sonnets ("To the onlie begetter of these insuing sonnets Mr. W. H. . . ."), was a lovely boy-actor in Shakespeare's company to whom the poet was deeply devoted. "Working purely by internal evidence" (143),[6] the theory discovers the actual name of this boy—Willie Hughes—embedded in the sonnets' puns (many of which are sexual) on the words "Will" and "Hews."

The story does not present this theory solely as literary criticism; in what we might designate its creative mode, it embeds the theory in a nested series of narratives, where it is exchanged through successive pairs of desiring men. The tale's narrator recounts his acquaintance with an older friend, Erskine, who, in turn, relates the story of his own youthful friendship with another beautiful boy-actor, Cyril Graham. This boy originally developed the interpretation of the sonnets, but was unable to persuade Erskine of his theory until he presented him with a painting of Mr. W. H., clearly identified as the young man of the sonnets. Although initially convinced, Erskine soon discovers the portrait to be a forgery, and upon revelation of this fraud, Graham shoots himself. While Erskine still remains unconvinced, the narrator himself is enticed by the hypothesis; when he presents his own evidence to Erskine, the narrator manages at last to convince the older man, only to find that, in so doing, he has lost his own faith in the theory. Two years later, he receives a note from Erskine, in which the latter announces his intention to kill himself out of devotion to the theory. The narrator rushes to his side, only to learn from Erskine's mother that he is already dead—not, however, by his own hand, but instead from consumption, which he knew would kill him when he sent the false suicide note.

The defining and permanent indeterminacy that, according to Wilde's theory, enables the fusion of criticism and literature also links this whole aesthetic enterprise with the other topic designated by its availability to interpretation, sexuality. Such indeterminacy is the hallmark of the unspeakability that generates the propitious homology between literary writing and the discourse of sexuality in the later nineteenth century. This conjunction is productive for both, raising up eroticism to an aesthetic principle even in the course of camouflaging it, also raising up art

6. Unless otherwise noted, parenthetical references are to the 1889 version in Wilde's *Complete Shorter Fiction*, ed. Isobel Murray (London: Oxford University Press, 1979), 139–69.

by lending it an erotic charge—although always thereby risking that art will be debased (or made inconsequential) by being sexualized.

The Portrait of Mr. W. H. suggests that criticism concerns itself with finding a solution to the artistic object before it, as if it were a puzzle or a riddle, and that, in the case of Shakespeare's sonnets, the solution is a proper name. But this puzzle-solving does not represent the whole of the critical enterprise, and in this sense the novella answers to another of the interpretive principles set forth in "The Critic as Artist":

> The critic will certainly be an interpreter, but he will not treat Art as a riddling Sphinx, whose shallow secret may be guessed and revealed by one whose feet are wounded and who knows not his name. Rather, he will look upon Art as a goddess whose mystery it is his province to intensify, and whose majesty his privilege to make more marvellous in the eyes of men. . . . He will not be an interpreter in the sense of one who simply repeats in another form a message that has been put into his lips to say. . . . It is only by intensifying his own personality that the critic can interpret the personality and work of others, and the more strongly this personality enters into the interpretation, the more real the interpretation becomes, the more satisfying, the more convincing, and the more true. (1033)

The Portrait of Mr. W. H. draws on aesthetic theory not as a masquerade for some prior sexual program, as though sex were the critic's answer to the riddle posed by the Sphinx-like artistic object; instead, the work *discovers* the sexual potential within its conception of the literary at the same time that it identifies the literary dimension of sexuality.[7]

---

7. Even in the passage just quoted, the term *personality* has a sexual charge, as it does elsewhere in Wilde's oeuvre. In *The Picture of Dorian Gray,* Basil expresses the passion he felt when he first noticed Dorian in these terms: "When our eyes met, I felt that I was growing pale. A curious sensation of terror came over me. I knew that I had come face to face with some one whose mere personality was so fascinating that, if I allowed it to do so, it would absorb my whole nature, my whole soul, my very art itself" (in *Complete Works,* 21). Wilde was cross-examined in court about a similar passage expunged from the novel:

> "Do you mean to say that that passage describes the natural feeling of one man towards another?"
> "It would be the influence produced by a beautiful personality."
> "A beautiful person?"
> "I said 'a beautiful personality.' You can describe it as you like. Dorian Gray's was a most remarkable personality."

An analysis of Shakespeare's sonnets that focuses on encrypted proper names is, first of all, a project encouraged by the poems themselves: "Every word doth almost tell my name, / Showing their birth, and where they did proceed" (Sonnet 76). Such an interpretation understands its object to be a puzzle, a surface on which coded information is inscribed; the information is visible to the knowing reader, yet hidden from the untrained eye. The story's narrator enunciates just this method of reading as he gazes on the portrait of Willie Hughes for the first time: "I see there is some writing there, but I cannot make it out" (140). If the disguised referent of the sonnets is itself a proper name, then the poems are cast in a register different from the usual account of them as universalizable love poetry. In Wilde's reading, the sonnets attain their literary quality precisely because they encipher hidden meanings in the materiality of their writing.

The realm of proper names induces the belief that the ambiguity of ordinary language has been transcended: meaning seems anchored to identity when, for instance, "Will" can speak his own name (as in Sonnets 135 and 136). A unique human identity and its concomitant proper name appear mutually constitutive. Yet as deconstructive theory — no less than Wilde himself, most pointedly in *The Importance of Being Earnest* — suggests, the difference between common words and proper names is only illusory. Naming epitomizes the basic contradiction of language, the impossible striving after a univocal correspondence between signifier and signified. As the exemplary case of language's indexical capacity, the name can thus be understood as a false word that tells the truth about the falseness — that is, the arbitrary, unmotivated character — of language in general. And if, at the level of the signifier, language is deracinated and ambiguous, when it assumes literary proportions so much the more is it subject to various, unfixable interpretations.[8]

Quoted in H. Montgomery Hyde, *The Trials of Oscar Wilde* (New York: Dover, 1962), 112. Unless otherwise noted, further references to the trials will be made parenthetically to this edition.

8. I rely here on Fineman, *Shakespeare's Perjured Eye*, and "The Significance of Literature: *The Importance of Being Earnest*," *October* 15 (Winter 1980): 79–90. In the latter essay, Fineman writes that Ernest

> inherits his name only to the extent that its significance is restricted or promoted to its nominality, only to the extent, that is to say, that it becomes a signifier of itself *as* a signifier, not a signified. This is indeed a paradigm of literary language, of language that calls attention to itself as language. . . . Wilde's play or farce on names is

In *The Portrait of Mr. W. H.*, the name that serves as the keystone of the interpretation is encoded in specifically graphemic form: it is a written unit, abbreviated—as a name is only when written—by its initial letters. Initials are important in this text not only in what they stand for but in the *way in which* they signify: they are the truncated, synecdochical form of the material signification of a proper name. Hence the forged portrait of the story's title is the "perfect representation" not of some referential reality but of the name figured in the sonnets. Like the name hidden in the poems, moreover, the forgery itself must be extracted from its unlikely location. Erskine recounts the story to the narrator:

> "[Cyril] told me that he had discovered [the picture] by the merest chance nailed to the side of an old chest that he had bought at a farmhouse in Warwickshire. . . . In the centre of the front panel the initials W. H. were undoubtedly carved. It was this monogram that had attracted his attention. . . . Here was an authentic portrait of Mr. W. H., with his hand resting on the dedicatory page of the Sonnets, and on the frame itself could be faintly seen the name of the young man written in black uncial letters on a faded gold ground, 'Master Will. Hews.' " (149–50)

In the same way that the initials of the sonnets' epigraph lead Cyril Graham to discover the name in the poems, the initials "attract his attention" to the chest in which he supposedly discovers the portrait. Cyril is a consistent reader: he moves from obscuring exteriors to revealing initials and finally to discovering written names. Just as the secret to the interpretation lies hidden in "the frame itself" of the painting, so in Wilde's story does the frame narrative contain the key to its contents—though Wilde's critical enterprise always effaces the difference between the frame and what seems to lie within it.

The forgery is a visual representation not only of the sonnets' subject, but also of the cryptographic hermeneutic by which the theory discovers that subject. Yet if the forgery represents the theory in visual form, it is only *as* a counterfeit—not as a representation of the real—

---

itself so important, for we may say that the special propriety of a proper name with respect to common nouns corresponds precisely to the specialized charge of literature with respect to so-called ordinary language—"so-called" because there could no more be an ordinary language without its fictive complement than there could be a natural language bereft of its fantasy of the propriety of proper names. (83)

that it induces belief. In Wilde's larger aesthetic project, the forgery is a form of art higher than the vulgar imitation of reality, and it is therefore kindred to criticism: neither is "trammelled by any shackles of verisimilitude." In "The Decay of Lying," for instance, Wilde writes of the liar: "Nor will he be welcomed by society alone. Art, breaking from the prison-house of realism, will run to greet him, and will kiss his false, beautiful lips, knowing that he alone is in possession of the great secret of all her manifestations, the secret that Truth is entirely and absolutely a matter of style" (981). Similarly, in "The Truth of Masks" (1885), he claims: "Of course the aesthetic value of Shakespeare's plays does not, in the slightest degree, depend on their facts, but on their Truth, and Truth is independent of facts always, inventing or selecting them at pleasure" (1071). The forgery is as true as the name it represents, not only in lending it pictorial form, but in recapitulating the structure of the proper name. It is more self-consciously simulated—and therefore, in Wilde's scheme, closer to the ideals of art—than any genuine portrait could be.

In claiming to discover its theory of the sonnets in the poems themselves, The Portrait of Mr. W. H. demonstrates how the artistic object itself can be critical-interpretive. "This was Cyril Graham's theory, evolved as you see purely from the Sonnets themselves, and depending for its acceptance not so much on demonstrable proof or formal evidence, but on a kind of spiritual and artistic sense, by which alone he claimed could the true meaning of the poems be discerned" (147). Regardless of its own status as forged, the portrait represents the theory's validity; it is a tool for overcoming skepticism, as Cyril explains to Erskine: "I did it purely for your sake. You would not be convinced in any other way. It does not affect the truth of the theory" (151). As a means of showing literature to contain criticism, Cyril regularly develops his theory by literalizing images from the sonnets: the character Willie Hughes bodies forth Shakespeare's puns, just as the portrait itself is already figured across the sonnets.[9] Cyril's coffered forgery simply dramatizes in fiction Shakespeare's repeated image of his friend as an "up-locked treasure" in a "chest" (Sonnet 52): "Thee have I not lock'd up in any chest / Save where thou art not" (Sonnet 48).

If in this sense the literary object itself discloses the means of its own interpretation, when we turn to the surrounding narrative, we can wit-

9. The young man in Shakespeare's poems is described throughout in terms of painting: "Mine eye hath play'd the painter and hath stell'd / Thy beauty's form in table of my heart" (Sonnet 24); "my love's picture . . . the painted banquet" (Sonnet 47); "I never saw that you did painting need, / And therefore to your fair no painting set" (Sonnet 83).

ness the collapse between creative and critical work from the other side of the provisional divide. Like the theory, the frame narrative everywhere exhibits an attention to the graphic value of names. Proceeding by Wilde's own logic, we can apply to the object of interpretation the hermeneutic model that inheres within it. "His very name fascinated me. Willie Hughes! Willie Hughes! How musically it sounded! Yes; who else but he could have been the master-mistress of Shakespeare's passion . . . ?" (159). As the significantly unnamed narrator makes this gleeful exclamation, he entices us to attend to the names Wilde chooses for his own characters—particularly those, like the ones in this story, that he uses over again in different works, as if both to emphasize and to exhaust their suggestive possibilities. Secreted within themselves, these names yield the very strategies with which to decode them.

At the center of the story is Cyril Graham, instigator of the Willie Hughes theory and a near reproduction of Willie himself. Both young men are "of quite extraordinary personal beauty, though evidently somewhat effeminate" (140). Like Shakespeare's presumed catamite, Cyril is "very languid in his manner, and not a little vain of his good looks. . . . He was always dressing up and reciting Shakespeare" (142). Also like Willie, Cyril's name is overdetermined; not only does it signify multivalently, however, it signifies multivalence itself, doing so precisely in the register of the written letter. Cyril invokes Saint Cyril, originator of the eponymous alphabet, which, to the reader of English, is an unintelligible form of writing. Appropriately, the coded alphabet's namesake is the character capable of deciphering the alphabetically reduced inscription. Bearing in mind the alphabetic allusion, we can rearrange the letters c y r i l to produce lyric, which in its anagrammatic form comes to stand for the sonnet folded in on itself: encrypted in the decrypter's name is the object of interpretation.

To supplement the suggestion of foreign alphabetics and topsy-turvy poetry inherent in Cyril's first name is his surname, Graham—which we might understand as gram, the supplement itself. The Oxford English Dictionary defines a -gram as "something written, letter (of the alphabet)." The -gram is not a meaningful word by itself, but only a suffix, a subatomic linguistic unit that signifies the atomic unit of material signification: it gains value only when conjoined with other morphemes (diagram, anagram). In this literal reading of a name, we locate the order of written language, and it is from this figure of language in language that the story produces its literary reading of the sonnets.

Insofar as The Portrait of Mr. W. H. functions as literary criticism, it proceeds according to a determinable hermeneutic practice to which I want to lend the name "Cyril Graham." Cyril Graham denominates the operations of written language, originating the Willie Hughes theory: a Cyril Graham reading attends to the sonnets' literal signification, producing the name of the object of desire out of the printed matter of the poems. Insofar as Mr. W. H. functions as literature, though, it embodies and enacts this critical practice in the narrated story that constitutes the frame. While within Cyril's theory the hidden name "Willie Hughes" is manifested in a character, in Wilde's frame narrative a Cyril Graham reading—bound up as it is in the decoding of written text—is amplified and announced in the thematization of writing itself.

The novella is suffused with letters, signatures, and literature. It begins and ends in a library, as if to bind the narrative between the covers of a book, and from the opening—"when the question of literary forgeries happened to turn up in conversation" (139)—the written word is at issue. In the portrait there is "crabbed sixteenth-century handwriting" that can be detected only with a magnifying glass (141), and writing on its frame that is visible only once it is cleaned (150); there are two suicide notes as well as Cyril's initial invitation to Erskine to learn of the theory, by which the latter "was rather surprised at his taking the trouble to write" (143). Writing in the novella comes to seem like the displaced performance of its interpretive model, as if the story were compelled to keep secret its method of deciphering secrets by broadcasting that method everywhere in the image of writing.

The sonnet theory is committed to writing each time it is reinvented, until it takes the tangible form of a letter—though a letter that is by definition unrecoverable:

> I have not any copy of my letter, I regret to say, nor have I been able to lay my hand upon the original; but I remember that I went over the whole ground, and covered sheets of paper with passionate reiteration of the arguments and proofs that my study had suggested to me. . . . I put into the letter all my faith. (164)

To put the theory into a letter is not simply to transcribe it: more than its literal epistolary location, the Willie Hughes theory has the material qualities of a letter, in that only one person at a time can possess (that is, believe) it. It can be passed from one person to another, but it cannot be shared or divided.

The theory's circuit through the story illustrates its indissoluble unity as epistolary object. In the first exchange, when Erskine begins to convince the narrator, he states, "As I don't believe in the theory, I am not likely to convert you to it" (141). The next exchange takes place twenty years prior, when Erskine is the recent convert; having discovered Cyril's forgery, he exclaims, "You never even believed in [the theory] yourself. If you had, you would not have committed a forgery to prove it" (151). In the third exchange, as the narrator returns the theory to Erskine toward the end of the story, he confesses: "No sooner, in fact, had I sent [the letter] off than a curious reaction came over me. It seemed to me that I had given away my capacity for belief in the Willie Hughes theory of the Sonnets, that something had gone out of me, as it were, and that I was perfectly indifferent to the whole subject" (165). The theory's determining characteristic is that to convince someone else of it is no longer to believe in it oneself. Belief "goes out of one" only to lodge itself in the recipient.

The story's most explicit letters, however—the suicide notes—curiously subvert its insistence on writing as the solution to interpretive puzzles. Cyril kills himself after the forgery is discovered, leaving behind a note for Erskine that claims "he was going to offer his life as a sacrifice to the secret of the Sonnets" (152). The suicide note is a form of absolute writing, because it is unidirectional and unanswerable. Yet the note is peculiarly ineffective, for in this story a man's suicide testifies to the insincerity of his belief: Erskine responds to the death by saying, "a thing is not necessarily true because a man dies for it" (152), and after Erskine's death the narrator comments, "No man dies for what he knows to be true. Men die for what they want to be true, for what some terror in their hearts tells them is not true." [10] Like criticism in

---

10. From the 1893 version of the story, The Portrait of Mr. W. H., ed. Vyvyan Holland (London: Methuen, 1958), 89. Wilde expresses the same sentiment in numerous places; a letter to Harry Marillier from 1886, for instance, suggests a relation between unspeakable desire and the sacrifice of one's life for that which is not believed:

You too have the love of things impossible . . . l'amour de l'impossible (how do men name it?). Sometime you will find, even as I have found, that there is no such thing as a romantic experience; there are romantic memories, and there is the desire of romance—that is all. Our most fiery moments of ecstasy are merely shadows of what somewhere else we have felt, or of what we long some day to feel. . . . I myself would sacrifice everything for a new experience, and I know there is no such thing as a new experience at all. I think I would more readily die for what I do not believe in than for what I hold to be true. I would go to the stake for a sensation and be a sceptic to the last! Only one thing remains infinitely fascinating to me, the mystery of moods. To be master of these moods is exquisite, to be mastered

general, as Wilde argues in the essays on aesthetics, the sonnet theory is unhindered by its empirical unverifiability, and the deaths of its proponents only go to prove its beauty, not its truth. Cyril's suicide fails in a more important way, too, as the performance of his death covers over the very name that he had hoped to sustain by killing himself: "He shot himself with a revolver. Some of the blood splashed upon the frame of the picture, just where the name [Willie Hughes] had been painted" (151–52). Although the story's ubiquitous images of writing dramatize in literature the procedures of interpretation, the interpreter's ultimate act of writing traduces his interpretation by figuratively covering with blood the name it has worked to decipher.

If Cyril's interpretive methods finally undo themselves, how are we to account for Erskine's suicide note, at once a rehearsal and inversion of Cyril's? Cyril's tool for countering disbelief is the portrait, which, by virtue of being forged, truthfully represents the constitutive falseness of the name written into the poems. Erskine makes the same effort with his letter, which, as the narrator learns, is a counterfeit, since he had known for months before he sent it that he was to die. But while the false picture tells the truth about the ways in which language is arbitrary and metaphorical—and therefore endlessly open to interpretation—the false letter entails several logical contradictions. Were it a genuine suicide note, it would, like Cyril's, indicate its author's doubt, rather than his faith, in the theory; but as an *insincere* claim to sacrifice his life for the theory, Erskine's letter is paradoxically effective. At the same time, insofar as it relies on the temporal and spatial displacements of writing in order to falsify (and thereby make persuasive) its case for an interpretation of the sonnets based on their written matter, Erskine's note—by contrast with Cyril's forged portrait—must lie with regard to the truth it tells about writing's falseness. Working in both cases like the liar's paradox, which motivates much of Wilde's characteristic wit (most notably the puns on "earnest" in his farce), Erskine's false letter goes Cyril one better, both in literalizing (making written) his forgery and in falsifying his suicide note.

The complications raised by Erskine's suicide note suggest that another

---

by them more exquisite still. Sometimes I think that the artistic life is a long and lovely suicide, and am not sorry that it is so.

The Letters of Oscar Wilde, ed. Rupert Hart-Davis (New York: Harcourt, Brace, 1962), 185; further references to this edition will be made parenthetically.

mode of interpretation is at work in the story, besides the graphemically based one associated with Cyril Graham. For in the process of staking out a terrain for literature that is codified and enigmatic, Wilde simultaneously proposes that certain sexual secrets provide a key to the interpretive puzzle just as plausibly as do the literary ones. I want to mark this shift in hermeneutic strategy, from deciphering written language to discovering homoerotic desire, by nominally designating the latter an "Erskine" reading, which is distinct from Cyril Graham's and linked in certain ways to Wilde himself. When he comes to narrate the theory, Erskine occupies the position of the sonneteer, adorer of his "very fascinating, and very foolish, and very heartless" friend (140); he might thereby stand in for the poets, Will and Oscar, themselves admirers of lovely boy-actors. By name he is kin of the Ers, which the OED defines as follows: "In 18th c., Erse was used in literary England as the ordinary designation of the Gaelic of Scotland, and occasionally extended to the Irish Gaelic; at present [1893] some writers apply it to the Irish alone. Now nearly obsolete." If Erse was nearly obsolete by this point, its homophone, arse, was out of fashion only in "polite use," according to the OED. And who more than Wilde is kin of the Erse and of the arse? As Terry Eagleton, among others, has suggested, the perversity of Wilde's Irishness in England was indissoluble from his heterodox sexual practice. In the play Saint Oscar, Eagleton's Wilde states, "I'm a racial hybrid; I might as well be a sexual one too." [11] The Portrait of Mr. W. H., the work that announces the arrival of Wilde's homosexuality according to many critics, [12] is the pivot between the public perception of him as a trouble-

---

11. Terry Eagleton, Saint Oscar (Derry: Field Day, 1989), 12. Eagleton links Wilde's politics in different realms—nation, class, sexuality, and gender—to his "proto-deconstructionist" (viii) linguistic practice and to his construction of his own identity as entirely performative. The English, he says, "can't tell whether it's praise or parody. I subvert their forms by obeying them so faithfully" (25). Commenting on his work, Eagleton states in the foreword to the play, "It seems to me vital to put that particular [sexual] ambiguity or doubleness back in the context of a much wider span of ambivalences. Wilde was perverse in much more than a sexual sense, and his sexual, social and artistic perversities are deeply interrelated" (xi). See also Neil Sammells, "Oscar Wilde: Quite Another Thing," in Paul Hyland and Sammells, ed., Irish Writing: Exile and Subversion (New York: St. Martin's, 1991), 116–25.

12. Rupert Croft-Cooke writes in The Unrecorded Life of Oscar Wilde (New York: David McKay, 1972) that Wilde's "comparatively discreet manner of existence during the years following his marriage [in 1884] was disturbed by a number of factors in 1889 and 1890, including [his] wilful and deliberate rashness in publishing a short story of homosexual

some Irish nationalist [13] and the image of him as a scandalous pederast. The peculiar conjunction of Irish and homosexual discourses produces a poetics that the work calls "Erskine"—a name as well for what Wilde represented to the English public.

The affinity between Wilde and Erskine becomes clearer if we consider the national and personal account he gave of language itself. In a letter to Edmond de Goncourt dated December 17, 1891, Wilde apologizes for having previously been misunderstood in French, for he is quick to admit "sans doute c'était de ma faute": "On peut adorer une langue sans bien la parler, comme on peut aimer une femme sans la connaître. Français de sympathie, je suis Irlandais de race, et les Anglais m'ont condamné à parler le langage de Shakespeare" (Letters, 304). It is, appropriately, only in a foreign tongue that Wilde can name the language he is condemned to speak: not English, bien sûr, but "the language of Shakespeare." He worships French without speaking it too well, just as he could love a woman without knowing her: this French heterosexual discourse (which he would go on to use in Salomé) is reserved for objects that are admired from afar, never really loved by intimate knowledge. The passage neatly condenses Wilde's association of the erotic and the literary, for it is ambiguous about whether his "condemnation" to speak the language of Shakespeare results from his literary profession or from his alienation with respect to English national and sexual mores. Shakespearean discourse takes on the value of Wilde's homoerotics, by contrast with the heterosexual terms in which he imagines French. When an Irishman speaks in this Shakespearean tongue—a lan-

---

interest called The Portrait of Mr. W. H. in Blackwood's Magazine" (111). Introducing the story, Isobel Murray writes: "At a time when homosexuality was considered one of the vilest human aberrations, severely punishable by law, to suggest that Shakespeare wrote his Sonnets to a boy actor whose personality dominated him was courting disaster. William Blackwood was either brave or a little out of touch when he wrote to Wilde accepting it" (Complete Shorter Fiction, 13). Likewise, in his introduction to The Portable Oscar Wilde, rev. ed. (New York: Penguin, 1981), Richard Aldington cites allusions to a work of Virgil's in Mr. W. H., "an exquisitely beautiful poem but flagrantly homosexual. To anyone who had read Virgil—and at that time most upper-class Englishmen had—The Portrait of Mr. W. H. was an unequivocal declaration and an insolent defiance. Prudent men began to drop Mr. Wilde's acquaintance" (23).

13. See, for instance, the Scots Observer review that compares Dorian Gray to a fine performance of an offensive song—namely, "God Save Ireland"; Oscar Wilde: Art and Morality, A Record of the Discussion which Followed the Publication of "Dorian Gray," ed. Stuart Mason [Christopher Millard], rev. ed. (London: Frank Palmer, 1912), 90–94.

guage different from the one that he adores like a woman—it has the sound of Erskine's voice.

The Portrait of Mr. W. H. both encrypts and strives to excavate homoerotic meanings, in much the same way that coded writing was both thematized and developed as a hermeneutic practice around Cyril Graham. Just as Cyril extracts the hidden painting from a chest in order to verify his theory, Erskine seeks "to unlock the secret of Shakespeare's heart," to provide "the only perfect key to Shakespeare's Sonnets that has ever been made" (152). The secret associated with Erskine is indignantly described by biographer Rupert Croft-Cooke:

> [The story] would have passed . . . if it had been put forward as a serious and rather boring literary theory, but to make a delightful spree of Shakespeare's homosexuality was unforgivable in the 1880s. It might fool the editor of Blackwood's who saw in it nothing but quaint antiquarian theorising, but it could not fool more knowing readers, who considered that Wilde was suggesting England's greatest poet was a bugger, and doing so by introducing as narrator "one of the pretty undergraduates who used to act girls' parts." [14]

Homoeroticism does pervade the story, often appearing in relatively explicit ways. Shakespeare's sonnets are called "strangely passionate poems" (144), and Willie himself is evoked in "passionate" language: "so well had Shakespeare drawn him, with his golden hair, his tender flower-like grace, his dreamy deep-sunken eyes, his delicate mobile limbs, and his white lily hands" (159). Erskine's initial gesture toward the narrator indicates a more-than-avuncular affection: "Erskine, who was a good deal older than I was, and had been listening to me with the amused deference of a man of forty, suddenly put his hand upon my shoulder" (139). And Erskine depicts his earlier and deeper attachment to Cyril in erotic terms:

> I was a year or two older than he was, but we were immense friends, and did all our work and all our play together. There was, of course, a good deal more play than work, but I cannot say that I am sorry for that. . . . I was absurdly devoted to him. . . . He certainly was wonderfully handsome. . . . I think he was the most splendid creature I ever saw. (141–42)

14. Croft-Cooke, Unrecorded Life, 111–12.

Cyril clearly knows as much about himself: "He always set an absurdly high value on personal appearance, and once read a paper before our debating society to prove that it was better to be good-looking than to be good" (142).

The sonnet theory itself emanates from erotically charged pairs of men. The originary couple, Willie and Shakespeare, comes to be replaced by Erskine and Cyril; the latter relationship is reproduced by the narrator and Erskine, though now Erskine is the disbelieving purveyor of the theory rather than its credulous recipient. Since belief in the theory has the qualities of material text, it is not only *about* desire (the theory supplies the name of the erotic object), but it takes on the asymptotic language of desire itself: "It seemed to me that I was always on the brink of absolute verification, but that I could never really attain to it" (163). As in Lacan's account of the purloined letter, possession of the text (belief in the theory) constitutes the subjectivity of its owner. Yet when we augment this analogy with the specific erotics of the story, we find that—unlike the oedipal triangle in which psychoanalysis situates production of the subject—Wilde's text (as well as Shakespeare's, read in this way) posits subjectivity in a homoerotic duality. In his July 1889 letter to Robert Ross, which discloses the origin of *The Portrait of Mr. W. H.*, Wilde situates himself in the genealogy of the story's poet/interpreters with respect to his protégé and sometime lover: "Indeed the story is half yours, and but for you would not have been written. . . . Now that Willie Hughes has been revealed to the world, we must have another secret" (*Letters*, 247).

I have suggested that the Erskine interpretation encodes Wilde's authorial persona, if only for the fact of a name. Continuing along the same line of reasoning, we might expect evidence of this alliance to locate itself seriously in Wilde's so-called signature effect, as carefully tended as the sounding of "Will" in the works of Shakespeare.[15] We have seen with Dickens and Trollope how naming functions as a quintessentially literary device that works in the same way as—and frequently serves to convey—sexual meanings. Wilde invokes his own name three times in the story: first at a moment of uneasiness about gender, again at a point

15. For evidence of Oscar's self-conscious use of "wild" elsewhere, see Karl Beckson, "The Autobiographical Signature in *The Picture of Dorian Gray*," *Victorian Newsletter* 69 (Spring 1986): 30–32. Beckson's insights resonate in a literal way with the comment in the *Punch* review of July 12, 1890, that *The Picture of Dorian Gray* is "Oscar Wilde's Wildest and Oscarest work" (Mason, *Oscar Wilde*, 159).

of imminent revelation, and finally in a passage suggesting both the one and the other. In the first instance, Cyril Graham is, "of course, wild to go on the stage" (143)—that is, to transform himself into a woman, as he does so well ("Cyril Graham was the only perfect Rosalind I have ever seen" [143]). The second occurs at the moment Cyril presents his theory: "He told me that he had at last discovered the true secret of Shakespeare's Sonnets . . . had found out who Mr. W. H. really was. He was perfectly wild with delight" (143–44). The last occasion returns us to the unanswered question of how to interpret Erskine's false suicide. In the story's penultimate scene, when the narrator learns of the "horribly grotesque tragedy" that Erskine has died, he admits:

> I said all kinds of wild things, and the people in the hall looked curiously at me.
>   Suddenly Lady Erskine, in deep mourning, passed across the vestibule. (168)

The narrator still believes Erskine to have committed suicide when the latter's mother materializes. Here, around the representation of the only woman in the story, a kind of hysterical ("wild") self-reference arises. As if to perform the anxiety surrounding the most glaring absence from the Willie Hughes theory of the sonnets—the dark lady—Lady Erskine appears in funereal black, seeming to necessitate the sounding of Oscar's own name.[16] The fact that the dark lady in Mr. W. H. is so marginal as to be almost unnoticeable is testimony to her very significance, as the story itself teaches us with the close attention it devotes to figures that lie hidden in frames. In Wilde's aesthetic lexicon, moreover, a "woman of no importance" is never entirely "trivial."

The Cyril Graham reading of this scene would easily make reference

16. If it is objected that Wilde's self-reference is altogether too marginal to be of much significance, it need only be pointed out that this is precisely the complaint sounded by Shakespearean critics faced with the Willie Hughes theory (at least when it is based on "internal evidence" and not on historical data): "Why not 'Will Rose'?" some have replied, since *Rose* is capitalized and italicized in the sonnets as much as *Hews*. This reaction misses the point of Wilde's theory, which is compelling to the extent that its interpretation deciphers the name by reinscribing it in its own literary form. That Wilde's theory operates at the level of the letter should encourage us to read likewise. For a comprehensive account of proposals for the identity of Mr. W. H., see *The New Variorum Edition of Shakespeare: The Sonnets*, vol. 2, ed. Hyder Edward Rollins (Philadelphia: Lippincott, 1944), appendices, and, for a reincarnation of these debates, Donald Foster, "Master W. H., R.I.P.," PMLA 102, no. 1 (January 1987): 42–54.

to Shakespeare's play on words in Sonnet 132 about the dark lady in mo[u]rning. As with the depiction of Willie Hughes, it would understand the story to enact dramatically a pun that is purely graphic in the sonnets: the difference between "mourning" and "morning" is only a written letter, visually (not aurally) discernible. Its narrative representation takes the form of the figure across whose body the Shakespearean pun is executed. The Erskine reading, on the other hand, might discover an analogy between the undesirability of Shakespeare's dark lady—the paradoxically unattractive object of desire—and the unattainable dark mother as object of the dead son's desire. Insofar as she manifests the figure that forms the horizon for masculine desire in any version of psychoanalysis, we seem to have returned to an oedipal mythology, hard as this story tried to swerve from it.[17] Like Cyril's suicide, then, which upends his theory by spilling blood on the very name it discloses, Erskine's death disrupts his project of locating homoerotic desire in the text.

Before addressing the consequences of the story's doubly failed, and curiously self-sabotaging, account of literary and homoerotic interpretation, I want to reinforce the reading by turning for a moment to the pornographic novel *Teleny* (1890), whose composition has often been attributed in part to Wilde. Viewing *The Portrait of Mr. W. H.* through *Teleny* yields an overt rendition of the sexual aspect of this analysis, thanks to the fundamentally explicit nature of pornography. The narrative structures are strikingly similar: Des Grieux, the central character of *Teleny*, tells his story (like Erskine) to an unnamed narrator, relating his youthful relationship with a brilliant, beautiful young artist, Teleny, who (like Cyril) kills himself after a secret is revealed. The two men are much more nearly doubles ("I stared at myself within the looking-glass, and I saw Teleny in it instead of myself. . . . I could not feel him at all; in fact, it seemed to me as if I were touching my own body"),[18] their rela-

---

17. In the later version of the story, Wilde accounts for the dark lady sonnets by insisting that the sequence be rearranged so that the young man sonnets contain and are not superseded by them. The narrator proposes that Shakespeare initially feigns love for the dark lady only in order to draw her away from Willie Hughes, but "suddenly he finds that what his tongue had spoken his soul had listened to" (Holland ed., 63–64), and he is helplessly in love with her, despite her ugliness. Eventually he recovers, she departs, and the poet and actor are reunited. Ironically, then, what Mr. W. H. does as criticism—rewrite the plot of the sonnets to circumvent their usual heterosexual teleology—it undoes in its frame narrative, by reinscribing the oedipal drama with the appearance of Erskine's mother.
18. Oscar Wilde and Others, *Teleny*, ed. John McRae (London: GMP, 1986), 46, 110.

tionship is overtly sexual (to say the least), and the parallel between the narrator and the artist (Teleny) is clearly articulated ("I think I can see him leaning . . . as you are leaning now, for you have many of his feline, graceful ways"),[19] where the similarity between the narrator and Cyril Graham is only implied in Mr. W. H. The close association between the key to Shakespeare's art and homosexuality in Mr. W. H. is carried over to Teleny in the form of a clear correspondence between the sexual and the artistic: Teleny's brilliant pianism is always contingent upon the erotic link with Des Grieux. Teleny is especially revealing about the force of the mother in Mr. W. H. In the pornographic novel, Des Grieux's mother finally comes between the men, as she and Teleny carry on an affair behind Des Grieux's back. She is expressly an erotic force, and her sudden insinuation within the homosexual relationship serves the same purpose as the startling appearance of the dark lady in The Portrait of Mr. W. H.: she suggests the closing in of an oedipally driven heterosexuality, here made overtly sexual.

That Cyril's suicide should so definitively controvert his interpretation of the sonnets suggests the insufficiency of the literary solution — the name—to the sonnet puzzle. In reverting to a classically oedipal narrative that culminates in the appearance of the mother, rather than yielding a homoerotic object of desire, Erskine's forged suicide might by analogy indicate the failure of the story's gay interpretive project.[20] What are we to make of the collapse of both undertakings? In one sense, this failure might itself be understood to succeed: the demonstrable inadequacy of either interpretation on its own indicates a movement beyond what "The Critic as Artist" calls "these obvious modes of art that have but one message to deliver," and suggests the triumph of "imaginative

19. Teleny, 159.
20. The arrival of oedipal heterosexuality in the story's penultimate moment does not (especially in the minimal form it assumes in Mr. W. H.) cancel the affirmative homoeroticism that has, up until this point, impelled the narrative; but its insistent resurgence does need to be accounted for. In "Tales of the Avunculate," Sedgwick rightly points to the skewed emphases of critics who have focused excessively on the ending of The Importance of Being Earnest (where a recognizably oedipal/patriarchal machinery likewise asserts itself) at the expense of the richly evocative homoerotic material that precedes it; others wishing to locate the gay-positivity of Dorian Gray have similarly had to suspend examination of the conclusion. While the unresolved erotic muddle of the middle of these texts is not wholly canceled by their endings, the works themselves place significant formal emphasis on their closural moments (dramatic resolution and reconciliation in the farce, the pitch of gothic horror and exposure in the novel).

beauty [that makes] all interpretations true, and no interpretation final" (1031). To reveal a singular truth about the poems as if they were a riddle would itself be to gainsay the spirit of the piece, which promotes an enfolding of literature and criticism around a common indeterminacy. The triumph of either the Cyril Graham reading or the Erskine one would also therefore upset the balance between literary and sexual forms of ambiguity, which the story works so carefully to arrange.[21]

The ultimate resistance of Mr. W. H. to the homoeroticism of the Erskine reading must nonetheless remain a problem for readers who want to see Wilde as the foundation upon which modernist gay self-identification is built. The story's reluctance in this respect corresponds with the protohomophobic retractions in Wilde's work elsewhere: male characters who are, in recognizable ways, sexually unorthodox typically either pay for their proclivities with their lives (as in The Picture of Dorian Gray) or conform to a superficially normative heterosexuality (as in The Importance of Being Earnest)—though this, it need hardly be stated, is true in general of public writing before the 1970s. If Wilde is to be celebrated as the founder of a gay male literary canon, it is crucial not to overlook the finally pessimistic representation of evidently gay figures, and of sexual heterodoxy generally, in his work. Wilde's literary project of sexual suggestiveness is so self-conscious that the exuberance of its content may necessitate the punitive retractions of its closural moments: in knowing what he is doing, Wilde also recognizes that he ought not to be doing it, and he inscribes this recognition at the level of plot. Yet if we are tempted to see this resistance, like Wilde's recantation of homosexuality in court and in jail, as homophobic, we need to beware of letting anachronism distort our apprehension of his aims. Wilde's aversion to an unequivocal

21. The difference between the two interpretive projects also structures the textual history of Mr. W. H. After the story appeared in Blackwood's magazine in July 1889, Wilde continued to work on it, completing an expanded version in 1893. The longer edition elaborates and deepens the invented biography of Shakespeare, introduces a history of boy-actors, and adds an essay on Platonic friendship and the homoerotic poetry of Michelangelo, Montaigne, and others. The effect of the later version is to alter the balance between frame narrative and sonnet theory greatly in favor of the latter. The only significant deletion in the 1893 edition is the compressed image of Cyril's blood spilling onto the name etched in the portrait's frame. If we recall that, between 1889 and 1893, Wilde's erotic preferences seem to have altered significantly as well, we might then suggest that the first version—with its bloodied writing—is more nearly allied with what I have called the Cyril Graham reading, while the second—as a clearly identified treatise on homosexual poetry—is strongly weighted toward the Erskine interpretation.

affirmation of homoeroticism has less to do with an intentional negativism about sex than with his positive program for literature. In the complementary text for considering this problem, Wilde's scandal, to which I now turn, instead of a literary project disclosing its sexual affinities, a criminal sexuality claims to draw upon literature as its raison d'être.

In both his critical and his literary practice, I have been arguing, Wilde develops an aesthetic theory in which literature, by virtue of its indeterminacy, appears both structurally analogous and conceptually contiguous with sexuality. The relationship between literariness and sexuality is not simply unidirectional, as if a prior, secret sexual meaning takes refuge beneath the guise of literature. Although such a case might be argued according to an Erskine reading, that interpretation, as The Portrait of Mr. W. H. shows, is only half the story; in the complementary Cyril Graham reading, the erotic is itself the occasion for exploring more fundamental literary questions. While one form of ambiguity supplies the latent meaning and the other its manifest expression, neither the literary nor the sexual can be considered primary. As a result, the imperative to interpret—and to sustain interpretability—becomes paramount in both endeavors, which perpetually require each other.

In the courtroom, however, where sexual meanings must be established unequivocally, literature serves as their principal alibi and interpretation determines criminal culpability. While Wilde's 1895 trials have been seen as both the nadir and the point of origin for the contemporary struggles of sexual nonconformists, the way in which literature— both specific literary works and the notion of the literary in general— also went to court in his trials has often gone unnoticed.[22] In the legal battle over interpretation, Wilde avers that all his writing is literary,

22. There is a tendency in some recent scholarship to forget that Wilde was by profession a literary man, and that it was his writing as much as his conduct that got him into trouble. The thing for which Wilde continues to be known best—his writing, not his imprisonment—tends to figure very little in such accounts. This is not to argue that one should focus on Wilde's literary output to the exclusion of his position in the history of homosexual persecutions; but if Wilde is to be elevated as the embodiment of the homosexual at the end of the nineteenth century, there must be an explanation for why he, and not anyone else, was so distinguished. Cohen's account in Talk on the Wilde Side, for instance, does not explain why the major homosexual scandals that preceded Wilde's did not likewise do the work of embodiment, since they concern far more than evidence of sexual acts, or why, say, Roger Casement, who followed Wilde, is so much less known today.

even when it appears explicitly erotic; the opposing counsel portrays it all as sexually coded, even when it seems legitimately literary. The incompatibility of these two accounts does not come down merely to a question of which one is true. For as in his essays on aesthetics, Wilde argues in court on behalf of interpretation as such, seeking to ensure that meanings remain unfixable.[23] Yet the ambiguity for which Wilde affirmatively stakes a claim also reinvigorates the moral suspicion with which literary culture had long been regarded, now through its association with criminal homosexuality. The reason why something is going unsaid may well be that it is unspeakable—which is to say, sexual.

Although Wilde's sexual conduct was officially at issue, at least in his second and third trials, it proved surprisingly difficult to demonstrate decisively, and both the defense and the prosecution had repeatedly to turn to literary evidence—the representation and interpretation of sexual activity in fiction and letters—through the course of the proceedings. As in the Boulton and Park case, legal claims about private sexual acts came to depend upon the interpretation of public personae, but while conspiracy charges provided the opening for examining the costumes, behavior, and correspondence of the defendants in 1870, it was the charge of "posing" that admitted literary evidence for Wilde.[24] Wilde's public, literary presentation of homosexual meanings, I want to argue, ultimately proved even more important and dangerous than his private sexual activities. His mistake was to suppose that aristocratic literary prerogatives could exonerate him: to say that potentially gay-

23. Bartlett likewise writes: "What Wilde and the court were contesting was not the evidence, but who had the right to *interpret* that evidence. . . . What was on trial was the right to speak (invent and articulate) the name of that love ['that dare not speak its name']" (*Who Was That Man?* 149; emphasis in original).

24. The differences between Wilde's case and the Boulton and Park scandal are instructive about the changes that twenty-five years made in the status of both sexual and literary evidence. The association of the drag queens with gentry in 1870 tended to exonerate them, while Wilde's cross-class connections—both his aristocratic pretensions and his liaisons with working-class youths—damaged his case. While the two cases rely on a similar confusion between public and private actions, differences between them are significant: before the respective scandals, Wilde was already a public figure with a literary career, while Boulton and Park were relatively unknown; Wilde was an Irishman of ambiguous class standing, while Boulton and Park were English youths from middle-class families; Wilde, for all his perceived effeminacy, was still superficially a family man, while Boulton and Park were semi-professional drag queens; and Wilde was convicted under the 1885 law for misdemeanor "gross indecency," while Boulton and Park were acquitted of the felony of conspiring to commit buggery (and negotiated a settlement on common-law misdemeanor charges of outraging public decency).

identified writing was literary convicted rather than absolved it, since it put such material into the hands of a general readership. At the same time, this argument secured sexual meaningfulness as a recognizable feature of literature, exposing the rhetoric of unspeakability common to sexual and literary discourses.

Wilde's scandal, then, might be understood to circulate around a question of literary interpretation, or, more properly, of what constitutes literature. Wilde himself initiated the first trial after the Marquess of Queensberry (the father of Wilde's companion, Lord Alfred Douglas) culminated a series of insults by leaving a card at Wilde's club accusing him of "posing [as a] somdomite [sic]." At the urging of a spiteful Lord Alfred, Wilde sued Queensberry for criminal libel, and it became the task of the defense to prove that Wilde had indeed posed as a sodomite, and that the libel was therefore justified. When it became evident, midway through the proceedings, that the defense had a strong case not only for Wilde's posing, but for his illicit sexual activities with other men, the prosecution withdrew and Queensberry was acquitted. Then the tables turned, as the evidence for the defense in the first trial became that of the Crown in both the second, which resulted in no verdict, and the third, in which Wilde was convicted and sentenced to two years in prison with hard labor.[25]

The most overtly literary evidence, concerning Wilde's novel, arose in response to Queensberry's Plea of Justification against the charges of libel. This plea first claims that Wilde "did solicit and incite" numerous young men "to commit sodomy and other acts of gross indecency and immorality with him . . . and did then and there commit the said other acts" (323–24). Specifically with respect to the accusation of posing, it charges:

> [Wilde] did write and publish and cause and procure to be printed and published with his name upon the title page thereof a certain immoral and obscene work in the form of a narrative entitled *The Picture of Dorian Gray* which said work was designed and intended by

25. Like others who have written on Wilde's scandal, I rely on H. Montgomery Hyde's redaction of the trials. As Cohen usefully reminds us in *Talk on the Wilde Side*, Hyde's dramatic narrative is not based on trial transcripts (such transcripts are not extant), but is instead a compilation of newspaper accounts and recollections, which are always tendentious. The absence of documentary evidence means that the kind of comparison between court proceedings and news reports possible with the Boulton and Park case cannot be done with Wilde, and testimony that was unreportable in the papers has now lapsed permanently into silence.

the said Oscar Fingal O'Flahertie Wills Wilde and was understood by the readers thereof to describe the relations intimacies and passions of certain persons of sodomitical and unnatural habits tastes and practices. (326)

In this so-called literary portion of the trial, Wilde's "Phrases and Philosophies for the Use of the Young" was also indicted; in itself, this text was relatively inoffensive, but it had been published in The Chameleon, a single-issue Oxford undergraduate paper that contained other clearly gay-identified material.

As a result of having been cited in the plea, The Picture of Dorian Gray figured prominently in the first trial, where posing became a particularly literary question, since Wilde was understood to represent himself — that is, to pose — in his literary persona.[26] In his celebrated exchange with Queensberry's counsel, Edward Carson, Wilde defended the novel against charges of perversion and immorality. Carson accused the novel of "putting forward perverted moral views" and inquired, with respect to a passage portraying the artist Basil Hallward's infatuation with young Dorian Gray, whether Wilde "consider[ed] that that description of the feeling of one man towards a youth just grown-up was a proper or an improper feeling?" (111). He quickly moved to asking whether Wilde himself had ever experienced a similar feeling ("Have you ever adored a young man madly?" [112]). Wilde maintained that it was purely a description of artistic fascination, and throughout the trials insisted that the novel contained no suggestions of unnatural vice.

Despite his testimony, Wilde was clearly aware of the sexual construction that could be put on his novel. He had originally published Dorian Gray in Lippincott's Monthly Magazine in July 1890, and within two months he

---

26. Wilde did little to dispel this myth, even at one point provocatively writing, "That strange coloured book of mine . . . contains much of me in it. Basil Hallward is what I think I am: Lord Henry what the world thinks me: Dorian what I would like to be — in other ages, perhaps" (Letters, 352). The novel itself makes contradictory statements about the relation between the creator and the work of art: "To reveal art and conceal the artist is art's aim" (Dorian Gray, preface, in Complete Works, 17); "Every portrait that is painted with feeling is a portrait of the artist, not of the sitter. . . . It is not he who is revealed by the painter; it is rather the painter who, on the coloured canvas, reveals himself" (21); "An artist should create beautiful things, but should put nothing of his own life into them. We live in an age when men treat art as if it were meant to be a form of autobiography. We have lost the abstract sense of beauty" (25).

claimed to have counted 216 reviews of the novel.[27] Although some of the notices were favorable, many were full of viciousness and invective; the review in the *Daily Chronicle*, for example, begins:

> Dulness and dirt are the chief features of *Lippincott's* this month. The element in it that is unclean, though undeniably amusing, is furnished by Mr. Oscar Wilde's story of *The Picture of Dorian Gray*. It is a tale spawned from the leprous literature of the French *Déca-dents*—a poisonous book, the atmosphere of which is heavy with the mephitic odours of moral and spiritual putrefaction—a gloat-ing study of the mental and physical corruption of a fresh, fair and golden youth, which might be horrible and fascinating but for its effeminate frivolity, its studied insincerity, its theatrical cynicism, its tawdry mysticism, its flippant philosophisings, and the contami-nating trail of garish vulgarity which is over all Mr. Wilde's elabo-rate Wardour Street aestheticism and obtrusively cheap scholar-ship.[28]

While this review is more malicious than most, much of its language— the "poisonousness" of the work, its "corruption," "effeminacy," "vul-garity," and "putrefaction"—was repeatedly invoked in criticism as an implicit attack on the novel's sexual perversion.[29] The review indicates that the sexual codes of Wilde's work had become legible to hostile as well as to sympathetic readers—but also that critics were as incapable as Wilde of making these suggestions explicit, regardless of their anti-thetical reasons for wishing to do so. The novel had to await a court of law for its sexual insinuations to be articulated outright.

Partly in response to the reviewers' moral outrage, Wilde revised his novel before publishing it in book form nine months later. His changes consisted largely of additions to bulk the slender volume and alterations intended to "obscure its moral," but he also excised the most obviously homoerotic passages, particularly those in which Basil proclaims his

27. Wilde makes the claim in a letter to *The Scots Observer*, August 13, 1890; quoted in Mason, *Oscar Wilde*, 113.

28. *Oscar Wilde: The Critical Heritage*, ed. Karl Beckson (London: Routledge & Kegan Paul, 1970), 72.

29. Similarly, in its review, which sparked a controversy that raged for months, the *St. James's Gazette* states, "Not being curious in ordure, and not wishing to offend the nostrils of decent persons, we do not propose to analyse *The Picture of Dorian Gray*" (Beckson, *Criti-cal Heritage*, 68).

love for Dorian in romantic terms.[30] The revisions came too late, however, for it was from the *Lippincott's* version that the opposing counsel
read out portions of *Dorian Gray* during the trials—and it was precisely
those passages that Wilde had cut (or, as his antagonist put it, "purged"
[111]) from the text.

Dorian Gray arose again in the second trial, although it was ostensibly
of less concern than the prosecution's witnesses (the young men who
claimed to have been solicited by and had sex with Wilde). While the
literary portion of the case was officially exhausted by the end of the
second trial, literature persisted in the proceedings, largely as a result of
the defendant's own efforts to keep it in view. Central to the case against
Wilde were two letters of his to Lord Alfred, which manifested such
recognizable signs of eroticism that readers could not ignore their corruption. The first is Wilde's reply to a poem Lord Alfred had sent him:

> My Own Boy,
>   Your sonnet is quite lovely, and it is a marvel that those red rose-
> leaf lips of yours should have been made no less for music of song
> than for madness of kisses. Your slim gilt soul walks between pas-
> sion and poetry. I know Hyacinthus, whom Apollo loved so madly,
> was you in Greek days.
>   Why are you alone in London, and when do you go to Salis-
> bury? Do go there to cool your hands in the grey twilight of Gothic
> things, and come here whenever you like. It is a lovely place—
> it only lacks you; but go to Salisbury first. Always, with undying
> love, yours,
>
> OSCAR
> (Letters, 326)

Wilde and his counsel, Sir Edward Clarke, consistently defended this letter by arguing that it was "a kind of prose poem." (It had in fact been
loosely translated into French as a sonnet by Pierre Louÿs and published.) In his opening speech at the first trial, Clarke stated:

> The words of that letter, gentlemen, may appear extravagant to
> those in the habit of writing commercial correspondence, or those
> ordinary letters which the necessities of life force upon one every

---

30. For a record of the additions, deletions, and emendations to the original version,
see Donald L. Lawler, *An Inquiry into Oscar Wilde's Revisions of "The Picture of Dorian Gray"* (New
York: Garland, 1988).

day. But Mr. Wilde is a poet, and the letter is considered by him as a prose sonnet, and one of which he is in no way ashamed and is prepared to produce anywhere as the expression of true poetic feeling, and with no relation whatever to the hateful and repulsive suggestions put to it in the plea in this case. (101–2)

Although the suggestions of homoeroticism were patent, Wilde maintained, "It is a beautiful letter. It is a poem. I was not writing an ordinary letter. You might as well cross-examine me as to whether *King Lear* or a sonnet of Shakespeare was proper" (115). To claim a literary provenance for this letter is not exactly to deny its sexual connotations, but rather to insist upon its nonreferentiality: construed as literature, the letter is, if open to being read as corrupt, also comprehensible simply as a beautiful and evocative combination of words. The ambiguity essential to its literariness also makes available its sexual suggestions, but the congealing of sexual meanings into a self-conscious language now threatens literature rather than being exculpated by it.

Wilde found the second of his letters harder to contain within a literary rubric:

> Dearest of all Boys,
>   Your letter was delightful, red and yellow wine to me; but I am sad and out of sorts. Bosie, you must not make scenes with me. They kill me, they wreck the loveliness of life. I cannot see you, so Greek and gracious, distorted with passion. I cannot listen to your curved lips saying hideous things to me. I would sooner be blackmailed by every renter in London than have you bitter, unjust, hating. I must see you soon. You are the divine thing I want, the thing of grace and beauty; but I don't know how to do it. Shall I come to Salisbury? My bill here is £49 for a week. I have also got a new sitting-room over the Thames. Why are you not here, my dear, my wonderful boy? I fear I must leave; no money, no credit, and a heart of lead.
>   YOUR OWN OSCAR
>   (*Letters*, 336–37)

Despite the affinity of this letter's financial complaints with the disavowed "commercial correspondence," Wilde stated with regard to it: "Everything I wrote is extraordinary. I do not pose as being ordinary, great heavens! . . . It was a tender expression of my great admiration for Lord Alfred Douglas. It was not, like the other, a prose poem" (117). Even if this letter is not itself literary, Wilde nonetheless claims an artist's exemption, for to acknowledge that his writing expresses "sodomitical" phrases would indeed be to "pose as . . . ordinary."

By his closing speech to the third trial, the prosecutor condemns the letters in the harshest language yet:

> I contend that such a letter found in the possession of a woman from a man would be open to but one interpretation. How much worse is the inference to be drawn when such a letter is written from one man to another! It has been attempted to show that this was a prose poem, a sonnet, a lovely thing which I suppose we are too low to appreciate. Gentlemen, let us thank God, if it is so, that we do not appreciate things of this sort save at their proper value, and that is somewhat lower than the beasts. If that letter had been seen by any right-minded man, it would have been looked upon as evidence of guilty passion. And you, men of pride, reason, and honour, are tried to be put off with this story of the prose poem, of the sonnet, of the lovely thing! (257–58)

This attack on the letters indicates that the evocation of homosexuality in writing is as reprehensible as the act itself; the correspondence in this sense represents only a more explicit version of the suggestions made in *Dorian Gray*. In court, the literary becomes evidential because of its susceptibility to perverse readings. In Wilde's mind, however, this interpretability is precisely what redeems his writing, for when "the noblest form of affection" is indited in the hand of an artist, it rises to an aesthetic principle.

When he comes to narrate the story of how his letters were misread—in yet another missive to Lord Alfred, the one from Reading prison, eventually published under the title *De Profundis*—Wilde still associates his love poetry with Shakespeare's, and again finds that literature provides the occasion for expressions of homoerotic desire:

> You send me a very nice poem, of the undergraduate school of verse, for my approval: I reply by a letter of fantastic literary conceits: I compare you to Hylas, or Hyacinth, Jonquil or Narcisse, or someone whom the great god of Poetry favoured, and honoured with his love. The letter is like a passage from one of Shakespeare's sonnets, transposed to a minor key. It can only be understood by those who have read the *Symposium* of Plato, or caught the spirit of

a certain grave mood made beautiful for us in Greek marbles. It was, let me say frankly, the sort of letter I would, in a happy if wilful moment, have written to any graceful young man of either University who had sent me a poem of his own making, certain that he would have sufficient wit or culture to interpret rightly its fantastic phrases. (*Letters*, 440–41)

Wilde is not exaggerating here or making excuses, as he might have been suspected of doing in court: he contends that the poetry and music of the letter's language constitutes it as literature, and puts it beyond reproach, regardless of the illegality of the eroticism it expresses. It does not occur to him that he appears in the letter to be "posing as a sodomite"; he is, rather, *being* literary.

The sexual significations of Wilde's letter to Lord Alfred, moreover—exactly like those of *The Portrait of Mr. W. H.*—take refuge in a layering of literature upon literary criticism. The indeterminacy requisite to making sexual meanings legible as literary ones arises precisely at a moment when a letter of commentary upon a sonnet itself *becomes* "like a sonnet": with its "fantastic literary conceits," the pederast's letter about a poetaster's sonnet is more poetic than the poem to which it replies. In privileging interpretation over literature, this sequence of poems and letters recapitulates the structure of *Mr. W. H.*, facilitating a further confusion between literary and sexual meanings.

Wilde insinuates his writing into a revered literary tradition, claiming that, as an artist, he has access to emotions and expressions denied "those in the habit of writing . . . ordinary letters." If, in the first trial, literature is converted into evidence, the unsuccessful strategy of the second and third trials is a conversion of evidence into literature. In this context, one can make sense of the ways in which Wilde's famous oration, justifying relations between men, has to deny the very eroticism it is usually imagined to vindicate:

> "The love that dare not speak its name" in this century is such a great affection of an elder for a younger man as there was between David and Jonathan, such as Plato made the very basis of his philosophy, and such as you find in the sonnets of Michelangelo and Shakespeare. It is that deep, spiritual affection that is as pure as it is perfect. It dictates and pervades great works of art like those of Shakespeare and Michelangelo, and those two letters of mine, such as they are. It is in this century misunderstood . . . and on account

of it I am placed where I am now. It is beautiful, it is fine, it is the noblest form of affection. There is nothing unnatural about it. (201)

By promoting the "beauty," "purity," and "nobility" of these affections, Wilde raises them to the level of an aesthetic—that is to say, not a sexual —experience. Although often read as a defense of homosexuality, this speech works only by subsuming eroticism to an aesthetic or literary discourse. The affiliation of this form of affection with Shakespeare's sonnets, initiated in *The Portrait of Mr. W. H.*, carries through the trials. To the prosecutor's inquiry, "I believe you have written an article to show that Shakespeare's sonnets were suggestive of unnatural vice," Wilde replies, "On the contrary, I have written an article to show that they are not. I objected to such a perversion being put upon Shakespeare" (113). In his defense, Wilde draws on an outmoded association as much to cover up his illegal sexual practice as genuinely to propound his literary theories.

Wilde's disavowal of homosexual activity continues to exercise commentators on the trials, and two of the most acute recent accounts differ starkly in their reading of this evidence. Although sympathetic to what he sees as the necessity of Wilde's renouncing homosexuality on the witness stand, Neil Bartlett, reading Wilde in the context of London's fin-de-siècle gay male subculture, nonetheless expresses a certain gay rage about the denials:

> It is important to remember that Wilde, throughout his three trials, was lying all the time. He denied or distorted the significance of the texts, incidents and relationships described in evidence against him, knowing all the time what was their "true meaning." He *was* a sodomite.... The court was not entirely ignorant of twenty years of London's culture and daily life; they read the papers.... What is remarkable, in the face of all the evidence, is that Wilde contested the case at all, or that the verdict was not announced on the first day.[31]

By contrast with this picture of Wilde as a self-identified—if self-denying—modern gay subject, Linda Dowling discusses Wilde's language in terms of the Oxford-based classical studies in which he had been tutored. Dowling understands Wilde's discourse in court, as elsewhere, to draw upon a particular set of classical codes, not as a screen for criminal sexuality but as an aesthetic project that he actually lived.

31. Bartlett, *Who Was That Man?* 148–49.

Wilde's defense of Lord Alfred's "love that dare not speak its name" line, Dowling writes,

> call[ed] upon the language of Oxford Hellenism to contest and dis-
> arm the enormous residual power of the ideological traditions so
> massively marshaled against him. Charged with corrupting youth,
> Wilde invokes Plato's pedagogic eros. Confronted with the sordid
> evidence of sodomic indecency, he appeals to a "pure" procreancy
> of the spirit. Condemned as effeminate and degenerate, he shows
> the intellectual fearlessness and commanding flexibility of mind so
> celebrated in Victorian liberal Hellenism as the only vitally regen-
> erative powers still capable of saving England. . . . When Douglas's
> poem is cited in court as evidence of a spreading sexual indecency
> at Oxford and elsewhere, Wilde, loyal to him even in this ex-
> tremity, summons himself to defend Douglas's lame verse. Speak-
> ing his mighty peroration, Wilde briefly embodies the power of
> a mind saturated in Greek thought and Oxford Hellenism to stave
> off the invading horror, to overcome another man's intellectual in-
> dolence and imaginative vulgarity, and to transfigure even vapidity
> into something eloquent and fine. . . . Even Wilde's frankly com-
> mercial relations with male prostitutes were conducted within the
> transforming frame of the Socratic eros.[32]

While this last sentence betrays an ingenious, perhaps overly ingenuous reading of Wilde's sexuality, Dowling's account has the merit of taking seriously Wilde's claims for literary impunity against the accusation that his writing expressed criminal homoeroticism. Although Dowling's argument might also be faulted for recapitulating Wilde's courtroom renunciation of homosexuality, it nonetheless usefully explicates the intellectual framework in which he could make his defense, avoiding the prosecutorial interrogation that critics have had to undertake when approaching Wilde's literary work in search of sexual meanings. We can finally understand that Wilde's testimony in court exemplifies the ambition of his literary aesthetic to serve simultaneously—not merely incidentally—as a justification for his sexual conduct.

Although the literary evidence purportedly diminished in importance as the trials progressed, the letters in fact became increasingly central

---

32. Linda Dowling, *Hellenism and Homosexuality in Victorian Oxford* (Ithaca: Cornell University Press, 1994), 142–43, 145.

to the prosecution's case. Despite the apparent strength of the evidence against Wilde, according to H. Montgomery Hyde, "it is perhaps not generally realized how near Sir Edward Clarke was to getting his client off altogether."[33] At the point when the jury was to reach a final verdict, much of the prosecution's case had been significantly discredited: by the third trial, the serious charge of conspiracy with Alfred Taylor had been dropped, one of the witnesses had perjured himself so severely that he could not be retained, another insisted that no indecencies had occurred with Wilde, and the Crown's two remaining principal witnesses were confessed blackmailers. More than the revolting suggestion that Wilde had carried on with young men of the lower classes, the most serious charge against him, in the eyes of the court and the press, was that of corrupting Edward Shelley, the case's only "youth of good education and character" (240)—though this was the single count on which he was acquitted. All of this is to suggest that the letters—one a "prose poem," the other "an expression of great admiration"—were finally among the most damaging and unassailable pieces of evidence against Wilde. As Wilde himself said in the third trial, with respect to the first one, "It was entirely about literature, and it was represented to me that I could not get a verdict because of those two letters you have read" (247). And as the following narrative from De Profundis demonstrates, Wilde felt that his letter to Lord Alfred, more than any of his liaisons with working-class youths, was the keystone to his incrimination:

> Look at the history of that letter! It passes from you into the hands of a loathsome companion: from him to a gang of blackmailers: copies of it are sent about London to my friends, and to the manager of the theatre where my work is being performed: every construction but the right one is put on it: Society is thrilled with the absurd rumours that I have had to pay a huge sum of money for having written an infamous letter to you: this forms the basis of your father's worst attack: I produce the original letter myself in Court to show what it really is: it is denounced by your father's Counsel as a revolting and insidious attempt to corrupt Innocence: ultimately it forms part of a criminal charge: the Crown takes it up: the Judge sums up on it with little learning and much morality: I go to prison for it at last. That is the result of writing you a charming letter. (Letters, 441)

33. H. Montgomery Hyde, The Trials of Oscar Wilde, Notable British Trials (London: William Hodge and Co., 1948), 85.

The Picture of Dorian Gray, along with the other texts associated with it, was at least as consequential as the nonliterary evidence in the trials. The case came down to a battle over the interpretation of texts, with the two sides arrayed along lines not only of sexual propriety but of class as well: the pugnacious, hypermasculine Marquess, with his insistence on the texts' effeminacy, provided the literal, common reading; the effeminate dandy Wilde had to argue for an elite interpretation of the texts as well as for their unremitting interpretability.[34]

In his effort to defend his language against the charge of criminal sexuality by designating it literary, Wilde also aimed to recuperate it from scandal. His case again demonstrates the reliance of scandal upon a fantasy of exposing private life: if his letters could be recognized as literature then they were by definition within the public purview, and there would be no scandal in having them exposed. Like the arguments made in court about Boulton and Park's public performances as exculpatory of their private life, the claims put forward that Wilde imagined a public audience for his private letters—as well as for his novel, when it came under scrutiny—flaunted a lack of embarrassment by broadcasting the letters' otherwise damaging messages. While the court enforces a hermeneutic of one-for-one correspondence between representation and reality, however, the operations of scandal, principally through the agency of the press, are not entirely antagonistic to uncertainty. Indeterminacy sustains Wilde's aesthetic project, and troubles the judicial proceedings; but scandal requires both the promise of eventual resolution into meaningfulness and a suspension, for as long as possible, of that result. The playful unspeakability that permeates Wilde's fiction, drama, and criticism is the very feature that enabled the scandal to explode. While veiled sexual meanings serve him as a rich literary resource, however, the scandal both strives after a literal determination of those meanings and avoids a premature foreclosure on them, inviting spectatorial pleasures in the process of striving itself.

It may seem odd that Wilde, who is best known as a playwright and socialite, who wrote only one novel, which is neither realist nor long, has been included in this study. In part, the preeminence of Wilde's scandal makes him the cynosure of any study of the phenomenon, particu-

---

34. On the class politics surrounding the reception of Wilde's work and reporting of the trials, see Regenia Gagnier, *Idylls of the Marketplace: Oscar Wilde and the Victorian Public* (Stanford: Stanford University Press, 1986).

larly one concerned to suggest its relation to literature. Moreover, the change in the discursive status of sexuality exemplified by Wilde's writing itself formally precluded the continuing production of long realist narratives as a primary literary mode. The Victorian novel, that is to say, so long goaded into prolixity at least in part by its simultaneous fascination with and disbarment from sexual topics, is made obsolete by a literary practice of sexual encoding that, like Wilde's, knows full well what it is doing.[35] Of course, long realist novels continued to be written after Wilde's demise, and they reached new levels of accomplishment with works such as those of Henry James. But an achievement like James's develops precisely out of his alternative solution—a purely literary one—to the discursive problem of sexual unspeakability, which Wilde had addressed through writing cognizant of its own erotic potential.

In the historical moment of Wilde's scandal, the other direction in which the shared indeterminacy of literary and sexual language could lead was to the utter denial of scandal, through the exaltation of literature as high artistic expression and the occlusion of sexual content. James articulates this alternative in two of his tales most explicitly concerned to demarcate the realm of the literary, *The Figure in the Carpet* (1896) and *The Aspern Papers* (1888). I take up these novellas, rather than James's full-length novels, both because of their overt interest in literature and criticism and because of their instructive affinities with Wilde's analogous literary-critical work, *The Portrait of Mr. W. H.*[36] While for Wilde sexu-

---

35. A similar conclusion might be drawn from the career of Thomas Hardy, who claimed that he found attacks on his work for its sexual suggestiveness so intolerable that he simply ceased writing novels. Indicating the obsolescence of the genre, Hardy (writing of himself in the third person) states that this

> turned out ultimately to be the best thing that could have happened; for [the attacks] well-nigh compelled him, in his own judgment at any rate, if he wished to retain any shadow of self-respect, to abandon at once a form of literary art [the novel] he had long intended to abandon at some indefinite time, and resume openly that form of it [poetry] which had always been more instinctive with him, and which he had just been able to keep alive from his early years, half in secrecy, under the pressure of magazine-writing. He abandoned it with all the less reluctance in that the novel was, in his own words, "gradually losing artistic form, with a beginning, middle, and end, and becoming a spasmodic inventory of items, which has nothing to do with art."

The Life and Work of Thomas Hardy, ed. Michael Millgate (Athens: University of Georgia Press, 1985), 309.

36. On the biographical, social, and intellectual context of the relations between James and Wilde, and each man's efforts to distinguish himself from the other, see Jonathan

ality is encoded in and as the literary, for James the sexual simply gives over its place to literature: the affect and the form of sexual unspeakability are transferred directly onto literature itself in James's tales, and literary secrets are invested with an energy ordinarily reserved for sexual objects. By contrast with Wilde's effort to justify sexual meanings in literary terms, James, by virtue of refusing sexuality, can lend its value to literature. And where Mr. W. H. explores characters' *belief* in a literarily inscribed sexual secret whose substance is known (the name of the homoerotic sexual object), the problem for James's narrators is their incapacity even to *know* the content of a (sexually transmissible) literary secret.

Wilde's deliberately indeterminate language, whose meanings can be equally literary or sexual, relies on an antecedent ambiguity, I have argued, about the distinction between literature and criticism. In highlighting interpretability as such, Wilde's writing is always open to—and in danger of—being read as sexual. While Wilde argues for the endless openness of literary writing to interpretation, James instead insists on its closed integrity. James's stories of literary detection belittle criticism by making the narrators' quests appear ridiculous and misguided, and reassert the priority of art over criticism. James mystifies literary art, holding out for it an inaccessible, untranslatable sphere of pure aesthetics where there is no danger of being tainted with sexuality. So while sexual cathexes are transposed onto literature, this project ultimately makes attempts at deciphering hidden sexual meanings seem insupportable.

Like Wilde, James recognizes that an indeterminate literary meaning is always a potentially sexual one. But while this realization results in a playful and affirmative homoerotics in Wilde, James's castigation of the literary critic is by contrast bound up in a negative erotics—an acute erotophobia grounded in an intensive antiheterosexuality. While the stories bear indications of sexual desire, including the non-normative, sexuality is so aggressively repudiated that to read these traces as encoding otherwise proscribed forms of eroticism is not entirely adequate.[37]

Freedman, *Professions of Taste: Henry James, British Aestheticism, and Commodity Culture* (Stanford: Stanford University Press, 1990).

37. My argument has affinities with that of Sedgwick on "The Beast in the Jungle" (*Epistemology of the Closet*, chap. 4), which proposes that, "to the extent that Marcher's secret has a content, that content is homosexual" (201), and, more fully, "that the outer secret, the secret of having a secret, functions, in Marcher's life, precisely as *the closet*. . . . It is the closet of, simply, the homosexual secret—the closet of imagining *a* homosexual secret"

Instead, James's tales transvalue the force of desire into a literary quest. When these bachelor narrators refuse obvious heterosexual solutions to their literary conundrums, it is neither because they are gay nor because they are impotent. Rather, it is inconceivable for the narrators to marry women in order to answer the literary questions that obsess them because sexual desire has been subsumed by what might be termed literary desire. Literary rather than sexual meanings take the value of the inscrutable—the unspeakable—in these stories. While the explanations are communicable within conventional marriages, the characters with whom the literary quests are primarily identified—the narrators—recognize that heterosexual revelation is for them an impossible solution: they seek, and cannot attain, answers to their questions in entirely literary terms.

The narrator of The Figure in the Carpet [38] tells of his search for the "general intention" (313) that inheres in the works of Vereker, an author whom he admires and who has told him of the existence of such a "secret" (283). This "idea" or "intention" (281) is virtually ineffable and can be indicated in the narrative only in the form of a hypertrophic catalogue of displacements: "The thing's as concrete there as a bird in a cage," Vereker says, "a bait on a hook, a piece of cheese in a mousetrap. It's stuck into every volume as your foot is stuck into your shoe. It governs every line, it chooses every word, it dots every i, it places every comma" (283–84). The narrator fails to unravel the secret, but he puts his friend Corvick, and Corvick's fiancée, Gwendolen, onto the track; Corvick eventually discovers the solution to the puzzle, transmits it to Gwendolen after their marriage, and then dies. Gwendolen retains possession of the secret, refusing to pass it on either to the narrator or to her second husband.

The story presents abundant evidence for an association of the literary secret with a concealed sexual content, and an interpretation that identified the sexual meaning of such hints would align with readings I

---

(205). Sedgwick makes this case on the basis of a relationship between a general discourse of unspeakability and homosexual signification in particular (202). In the stories under consideration here, James's concern with writing, as the literal register of the unspeakable, self-consciously evacuates the sexual content that might be attributed to the secrets, and this evacuation precedes even the homo/hetero distinction.
38. In The Complete Tales of Henry James, ed. Leon Edel, 12 vols., 9:273–315 (Philadelphia: J. B. Lippincott, 1962–64); parenthetical references are to this edition.

have presented elsewhere in this study. The logic of those readings has, in several cases, been to heed the Freud of *Dora* in recognizing sexuality in the very signs of its absence, negation, or denial—to understand that these various ways of saying "no" to sex sustain a "yes" in a different register. Yet the refusal of sexuality in James's literary detection stories is so assertive and conspicuous that to read it simply as a disavowal which attests to the repression or closeting of sexual material would not suffice. An insistently Freudian reading might seek to assimilate refusal itself to sexual meaningfulness by taking it to indicate sexual inadequacy. But the "yes" to which this "no" gives way is literary *rather than*—not a cover for—the sexual. Unlike Wilde, who valorizes an indeterminacy available to sexual meanings, James holds out the literary object as that which abrogates the critic's very capacity to derive meanings.

Where is this evidence for sexuality in *The Figure in the Carpet?* In its primary, negative mode, it takes the form of the narrator's acute awareness that his exclusion from comprehending the "general intention of [Vereker's] books" (313) aligns with his alienation from heterosexual romance—romance with respect to which he feels himself "a kind of coerced spectator" (303). "Was the figure in the carpet traceable or describable only for husbands and wives—for lovers supremely united?" (306). Vereker suggests as much, and Corvick makes marriage with Gwendolen the condition for telling her the secret. The narrator is ostentatiously barred from this marriage plot that makes the literary one accessible. In case he does not feel the smart of that isolation strongly enough himself, his exclusion is flaunted by the couple's brandishing the privilege of the heterosexual "we": explaining how Corvick solved the riddle while alone in India, Gwendolen says to the narrator, "I suppose I may tell you now—why he went and why I consented to his going. We knew the change would do it . . . would give the needed touch" (297). And then to drive home the point:

> "Did you hear in those few days of your blighted bliss," I wrote, "what we desired so to hear?" I said, "we" as a little hint; and she showed me she could take a little hint. "I heard everything," she replied, "and I mean to keep it to myself!" (305)

Finally, when he entertains, for a moment, the idea of marrying the widowed Gwendolen for the purpose of obtaining knowledge of the figure, the narrator immediately recognizes the erotic impossibility of this prospect: "There was enough to make me wonder if I should have

to marry Mrs. Corvick to get what I wanted. Was I prepared to offer
her this price for the blessing of her knowledge? Ah! that way madness
lay—so I said to myself at least in bewildered hours" (306).

Beyond the narrator's repudiation of heterosexuality, other erotic possibilities seem as little promising. In light of Corvick's requirement that
Gwendolen marry him to obtain the secret, the notion of a comparable
homosexual arrangement with the narrator is raised only to be rendered preposterous: "It seemed more than a hint that on me as well he
would impose some tiresome condition" (300)—though what that condition might be is never determined. The relationship most infused with
homoerotic potential is the narrator's flirtation with Vereker, whom he
hopes to charm with his critical essay: "The only effect I cared about
was the one it would have on Vereker up there by his bedroom fire"
(277). Indeed, the initial literary enticement—when Vereker first alerts
the narrator to the existence of the figure—takes the form of a seduction, late at night in a bedroom:

> "My dear young man," he exclaimed, "I'm so glad to lay hands on
> you! I'm afraid I most unwittingly wounded you by those words
> of mine at dinner." . . . I protested that no bones were broken; but
> he moved with me to my own door, his hand, on my shoulder,
> kindly feeling for a fracture; and on hearing that I had come up to
> bed he asked leave to cross my threshold and just tell me in three
> words what his qualification of my remarks had represented. (279)

In spite of all the suggestiveness of these passages, they amount to a
repudiation of homoeroticism to the same extent that the explicit rejection of marriage does of heterosexuality ("that way madness lay").
For the narrator identified with the writing position of this tale, the
only way to resolve a literary problem is with a literary solution, and
when the mystical quality of this literariness is designated by its sheer
ineffability, no space remains for an erotics similarly recognizable by
its unspeakability. When the narrator states, as he does several times, "I
sat up with Vereker half the night" (275), the line can only have reference to his reading, try as one might to bend its valence. Moreover, the
tale's most sexually suggestive moment indicates that marriage itself—
as much as less sanctioned forms of erotic transaction—devolves from
the literary enterprise. In describing the honeymoon revelation of the
literary enigma, the narrator suggests how even conventional heterosexual intercourse is bound up with the literary quest: "This was above

all what I wanted to know: had *she* seen the idol unveiled? Had there been a private ceremony for a palpitating audience of one? For what else but that ceremony had the previous ceremony [the wedding] been enacted?" (305). The usual wedding-night unveiling of sexual mysteries is subordinated to the disclosure of the literary secret—without, however, losing any of its erotic force. All the characters take for granted that marriage derives from a desire to apprehend and to convey the figure far more than it does from a wish to express passion or romance.[39]

The Aspern Papers reinforces the sense of sexual terror that results from an unanswerable literary quest. Another bachelor narrator tells a tale of literary pilgrimage—a search in Venice for undiscovered material on a long-dead poet, Jeffrey Aspern, whom he and a male friend back home, Cumnor, idolize. The narrator ingratiates himself to an elderly woman, Miss Bordereau, and her middle-aged niece, Miss Tita; the former was in her youth a lover of Aspern's, and the object of some of his poems. She is thought to possess a cache of love letters from him—papers the young critic feels a desperate desire to read and to publish. In order to get close to the women, he becomes their lodger and, only somewhat unwittingly, induces the niece to fall in love with him. The old woman dies and the niece offers to trade him the papers for a betrothal, but the suggestion is unthinkable to him. He soon repents his rejection of her, but she has already burned the letters, and so he must be satisfied with the miniature portrait of Aspern he has bought from her, which he keeps above his writing desk to remind himself of what his failure of desire has cost him.

As in *Figure in the Carpet*, the content of the literary secret remains hidden from the narrator as well as from the reader, and the heterosexual contract requisite to obtaining that knowledge is here even more vividly recounted and repudiated. Knowledge of a heterosexual romance (As-

39. While the eponymous figure remains entirely metaphorical, the figures in the story—the characters—are themselves embodiments of literality. Corvick, for instance, says of Gwendolen: "'She's quite incredibly literary, you know—quite fantastically!' I remembered his saying of her that she felt in italics and thought in capitals" (293). Desire derives from the characters being literary figures rather than deep psychological subjects, as the following privileging of "the book" over "the man" makes evident: the fact of the secret's existence "fell in . . . completely with the sense [Corvick] had had from the first that there was more in Vereker than met the eye. When I remarked that the eye seemed what the printed page had been expressly invented to meet he immediately accused me of being spiteful because I had been foiled" (286–87). The story's overarching pun on the trope of "the figure" generates both its untranscendable metaphoricity and the figurality (personification) of the literary.

pern and Miss Bordereau) is available only *through* such a romance (the narrator and Miss Tita); yet this exchange is rendered impossible by the narrator's appetite for information about the literary figure having entirely nullified his capacity for sexual desire. The former desire, forged in confederation with Cumnor, itself takes the form of romance, but romance that again falls fully under the aegis of literary detection. As he explains his preoccupation with Aspern to his patroness, Mrs. Prest, the narrator notes:

> I could see that she was amused by my infatuation, the way my interest in the papers had become a fixed idea. "One would think you expected to find in them the answer to the riddle of the universe," she said; and I denied the impeachment only by replying that if I had to choose between that precious solution and a bundle of Jeffrey Aspern's letters I knew indeed which would appear to me the greater boon. She pretended to make light of his genius and I took no pains to defend him. One doesn't defend one's god: one's god is in himself a defence. . . . The most I said was that he was no doubt not a woman's poet. (276–77)[40]

The narrator's "infatuation" with the dead poet is overwhelming, but rather than enabling him to surmount all obstacles and throw himself before the "piece of middle-aged female helplessness" (369) that is Miss Tita, this literary obsession obviates such a prospect. There is no chance for a positively charged sexual passion in one so literarily preoccupied; the narrator's defensive repulsion, articulated in frankly misogynistic terms, testifies to the erotophobia induced by the literary question:

> What in the name of the preposterous did she mean if she did not mean to offer me her hand? That was the price—that was the price! And did she think I wanted it, poor deluded, infatuated, extravagant lady? . . . I had not given her cause—distinctly I had not. I had said to Mrs. Prest that I would make love to her; but it had been a joke without consequences and I had never said it to Tita Bordereau. I had been as kind as possible, because I really liked her; but since when had that become a crime where a woman of such an age and such an appearance was concerned? . . . Whether I had given cause or not it went without saying that I could not pay the price. I could

---

40. In *Complete Tales*, 6:275–382; parenthetical references are to this edition.

not accept. I could not, for a bundle of tattered papers, marry a ridiculous, pathetic, provincial old woman. (376–77)

Like *The Figure in the Carpet*, this tale circulates around an unknown and unknowable literary secret whose form recapitulates that of the usual, presumptively sexual, secret. The metaliterary aspect of these works — their object lessons in how *not* to read James's stories themselves — strives to shame readers into feeling that even an inquiry into the content of these secrets is inappropriate. The fact that such literary secrets are attainable through heterosexual unions only reinforces the point, for this heterosexuality is a wholly negative, radically unavailable alternative to the type of the literary critic concerned with such questions.

The contentlessness of the secrets in James's stories — by contrast with the secret in Wilde, which is discernibly sexual — enables these tales to pose problems of knowledge, rather than, as in Wilde, of belief.[41] The endings of the respective works bear out this difference between the yearning after knowledge and a quest for faith. The narrator of *The Portrait of Mr. W. H.* concludes by bemusedly pondering his own capacity for belief in the homoerotic account of the poems: "But sometimes, when I look at [the picture], I think that there is really a great deal to be said for the Willie Hughes theory of Shakespeare's Sonnets" (169). Belief in the theory of the sonnets constitutes the subjectivity of the proselyte, and while this faith serves as a conduit for desire between men, it also throws up a barrier to the realization of that desire: in the process of securing belief — committing it to writing, in the form of a letter — its possessor gives it over to the other, and the potential for a connection between them dissolves. As usual in Wilde's work, the narrator winds up renouncing the homoerotic possibility, or at best finds himself in a state of permanent irresolution about it.

41. James's tales mock the very sort of literary riddling in which Wilde's story engages, a search for information that appears to confuse the text for the person of the author. In each of the James stories, the narrator-critic's undertaking is at one point aligned precisely with a search for the meaning of Shakespeare's sonnets, and James alludes to such a search in order to indicate its absurdity. The narrator of *Figure in the Carpet* says of the author Vereker, "He was like nothing . . . but the maniacs who embrace some bedlamitical theory of the cryptic character of Shakespeare" (291). Likewise, the narrator of *The Aspern Papers* writes of Miss Bordereau: "It was incontestable that, whether for right or for wrong, most readers of certain of Aspern's poems (poems not as ambiguous as the sonnets — scarcely more divine, I think — of Shakespeare) had taken for granted that Juliana had not always adhered to the steep footway of renunciation" (309).

The narrator of *The Aspern Papers* ends similarly gazing upon a literary portrait—though here the portrait reflects the failure of his desire to obtain the knowledge he sought, rather than the failure of his faith to sustain that desire. The literary question of the story is left unanswered, not undecided, and he remains isolated in his self-recrimination: "When I look at [the picture]," the last sentence reads, "my chagrin at the loss of the letters becomes almost intolerable" (382). *The Figure in the Carpet* finishes on a more mean-spirited note, for this narrator attains a measure of relief by spitefully transferring the irresoluble quest onto someone else—Gwendolen's widower: "I may say that to-day as victims of unappeased desire there isn't a pin to choose between us. The poor man's state is almost my consolation; there are indeed moments when I feel it to be almost my revenge" (315). Having been punished and excluded by the institutions of heterosexuality, this narrator exacts his vengeance upon it. It is all the more invidious for being a pyrrhic victory: rather than smashing the privileges of matrimony, the narrator simply recruits one of its former adherents for the cause of sexually debilitated literary compulsion.

No doubt this denial of the sexual affirms its continued importance to, and its ongoing conditioning of, literature as the location of unspeakability. By considering the fundamental question about literary meaning as one of knowledge rather than as one of faith, James asserts the unassailable inscrutability of the literary object as a powerful defense against the encroachment on literature of sexual indeterminacy. The literary may be deeply intertwined with the sexual, he seems to say, but that relationship is unfathomable, and one had best avoid looking into it too deeply. The literary quest itself forms the site of self-constitution for James's narrators, blocked as they are from erotic attachments; but the subjectivity thus produced is fearsomely atomized and abjected, disengaged in solipsism and "unappeased desire." While literature sustains irresolution for Wilde, in James it is disfiguring and self-consuming.

What consequences does the difference between Wildean and Jamesian literary unspeakability have for the construction of scandal? In both cases scandal is displaced away from the literary, but in different directions. In Wilde's case, the literary *object* becomes scandalous: hence the reception of *Dorian Gray* both at its publication and in the trials. In James's literary-critical stories, the scandal is never permitted to blossom—it is preempted, held in abeyance, or dissipated. Even the James narratives less overtly preoccupied with the epistemological status of literature manage at once to engage the usual theme and structure of the Victorian scandal story and to refuse the full efflorescence of that scandal. To take the most familiar example, in *The Portrait of a Lady* (1881), the scandal that drives the plot—the fact that Madame Merle is Osmond's lover and Pansy's mother—is exposed, but its effects are not realized. Madame Merle departs to avoid the scandal, and the novel ends before Isabel confronts Osmond. Missing from this famously truncated story is the public effect of the sexual revelation; it is as if Eliot had wrapped up *The Mill on the Floss* without showing us the reaction of the world's wife to Maggie's return. While Eliot's concern is with the ethical consequences of the scandal, James's evasion serves to transpose consideration of the scandal's effects back onto the aesthetic realm. Again, in *The Wings of the Dove* (1902), the scandal toward which the novel builds— of Merton Densher and Kate Croy's plot against Milly Theale—dissolves in the novel's termination. Where scandal actively contributed to sexual unspeakability in the works I have considered in prior chapters, for Wilde and James it falls into crisis, on the one hand collapsing into the literal scandal surrounding the author and on the other evaporating into an aesthetic of the self-regarding literary artifact.

If James's work represents a defense against scandal that functions by completely absorbing sexual into literary unspeakability, another writer on the brink of modernism, Sigmund Freud, develops a reverse strategy, which subsumes the literary to narratives that overtly place sex at their center. Freud's discovery of sexuality as the primum mobile, coupled with the narrative form of his case studies—the earliest of which, the *Studies on Hysteria* (1893–95), are contemporary with the stories I have considered here—reacts against the ideology of sexual unspeakability institutionalized in literature. Sex now explicitly drives narrative and outstrips self-conscious literary meaning, with which Wilde had so carefully sought to hold sexual signification in balance, and with which James had so sedulously obscured it. Psychoanalysis disdains the evasions and displacements in which literature had for so long found a stimulus, imagining as its task instead to speak openly about sexual meanings and motives. Its candid rebuttal of diffidence makes psychoanalysis look in one respect like pornography, which also renounces coy literary connotation. Both Freudian reading and pornographic representation castigate their imagined antagonists as repressed, but while the former aims to expose such evasion dispassionately, the latter counters repression with a garrulous sexuality whose end is arousal.

The imperative to interpret sexual meanings, which impels literary criticism like this work itself, derives from Freud's insistence on drawing out such significance. Despite Freud's urging that sexual reticence be overcome, the ongoing manufacture of scandal testifies to the durability of the epoch of repression. As both a site for the production of sexual meanings and a component of the ideology of sexual unspeakability, scandal, for all its punitive moralizing, exposes not only the costs but the capacities of sexual restraint. If this study is indebted for its proficiency at reading sexuality to a Freudian framework, it owes as much to a Wildean critical practice that knows itself to be in the presence of literature precisely when sexual meanings are being rendered unspeakable.

AFTERWORD

It might almost go without saying that we still belong within the culture of scandal. As much as ever, scandal today provides copious opportunities for making news out of sex, and for heating up the news by linking it to sex. The elusive language of scandal continues both to demarcate and to violate the realm of the unspeakable, to indicate what should not be spoken by giving it a hearing. Yet since literary writing has waned as the principal mode of bourgeois cultural expression over the past century, it can no longer be accounted the main beneficiary of the rhetorical quarry that is scandal. Other, now dominant, forms of mass cultural production—the television talk show, for example, and the internationally broadcast courtroom drama—partake of scandal, both for their plots and for the means by which they engross their audiences. The customary forms of engagement with scandal that I have explored also persist. Such reactions range from hand-wringing over others' prurience to claims for deterrence, from vindictive pleasure-taking to sanctimonious disavowal, from recognizing new possibilities to suave indifference.

If it seems gratuitous to stress contemporary culture's ongoing thralldom to scandal, we must nonetheless emphasize that the conditions for scandals, which in the nineteenth century facilitated the formation of sexual identities, have not abated. Present-day scandals persevere in both censuring and making visible the defining deviance of sexual minorities, frequently lesbians and gay men. Like those induced by Victorian scandals, today's public fantasies about non-normative sexual practices provoke crises over privacy, perversity, corporeal integrity, gender ideology, and the health of the body politic. For those who would require it, a history like Oscar Wilde's—of sexual misconduct resulting in imprisonment with hard labor—is consequently still necessary as proof that sexuality belongs within the domain of politics.

Valuable as this lesson is, moreover, it is not the only one available from such Victorian examples as I have presented. For to the extent that Wilde and his scandalous forebears made an impact, they did so as much through their cultivation of what is termed a literary sensibility as through their ignominious appearances in court. Wilde's political achievement was less the goal than the consequence of his literary work, and the culture industry, to which literary production belongs, continues down to the present to be the principal location at which political fights over sexuality are played out. Ongoing battles over morality in the arts suggest how incendiary representations of sex can still damage cultural institutions. So-called sexual deviants and the so-called cultural elite now serve mutually to discredit each other. But a century ago, the sexual and the literary could tactically and cannily promote one another. The linking of sexual to literary indeterminacy, which I have traced under the rubric of unspeakability, was consummated by Wilde, and it derived in part from the other figures I have considered: Dickens invigorated this strategy, Eliot elevated it, Trollope refined it, and the Boulton and Park trial both broadcast and nearly shattered it. Wilde's endeavor, of course, badly misfired, and this failure meant not only that literary culture would thereafter be used to denigrate the politics of sexuality, but that sexuality would serve as the cudgel with which to beat down artistic expression. Yet if in Wilde's judicial failure we see predicted the punitive reciprocal uses to which sexual meanings and cultural production are today put, we may also witness, in his literary successes, an avenue for other possibilities.

Despite the homophobic malevolence with which the scandalous and the literary converged in Wilde's trials, then, the tradition that culminated in his career remains suggestive for the ways in which sexual unspeakability might still be productive. The liberation battles of the past thirty years notwithstanding, a code of discretion continues to govern public discussions of sexuality, as the unrelenting proliferation of scandal stories attests. The Victorian lineage I have explored does not propose breaking free from these constraints as an ideal, for release is

hardly imaginable when such restrictions constitute the sexuality we experience as our own. Instead, this tradition suggests how the very conditions of sexual unspeakability generate resources for pleasure, both
aesthetic and erotic. Like the appropriation of handcuffs for an erotic
scene, which serves not to arrest sexual play but instead to eroticize the
tools of the policing trade, the incitement to arousal may lie more in
admitting restraint than in imagining it can be evaded. Recognizing that
an incapacity to shape our lips around certain words might open our
mouths to other sorts of incursions is hardly to capitulate to a regime of
sexual normalization. It is rather to suggest that risking the sticky mess
of a scandal might just make it worth clasping the arms in whose embrace we find ourselves locked.

WORKS CITED

Ackroyd, Peter. *Dressing Up: Transvestism and Drag, the History of an Obsession.* New York: Simon & Schuster, 1979.

Acton, William. *The Functions and Disorders of the Reproductive Organs.* 1857. 6th ed. London: Churchill, 1875.

Aldington, Richard, and Stanley Weintraub, eds. *The Portable Oscar Wilde.* Rev. ed. New York: Penguin, 1981.

Altick, Richard. *The English Common Reader.* Chicago: University of Chicago Press, 1957.

————. *Evil Encounters: Two Victorian Sensations.* London: John Murray, 1986.

Anderson, Benedict. *Imagined Communities: Reflections on the Origin and Spread of Nationalism.* Rev. ed. London: Verso, 1991.

The Annual Register: A Review of Public Events at Home and Abroad. London: Rivingtons, 1872.

apRoberts, Ruth. *The Moral Trollope.* Athens, Ohio: Ohio University Press, 1971.

Armstrong, Nancy. *Desire and Domestic Fiction: A Political History of the Novel.* New York: Oxford University Press, 1987.

Aronson, Theo. *Prince Eddy and the Homosexual Underworld.* London: John Murray, 1994.

Atlay, J. B. *Famous Trials of the Century.* London: Grant Richards, 1899.

Banfield, Ann. *Unspeakable Sentences: Narration and Representation in the Language of Fiction.* Boston: Routledge & Kegan Paul, 1982.

Barker, Francis. *The Tremulous Private Body: Essays on Subjection.* London: Methuen, 1984.

Barker-Benfield, G. J. *The Horrors of the Half-Known Life: Male Attitudes Toward Women and Sexuality in Nineteenth-Century America.* New York: Harper & Row, 1976.

Barthes, Roland. *S/Z.* Trans. Richard Miller. New York: Hill and Wang, 1974.

Bartlett, Neil. *Who Was That Man? A Present for Mr. Oscar Wilde.* London: Serpent's Tail, 1988.

Beck, Theodric Romeyn, and John B. Beck. *Elements of Medical Jurisprudence.* 10th ed. Albany: Little & Co., 1850.

Beckson, Karl. "The Autobiographical Signature in *The Picture of Dorian Gray.*" *Victorian Newsletter* 69 (Spring 1986): 30–32.

Beckson, Karl, ed. *Oscar Wilde: The Critical Heritage.* London: Routledge & Kegan Paul, 1970.

Beer, Gillian. *George Eliot.* Key Women Writers. Bloomington: Indiana University Press, 1986.

Bell, Sir Charles. *The Hand: Its Mechanism and Vital Endowments, as Evincing Design.* London, 1833.

Bevington, Merle Mowbray. *The Saturday Review, 1855–1868: Representative Educated Opinion in Victorian England.* New York: Columbia University Press, 1941.

Bingham, Madeline, Baroness Clenmorris. *Earls and Girls.* London: Hamish Hamilton, 1980.

Blyth, Henry. *The High Tide of Pleasure: Seven English Rakes.* London: Weidenfeld and Nicolson, 1970.

Bodenheimer, Rosemarie. *The Real Life of Mary Ann Evans: George Eliot, Her Letters and Fiction.* Ithaca: Cornell University Press, 1994.

Boumelha, Penny. "George Eliot and the End of Realism." *Women Reading Women's Writing.* Ed. Sue Roe. Brighton: Harvester, 1987. 13–35.

Boyle, Thomas. *Black Swine in the Sewers of Hampstead: Beneath the Surface of Victorian Sensationalism.* New York: Viking, 1989.

Braddon, Mary E. *Lady Audley's Secret.* 1862. London: Penguin/Virago, 1987.

Brailsford, Dennis. *Bareknuckles: A Social History of Prize-Fighting.* Cambridge: Lutterworth Press, 1988.

Breuer, Josef, and Sigmund Freud. *Studies on Hysteria.* 1893–95. Ed. James Strachey. New York: Basic, n.d.

Bridgeman, Harriet, and Elizabeth Drury. *Society Scandals.* Newton Abbot: David & Charles, 1977.

Brontë, Charlotte. *Jane Eyre.* 1847. New York: Norton, 1971.

Brooks, Peter. *Reading for the Plot: Design and Intention in Narrative.* New York: Alfred A. Knopf, 1984.

Brown, Lucy. *Victorian News and Newspapers.* Oxford: Clarendon Press, 1985.

Brun, Jean. *La main et l'esprit.* Paris: Presses Universitaires de France, 1963.

Carroll, David, ed. *George Eliot: The Critical Heritage.* London: Routledge & Kegan Paul, 1971.

Chester, Lewis, David Leitch, and Colin Simpson. *The Cleveland Street Affair.* London: Weidenfeld and Nicolson, 1976.

Clarke, George. *The Lives of Boulton and Park: Extraordinary Revelations.* London, 1870.

Cohen, Ed. *Talk on the Wilde Side: Toward a Genealogy of a Discourse on Male Sexualities.* New York: Routledge, 1993.

———. "Writing Gone Wilde: Homoerotic Desire in the Closet of Representation." *PMLA* 102, no. 5 (October 1987): 801–13.

Collins, Wilkie. *The Woman in White.* 1859–60. London: Penguin, 1974.

Conan Doyle, Arthur. *The Complete Adventures and Memoirs of Sherlock Holmes.* New York: Bramhall House, 1975.

Cotsell, Michael, ed. *Critical Essays on Charles Dickens's Great Expectations.* Boston: G. K. Hall, 1990.

Craft, Christopher. *Another Kind of Love: Male Homosexual Desire in English Discourse, 1850–1920.* Berkeley: University of California Press, 1994.

Croft-Cooke, Rupert. *The Unrecorded Life of Oscar Wilde.* New York: David McKay, 1972.

Crompton, Louis. *Byron and Greek Love: Homophobia in 19th-Century England.* Berkeley: University of California Press, 1985.

Cullen, Tom. *The Empress Brown: The Story of a Royal Friendship.* London: The Bodley Head, 1969.

Cvetkovich, Ann. *Mixed Feelings: Feminism, Mass Culture, and Victorian Sensationalism.* New Brunswick: Rutgers University Press, 1992.

Davidoff, Leonore. "Class and Gender in Victorian England: The Diaries of Arthur J. Munby and Hannah Cullwick." *Feminist Studies* 5 (Spring 1979): 86–141.

Davidoff, Leonore, and Catherine Hall. *Family Fortunes: Men and Women of the English Middle Class, 1780–1850.* London: Hutchinson, 1987.

Davis, Lennard. *Factual Fictions: The Origins of the English Novel.* New York: Columbia University Press, 1983.

Dellamora, Richard. *Masculine Desire: The Sexual Politics of Victorian Aestheticism.* Chapel Hill: University of North Carolina Press, 1990.

Derrida, Jacques. *Of Grammatology.* Trans. Gayatri Chakravorty Spivak. Baltimore: Johns Hopkins University Press, 1976.

de Salamanca, Don Felix [John H. Ingram]. *The Philosophy of Handwriting.* London: Chatto & Windus, 1879.

Dickens, Charles. *Bleak House.* 1852–53. London: Penguin, 1971.

———. *David Copperfield.* 1849–50. London: Penguin, 1966.

———. *Great Expectations.* 1860–61. London: Penguin, 1965.

———. *Hard Times.* 1854. New York: Norton, 1966.

———. *Little Dorrit.* 1855–57. London: Penguin, 1967.

———. *The Mystery of Edwin Drood.* 1870. London: Mandarin, 1991.

———. *The Old Curiosity Shop.* 1840–41. London: Penguin, 1972.

———. *Oliver Twist.* 1837–39. London: Penguin, 1966.

Dollimore, Jonathan. *Sexual Dissidence: Augustine to Wilde, Freud to Foucault.* Oxford: Clarendon Press, 1991.

Donoghue, Emma. *Passions Between Women: British Lesbian Culture, 1668–1801.* New York: HarperCollins, 1995.

Dowling, Linda. *Hellenism and Homosexuality in Victorian Oxford.* Ithaca: Cornell University Press, 1994.

Eagleton, Terry. *Saint Oscar.* Derry: Field Day, 1989.

Edelman, Lee. *Homographesis: Essays in Gay Literary and Cultural Theory.* New York: Routledge, 1994.

Eliot, George. *Essays.* Ed. Thomas Pinney. London: Routledge & Kegan Paul, 1963.

———. *Middlemarch.* 1871–72. London: Penguin, 1965.

———. *The Mill on the Floss.* 1860. Oxford: Oxford University Press, 1980.

————. *Selected Essays, Poems and Other Writings.* Ed. A. S. Byatt and Nicholas Warren. London: Penguin, 1990.

Ellis, Havelock, and John Addington Symonds. *Sexual Inversion.* Vol. 1 of *Studies in the Psychology of Sex.* 1897. New York: Arno, 1975.

Ellmann, Richard. *Oscar Wilde.* New York: Alfred A. Knopf, 1988.

Faderman, Lillian. *Scotch Verdict.* New York: Quill, 1983.

Farmer, John S. *A Dictionary of Slang.* 1890. 7 vols. in 2. Ware, Hertfordshire: Wordsworth, 1987.

Finch, Casey, and Peter Bowen. " 'The Tittle-Tattle of Highbury': Gossip and the Free Indirect Style in *Emma.*" *Representations* 31 (Summer 1991): 1–18.

Fineman, Joel. *Shakespeare's Perjured Eye: The Invention of Poetic Subjectivity in the Sonnets.* Berkeley: University of California Press, 1986.

————. "The Significance of Literature: *The Importance of Being Earnest.*" *October* 15 (Winter 1980): 79–90.

Flint, Kate. *The Woman Reader, 1837–1914.* Oxford: Clarendon Press, 1993.

Forker, Charles R. "The Language of Hands in *Great Expectations.*" *Texas Studies in Language and Literature* 3 (Summer 1961): 280–93.

Foster, Donald. "Master W. H., R.I.P." *PMLA* 102, no. 1 (January 1987): 42–54.

Foucault, Michel. *The History of Sexuality.* Vol. 1. Trans. Robert Hurley. New York: Vintage, 1978.

Freedman, Jonathan. *Professions of Taste: Henry James, British Aestheticism, and Commodity Culture.* Stanford: Stanford University Press, 1990.

Freud, Sigmund. *Civilization and Its Discontents.* 1930. New York: Norton, 1961.

————. "The Dissolution of the Oedipus Complex." 1924. *The Standard Edition of the Complete Psychological Works of Sigmund Freud.* Ed. James Strachey. 24 vols. London: Hogarth Press, 1953–74. 19:173–79.

————. *Dora: An Analysis of a Case of Hysteria.* 1905. Ed. Philip Rieff. New York: Collier, 1963.

Gagnier, Regenia. *Idylls of the Marketplace: Oscar Wilde and the Victorian Public.* Stanford: Stanford University Press, 1986.

Gallagher, Catherine. "George Eliot and *Daniel Deronda:* The Prostitute and the Jewish Question." *Sex, Politics, and Science in the Nineteenth-Century Novel: Selected Papers from the English Institute, 1983–84.* Ed. Ruth Bernard Yeazell. Baltimore: Johns Hopkins University Press, 1986. 39–62.

————. *Nobody's Story: The Vanishing Acts of Women Writers in the Marketplace, 1670–1820.* Berkeley: University of California Press, 1994.

Garber, Marjorie. *Vested Interests: Cross-Dressing & Cultural Anxiety.* New York: Routledge, 1992.

Garrigan, Kristine Ottesen, ed. *Victorian Scandals: Representations of Gender and Class.* Athens, Ohio: Ohio University Press, 1992.

Gilbert, Elliot L. " 'In Primal Sympathy': *Great Expectations* and the Secret Life." *Dickens Studies Annual* 11. New York: AMS, 1983. 89–113.

Gluckman, Max. "Gossip and Scandal." *Current Anthropology* 4 (June 1963): 307–16.

Goldberg, Jonathan. *Writing Matter: From the Hands of the English Renaissance.* Stanford: Stanford University Press, 1990.

Habermas, Jürgen. *The Structural Transformation of the Public Sphere: An Inquiry into a Category of Bourgeois Society.* Trans. Thomas Burger. Cambridge, Mass.: MIT Press, 1991.

Haight, Gordon S. *George Eliot: A Biography.* New York: Oxford University Press, 1968.

Hall, N. John. *Trollope: A Biography.* Oxford: Clarendon, 1991.

Hammond, H. H. *Of Scandall.* Oxford, 1644.

The Hand Phrenologically Considered: Being a Glimpse at the Relation of the Mind with the Organisation of the Body. London: Chapman and Hall, 1848.

Hardy, Barbara. *Particularities: Readings in George Eliot.* Athens, Ohio: Ohio University Press, 1982.

Hare, E. H. "Masturbatory Insanity: The History of an Idea." *Journal of Mental Science* 108, no. 452 (January 1962): 2–25.

Hart-Davis, Rupert, ed. *The Letters of Oscar Wilde.* New York: Harcourt, Brace, 1962.

Hazelwood, Robert R., et al. *Autoerotic Fatalities.* Lexington, Mass.: D. C. Heath, 1983.

Hocquenghem, Guy. *Homosexual Desire.* Trans. Daniella Dangoor. Durham: Duke University Press, 1993.

Holcombe, Lee. *Wives and Property: Reform of the Married Women's Property Law in Nineteenth-Century England.* Toronto: University of Toronto Press, 1983.

Hornback, Bert G. *Great Expectations: A Novel of Friendship.* Boston: Twayne, 1987.

Howe, Joseph W. *Excessive Venery, Masturbation and Continence.* 1887. New York: Arno, 1974.

Hughes, Winifred. *The Maniac in the Cellar: Sensation Novels of the 1860s.* Princeton: Princeton University Press, 1980.

Hyde, H. Montgomery. *The Cleveland Street Scandal.* New York: Coward, McCann & Geoghegan, 1976.

———. *A History of Pornography.* London: Heinemann, 1964.

———. *The Love That Dared Not Speak Its Name.* Boston: Little, Brown, 1970.

———. *A Tangled Web: Sex Scandals in British Politics and Society.* London: Futura, 1986.

———. *The Trials of Oscar Wilde.* Notable British Trials. London: William Hodge and Co., 1948.

———. *The Trials of Oscar Wilde.* New York: Dover, 1962.

Jacobus, Mary. "The Question of Language: Men of Maxims and *The Mill on the Floss.*" *Critical Inquiry* 8, no. 2 (Winter 1981): 207–22.

James, Henry. *The Art of Fiction and Other Essays.* New York: Oxford University Press, 1948.

———. *The Complete Tales.* Ed. Leon Edel. 12 vols. Philadelphia: J. B. Lippincott, 1962–64.

———. *The Portrait of a Lady.* 1881. Boston: Houghton Mifflin, 1963.

———. *The Wings of the Dove.* 1902. New York: Norton, 1978.

Jenkins, Roy. *Victorian Scandal.* New York: Pyramid, 1965.

Keeler, Christine, and Robert Meadley. *Sex Scandals.* London: Xanadu, 1985.

Kendrick, Walter M. *The Novel-Machine: The Theory and Fiction of Anthony Trollope.* Baltimore: Johns Hopkins University Press, 1980.

————. *The Secret Museum: Pornography in Modern Culture.* New York: Viking, 1987.

Kincaid, James R. *Child-Loving: The Erotic Child and Victorian Culture.* New York: Routledge, 1992.

————. *The Novels of Anthony Trollope.* Oxford: Clarendon, 1977.

Kingston, Charles. *Society Sensations.* London: Stanley Paul & Co., 1922.

Kopelson, Kevin R. *Love's Litany: The Writing of Modern Homoerotics.* Stanford: Stanford University Press, 1994.

Krueger, Christine L. "Naming Privates in Public: Indecent Assault Depositions, 1830–1860." *Mosaic* 27, no. 4 (December 1994): 121–40.

Kucich John. "Transgression in Trollope: Dishonesty and the Antibourgeois Elite." ELH 56, no. 3 (Fall 1989): 593–618.

Lanser, Susan Sniader. *Fictions of Authority: Women Writers and Narrative Voice.* Ithaca: Cornell University Press, 1992.

Laqueur, Thomas W. "Onanism, Sociability, and the Imagination." Unpublished essay, 1992.

————. "The Queen Caroline Affair: Politics as Art in the Reign of George IV." *Journal of Modern History* 54 (September 1982): 417–66.

Lawler, Donald L. *An Inquiry into Oscar Wilde's Revisions of "The Picture of Dorian Gray."* New York: Garland, 1988.

Leavis, F. R. *The Great Tradition.* London: Chatto & Windus, 1973.

Levine, M. H. "Hands and Hearts in *Great Expectations.*" *Ball State University Forum* 6 (Autumn 1965): 22–24.

Litvak, Joseph. *Caught in the Act: Theatricality in the Nineteenth-Century English Novel.* Berkeley: University of California Press, 1992.

Lumley, Edward. *The Art of Judging the Character of Individuals from Their Handwriting and Style.* London: John Russell Smith, 1875.

Lyon, Elisabeth. Introduction. "Unspeakable Images." *Camera Obscura* 24 (September 1990): 5–6.

Lyons, Paul. "The Morality of Irony and Unreliable Narrative in Trollope's *The Warden* and *Barchester Towers.*" *South Atlantic Review* 54, no. 1 (1989): 41–54.

Marcus, Steven. *The Other Victorians: A Study of Sexuality and Pornography in Mid-Nineteenth Century England.* 2d ed. New York: New American Library, 1974.

Martin, R. B. *Enter Rumour: Four Early Victorian Scandals.* London: Faber and Faber, 1962.

Mason, Stuart [Christopher Millard], ed. *Oscar Wilde: Art and Morality, A Record of the Discussion which Followed the Publication of "Dorian Gray."* Rev. ed. London: Frank Palmer, 1912.

McCalman, Iain. *Radical Underworld: Prophets, Revolutionaries and Pornographers in London, 1795–1840.* Cambridge: Cambridge University Press, 1988.

McKenzie, K. A. *Edith Simcox and George Eliot.* London: Oxford University Press, 1961.

McKeon, Michael. *The Origins of the English Novel, 1600–1740.* Baltimore: Johns Hopkins University Press, 1987.

Melville, Herman. *Pierre; or, the Ambiguities.* 1852. New York: Grove Press, 1957.

Mill, John Stuart. *On Liberty with The Subjection of Women and Chapters on Socialism.* Ed. Stefan Collini. Cambridge: Cambridge University Press, 1989.

Miller, D. A. "Anal Rope." *Representations* 32 (Fall 1990): 114–33.

———. *Narrative and Its Discontents: Problems of Closure in the Traditional Novel.* Princeton: Princeton University Press, 1981.

———. *The Novel and the Police.* Berkeley: University of California Press, 1988.

Miller, J. Hillis. *Charles Dickens: The World of His Novels.* Cambridge, Mass.: Harvard University Press, 1958.

Miller, Nancy. "Emphasis Added: Plots and Plausibilities in Women's Fiction." *The New Feminist Criticism.* Ed. Elaine Showalter. New York: Pantheon, 1985. 339–60.

Miller, William Ian. *Humiliation and Other Essays on Honor, Social Discomfort, and Violence.* Ithaca: Cornell University Press, 1993.

Millgate, Michael, ed. *The Life and Work of Thomas Hardy.* Athens: University of Georgia Press, 1985.

Moore, Jack B. "Hearts and Hands in *Great Expectations.*" *Dickensian* 61 (Winter 1965): 52–56.

Mort, Frank. *Dangerous Sexualities: Medico-Moral Politics in England Since 1830.* London: Routledge, 1987.

Neuman, R. P. "Masturbation, Madness, and the Modern Concepts of Childhood and Adolescence." *Journal of Social History* 8, no. 3 (Spring 1975): 1–27.

Newsom, Robert. "The Hero's Shame." *Dickens Studies Annual* 11. New York: AMS, 1983. 1–24.

Norton, Rictor. *Mother Clap's Molly House: The Gay Subculture in England, 1700–1830.* London: GMP, 1992.

An Official Report of the Cause Célèbre Mordaunt v. Mordaunt, Cole, and Johnstone. London: Evans, Oliver, 1870.

Poovey, Mary. "Figures of Arithmetic, Figures of Speech: The Discourse of Statistics in the 1830s." *Critical Inquiry* 19, no. 2 (Winter 1993): 256–76.

———. *Uneven Developments: The Ideological Work of Gender in Mid-Victorian England.* Chicago: University of Chicago Press, 1988.

Porter, Roy, and Lesley Hall. *The Facts of Life: The Creation of Sexual Knowledge in Britain, 1650–1950.* New Haven: Yale University Press, 1995.

Ragussis, Michael. *Acts of Naming: The Family Plot in Fiction.* New York: Oxford University Press, 1986.

Révész, Géza. *The Human Hand: A Psychological Study.* Trans. John Cohen. London: Routledge, 1958.

Roe, Michael. *Kenealy and the Tichborne Cause: A Study in Mid-Victorian Populism.* Melbourne: Melbourne University Press, 1974.

Rollins, Hyder Edward, ed. *The New Variorum Edition of Shakespeare: The Sonnets.* Philadelphia: Lippincott, 1944.

Roughead, William. *Bad Companions.* Edinburgh: W. Green & Son, 1930.

———. *Malice Domestic.* Edinburgh: W. Green & Son, 1928.

Rousseau, G. S. "The Pursuit of Homosexuality in the Eighteenth Century: 'Utterly Confused Category' and/or Rich Repository?" *'Tis Nature's Fault: Unauthorized Sexu-*

ality During the Enlightenment. Ed. Robert Purks Maccubbin. Cambridge: Cambridge University Press, 1987. 132–68.

Sammells, Neil. "Oscar Wilde: Quite Another Thing." *Irish Writing: Exile and Subversion.* Ed. Paul Hyland and Neil Sammells. New York: St. Martin's, 1991. 116–25.

Saul, Jack. *The Sins of the Cities of the Plain; or, the Recollections of a Mary-Ann, with Short Essays on Sodomy and Tribadism.* 2 vols. London: privately printed, 1881.

Scarry, Elaine. "Work and the Body in Hardy and Other Nineteenth-Century Novelists." *Representations* 3 (Summer 1983): 90–123.

Schmidgall, Gary. *The Stranger Wilde: Interpreting Oscar.* New York: Dutton, 1994.

The Secret Vice Exposed! Some Arguments Against Masturbation. New York: Arno, 1974.

Sedgwick, Eve Kosofsky. *Between Men: English Literature and Male Homosocial Desire.* New York: Columbia University Press, 1985.

———. *Epistemology of the Closet.* Berkeley: University of California Press, 1990.

———. *Tendencies.* Durham: Duke University Press, 1993.

Sharpe, Jenny. *Allegories of Empire: The Figure of Woman in the Colonial Text.* Minneapolis: University of Minnesota Press, 1993.

Sinfield, Alan. *The Wilde Century: Oscar Wilde, Effeminacy and the Queer Moment.* New York: Columbia University Press, 1994.

Sins of the Cities of the Plain. New York: Masquerade, 1992.

Smith, F. B. "Labouchère's Amendment to the Criminal Law Amendment Bill." *Historical Studies* (Melbourne) 17, no. 67 (October 1976): 165–75.

Sorell, Walter. *The Story of the Human Hand.* Indianapolis: Bobbs-Merrill, 1967.

Spacks, Patricia Meyer. *Gossip.* New York: Alfred A. Knopf, 1985.

Stang, Richard. *The Theory of the Novel in England, 1850–1870.* New York: Columbia University Press, 1959.

Steakley, James D. "Iconography of a Scandal: Political Cartoons and the Eulenburg Affair in Wilhelmin Germany." *Hidden from History: Reclaiming the Gay and Lesbian Past.* Ed. Martin Bauml Duberman, Martha Vicinus, and George Chauncey, Jr. New York: New American Library, 1989. 233–63.

Stockton, Kathryn Bond. *God Between Their Lips: Desire Between Women in Irigaray, Brontë, and Eliot.* Stanford: Stanford University Press, 1994.

Street-Porter, Janet. *Scandal!* London: Allen Lane, 1981.

Taylor, Alfred Swaine. *Medical Jurisprudence.* 3d ed. London, 1850.

Taylor, John Tinnon. *Early Opposition to the English Novel.* New York: King's Crown, 1943.

Tracy, Robert. "Reading Dickens's Writing." *Dickens Studies Annual* 11. New York: AMS, 1983. 37–59.

The Trial of Boulton and Park, with Hurt and Fiske. A Complete and Accurate Report of the Proceedings. Manchester: John Heywood, 1871.

Trollope, Anthony. *An Autobiography.* 1883. Oxford: Oxford University Press, 1980.

———. *The Eustace Diamonds.* 1871–72. 2 vols. in 1. Oxford: Oxford University Press, 1973.

Vaschide, N. *Essai sur la psychologie de la main.* Paris: Rivière, 1909.

Vernon, Patricia A. "The Poor Fictionist's Conscience: Point of View in the Palliser Novels." *Victorian Newsletter* 71 (Spring 1987): 16–20.

———. "Reading and Misreading in *The Eustace Diamonds.*" *VIJ* 12 (1984): 1–8.

Walkowitz, Judith R. *City of Dreadful Delight: Narratives of Sexual Danger in Late-Victorian London.* Chicago: University of Chicago Press, 1992.

———. *Prostitution and Victorian Society: Women, Class, and the State.* Cambridge: Cambridge University Press, 1980.

Weeks, Jeffrey. *Coming Out: Homosexual Politics in Britain, from the Nineteenth Century to the Present.* London: Quartet, 1977.

———. "Inverts, Perverts, and Mary-Annes: Male Prostitution and the Regulation of Homosexuality in England in the Nineteenth and Early Twentieth Centuries." *Journal of Homosexuality* 6, no. 1/2 (Fall/Winter 1980–81): 113–34.

———. *Sex, Politics and Society: The Regulation of Sexuality Since 1800.* 2d ed. London: Longman, 1989.

Welsh, Alexander. *George Eliot and Blackmail.* Cambridge, Mass.: Harvard University Press, 1985.

Wharton, Francis, and Moreton Stillé. *Treatise on Medical Jurisprudence.* Philadelphia: Kay & Brother, 1855.

Wilde, Oscar. *The Complete Shorter Fiction.* Ed. Isobel Murray. London: Oxford University Press, 1979.

———. *The Complete Works.* New York: Harper & Row, 1989.

———. *The Portrait of Mr. W. H.* 1893. Ed. Vyvyan Holland. London: Methuen, 1958.

Wilde, Oscar, and Others. *Teleny.* Ed. John McRae. London: GMP, 1986.

Williams, Linda. *Hard Core: Power, Pleasure, and the "Frenzy of the Visible."* Berkeley: University of California Press, 1989.

Williams, Raymond. *The Long Revolution.* New York: Columbia University Press, 1961.

Williams, Sherwood A. "The Perversion of Representation: Naturalism and Decadence in the Late Nineteenth Century." Ph.D. diss., University of California, Berkeley, 1990.

Wilson, Colin, and Donald Seaman. *Scandal! An Encyclopedia.* London: Weidenfeld and Nicolson, 1986.

Woodman, W. Bathurst, and Charles Meymott Tidy. *Forensic Medicine and Toxicology.* Philadelphia: Lindsay & Blakiston, 1877.

Yeazell, Ruth Bernard. "Podsnappery, Sexuality, and the English Novel." *Critical Inquiry* 9 (December 1982): 339–57.

INDEX

public, 15, 102–11, 128, 130–58, 179–
84; and sexuality, 61, 77–89, 103–10,
135–36, 148–58, 238
Generalization (rhetorical), 133, 138–39,
143–58, 184–89
Gilbert, Elliot L., 31n
Gluckman, Max, 14n
Goldberg, Jonathan, 39n
Goncourt, Edmond de, 206
Gossip: and femininity, 15, 137–45; and
scandal, 7n, 14, 15, 19, 22, 133–49,
179–89, 224–25

Habermas, Jürgen, 15n, 80n
Haight, Gordon S., 156n
Hall, N. John, 177n
Hammond, H. H., 4n
Hand: and female sexuality, 61–70; and
heterosexuality, 54–57, 63–64, 68–
69, 149–53; as labor, 37–40, 45, 62;
and male homosexuality, 45–61; and
male sexuality, 33–61, 70; and manners, 45–48, 54–58; as masturbatory,
33–45, 62, 71; in pugilism, 48–60,
64–65; shaking, 45–48, 54; in Victorian culture, 33–36; as writing, 32n,
34, 38–40, 63
Hardy, Thomas, 27, 173, 226n
Hastings, Lady Flora, 182n
Heterosexuality, 10–15, 17–18, 20, 41,
49, 54–57, 61, 63–64, 68–71, 104–
5, 108–10, 114, 118–19, 128, 132–58,
159–90, 205–7, 227–35
Hicklin Standard, 103
Hocquenghem, Guy, 81–82n
Homophobia, 54, 61, 89, 91–95, 97–110,
156, 191–92, 210–13, 221–24, 237–39
Homosexuality: female, 6, 65, 153–58,
237–39; male, 3n, 5, 8–12, 20, 22,
32n, 45–61, 73–129, 131–33, 152–53,
157–58, 191–93, 205–30, 237–39. See
also Gay
Howe, Joseph W., 26n, 35

Humiliation, 5, 16, 31, 36–40, 46–50,
64, 78, 130–31, 136–37, 140, 143, 148,
160, 190, 225, 237–38
Hyde, H. Montgomery, 2n, 14n, 17n,
74n, 75n, 85n, 92n, 103n, 124n, 198n,
215n, 224

Imperialism. See National identity
Indeterminacy, 22, 32, 70–71, 96, 116,
122, 192–236, 238. See also Sexual
unspeakability
Interpretation, 116–21, 159–62, 191–236
Ireland, 10, 123, 205–6
Irony, 133, 141–42, 146–47, 149, 188–90

Jacobus, Mary, 145n
James, Henry, 3n, 19, 25, 193; "The Art
of Fiction," 104n; The Aspern Papers,
226–28, 231–34; The Figure in the Carpet,
226–34; The Portrait of a Lady, 235; The
Wings of the Dove, 235
Jenkins, Roy, 11n, 12n
Jewels, 159, 161–79
Jonathan (Biblical), 157, 221

Kendrick, Walter M., 27n, 103n, 123n,
177n, 185–86n, 186
Kincaid, James R., 2n, 185n
Krueger, Christine L., 121n
Kucich John, 188n

Labouchère amendment, 75n, 76, 84,
85–86n, 214n
Lacan, Jacques, 208
Lanser, Susan Sniader, 146n
Laqueur, Thomas W., 17n, 27n, 42n
Law: property, 167–75, 181; as regula-
tion of sexuality, 10, 12, 74–90, 192,
213–25
Leavis, F. R., 135n
Lesbianism, 6, 65, 153–58, 237–39
Lewes, George Henry, 20, 153
Libel, 11, 215

William A. Cohen is Assistant Professor of English at the
University of Maryland at College Park.

Library of Congress Cataloging-in-Publication Data
Cohen, William A.
Sex scandal : the private parts of Victorian fiction /
by William A. Cohen.
p.   cm. — (Series Q)
Includes bibliographical references and index.
ISBN 0-8223-1856-3 (alk. paper). — ISBN 0-8223-1848-2
(pbk. : alk. paper)
1. English fiction—19th century—History and criticism.
2. Scandals in literature.   3. Literature and society—
Great Britain—History—19th century.
4. Homosexuality and literature—Great Britain—
History—19th century.   5. Scandals—Great Britain—
History—19th century.   6. Great Britain—History—
Victoria, 1837–1901.   7. Sex in literature.   I. Title.
II. Series.
PR878.S317C64   1996   823'.8093538—dc20
96-7641 CIP